"Andrew Perrin's book is an excellent and reliable introduction to the Dead Sea Scrolls and the site of Qumran. It has just the right combination of scholarly knowledge and engaging public outreach. It provides up-to-date research by the author in fields not usually surveyed, all in an enjoyable, often amusing way."

JONATHAN BEN-DOV,
Professor, Department of Biblical Studies,
Tel Aviv University

"This lively presentation of the Dead Sea Scrolls highlights in many fresh ways both their significance for the better understanding of the past and also their implications for the present. Every alliterative subheading resonates with intriguing insight. The whole is easy-access illumination of a truly fascinating subject."

GEORGE J. BROOKE,
Rylands Professor Emeritus of Biblical Criticism and Exegesis,
University of Manchester

"This is a lively and engaging introduction to the Dead Sea Scrolls for the non-specialist. It is noteworthy for its discussion of forgeries and of the Aramaic texts, issues that are often overlooked in standard introductions."

JOHN J. COLLINS,
Holmes Professor of Old Testament Emeritus,
Yale Divinity School

"Are you intrigued by the Dead Sea Scrolls and eager to learn their relevance to the Bible and the ancient world? Look no further than Andrew Perrin's *Lost Words and Forgotten Worlds*. Perrin offers a scholarly yet accessible exploration into the significance of the Dead Sea Scrolls, encouraging us to uncover their enduring influence on our understanding of ancient texts and history. Departing from conventional approaches, Perrin infuses his work with wit, humor, and scholarly analysis, resulting in a delightful and engaging journey through the fascinating world of the Dead Sea Scrolls."

DOMINICK S. HERNÁNDEZ,
Associate Professor of Old Testament and Semitics,
Talbot School of Theology;
Director of Talbot en Español, Biola University

"Andrew Perrin's book is more than a mere introduction and survey of the Dead Sea Scrolls; it is an insightful and up-to-date revelation of the real meaning of the Scrolls and the various controversies surrounding their discovery and—in some cases—their authenticity. It's also a fun read!"

CRAIG A. EVANS,
John Bisagno Distinguished Professor of Christian Origins,
Houston Christian University

"If you've ever wondered about those strange books called the Dead Sea Scrolls, Perrin's new book is for you! Perrin's book is full of Indiana Jones-esque stories of the DSS discovery, tales of clever forgeries, and depictions of different Jewish groups in Jesus's day. Grounded in excellent scholarship, Perrin uses engaging stories and his welcoming tone to make the Dead Sea Scrolls feel friendly, rather than remote."

BETH M. STOVELL,
Professor of Old Testament,
Ambrose University

"Andrew Perrin grabs the regurgitated conversations of the ivory towers, marches down the spiral stairs, emerging in the light of day below in order to reimagine what it means to introduce the Dead Sea Scrolls to the interested, and soon to be curious, reader. Perrin has proven that there is such a thing as an informative page-turner that offers breadth, depth, and insights to the most contemporary of debates on Qumran scrolls."

BENJAMIN WOLD,
Associate Professor of Ancient Judaism,
Trinity College Dublin

LOST WORDS AND FORGOTTEN WORLDS

REDISCOVERING THE DEAD SEA SCROLLS

LOST WORDS AND FORGOTTEN WORLDS

REDISCOVERING THE DEAD SEA SCROLLS

ANDREW B. PERRIN

Lost Words and Forgotten Worlds: Rediscovering the Dead Sea Scrolls

Lexham Academic, an imprint of Lexham Press
1313 Commercial St., Bellingham, WA 98225
LexhamPress.com

Print ISBN 9781683597957
Digital ISBN 9781683597940

Lexham Editorial: Derek R. Brown, Katrina Smith, Abigail Stocker
Cover Design: Sarah Brossow
Typesetting: Abigail Stocker

24 25 26 27 28 29 30 / IN / 12 11 10 9 8 7 6 5 4 3 2 1

For Emma, my first great adventure.

For Jude, my second.

Contents

Acknowledgments

The Perrin home team (Tanya, Emma, and Jude) are my reason for everything. When I first had the idea for this volume, I penned the dedication in a blank Word document, then slogged along from there, word by word, regularly looking back to my "why" on page one. Emma and Jude, being your dad is among my greatest pleasures in life. Thanks for being my North Star. This one's for you.

Many scholars have shaped my understanding of the scrolls—too many to list here. More than any, I am indebted to Martin Abegg, Peter Flint, Daniel Machiela, Eileen Schuller, and Loren Stuckenbruck. Your scholarship and generous spirits inspire my work in the scrolls. Thanks for both teaching me and living out what a scholar can be. I am particularly grateful to Eileen Schuller, who read and reviewed this manuscript in full. Thanks also to Årstein Justnes for being a thought partner and reviewer of chapter 3.

The early content of this book was developed and test-driven in my Dead Sea Scrolls classes at Trinity Western University. Thanks to the undergrads there who read sample chapters for bonus marks, and thanks to my talented graduate students—Shelby Bennett, Brian Felushko, Matthew Hama, and Kyle Young—who reviewed and ripped apart earlier draft chapters.

I am grateful to my editor at Lexham Press, Derek Brown, for his support, enthusiasm, and patience in this project that was disrupted by the pandemic, among other delays mostly of my making. Thanks to Katy Smith at the press for her support on image permissions. The creativity and commitment of the Lexham team to publishing meaningful works in innovative ways is much needed in the academic guild. I appreciate you all for thinking outside the box with me.

To everyone else—family and friends—sorry my last few books have been so long, dull, and expensive. My hope is that this one is a way of, at last, inviting you into this world of scribes, scrolls, and scriptures that has occupied more than half my life.

Last but not least, I am glad to contribute 10 percent of the royalties from this volume to Autism Canada in support of folks and families journeying with life on the spectrum. You can find out more about their important work at www.autismcanada.org.

Now, on to the scrolls.

Andrew B. Perrin
Copenhagen, Denmark
August 17, 2023

Preface

How to Read a Dead Sea Scroll

One of the exciting and frustrating things about the Dead Sea Scrolls (DSS) is that they are often tattered and torn manuscripts. At the best of times, they are nearly complete scrolls, but at the worst, they are Dead Sea scraps, deteriorated with age. This means the way texts are deciphered and represented is often confusing. This short guide will help you understand *what* text or composition you are reading, as well as *why* the text is referred to or presented in a certain way. Note that this guide strives for simplicity. There is some variety in how scholars or other publications might refer to the materials.

Names and Titles *for* Scrolls

Very few scrolls actually include the titles of the work on the scroll itself. In most cases, titles are assigned by modern editors. Many writings are attested in multiple manuscripts. When you come across something like 11QTemṗleScroll[a] or 11QT[a], these are modern shorthand references for the Qumran Cave 11 copy of the *Temple Scroll.* Superscript letters indicate the first (a), second (b), third (c) copy, and so on, found in a particular cave. You may also come across a strictly numerical system for these references, which in this case would be 11Q19. In this book, when referring to the composition represented by one or more manuscripts, I will do so using its title in italics. In some cases, there is variety, disagreement, and multiple modern titles.

In general, I pick or provide the ones that are most common or make the most sense. Confused yet? It's not as tough as it sounds.[1]

References to Content *in* Scrolls

Ancient scrolls are generally made up of several sheets of leather or papyrus. These were stitched together and then inscribed in columns. Scrolls can range from about the size of a cigarette butt to several meters in length. Unfortunately, in most cases, the DSS are in various states of decay. Whether scroll or scrap, the referencing system is essentially the same. When referring to a column or fragment number and line of text, I will do so by separating the two by a colon. Note that, like biblical verses, this numbering is not inherent to the texts; rather, it is a system developed to locate and refer to sections or lines. For example, 11Q19 52:1 refers to the fifty-second column and first line of the specific copy of 11Q19 or 11QTempleScroll[a] of the *Temple Scroll.* Works that are known only by puzzle pieces of fragments are also numbered, even if the structure in columns is not known. When the columns are known in fragmentary texts, they are referenced by Roman numerals after the manuscript and fragment number (for example 4Q542 1i: 4–7). For simplicity's sake, in this book I will provide the manuscript number, column or fragment number, and line number when quoting or referencing a specific point in a DSS text. Don't worry—you don't need to look anything up. All the texts we work with will be right here in this book.

Transcriptions and Translations *of* the Scrolls

There are many places where the text of the DSS is lost or damaged, making it difficult to decipher. For original language transcriptions or English translations, any content that comes between square brackets is lost but reconstructed. Occasionally, I will include a word, phrase, or reference in regular brackets or parentheses. This content is to help smooth out translations or make clear for a modern reader when a biblical text is being cited but does not reflect the actual content of the scroll. Ellipses in translations indicate a larger stretch of damaged material. If it feels like some of the translations are glitchy sentence fragments strung together, that's because in many instances they are. The word *vacat* is also included within transcriptions or translations to signify where scribes left an intentional blank space in between words in a paragraph.

I won't quote the original language texts of the DSS (Hebrew, Aramaic, or Greek) very often in this book. When I do, I'll always provide translations and make sense of what is going on in the original language texts. But there is also a system for reflecting the degrees of certainty of a given character. If a closed dot appears above a letter (אׄ), this means it is *probable*. If a small open circle appears above the letter (אֺ), this means it is *possible* but not certain. If a big open circlet appears in line with the text (◦), this means there are remains of some lost letter but not enough to hazard a best guess. If there is no dot or circlet above the figure (א), the character is clear and uncontested.

That's a bit about scroll texts and translations. Next up: where to find them.

A Note on Primary Sources

Dead Sea Scrolls English translations are primarily from *The Dead Sea Scrolls: A New Translation* (revised edition) by Michael Wise, Martin Abegg Jr., and Edward Cook. When citing original language materials from the DSS, I draw primarily on the volumes of the Discoveries in the Judean Desert (DJD) series, with a few exceptions. Most renderings of the Aramaic DSS are my own, save for those of the *Genesis Apocryphon*, the English and Aramaic of which I have drawn from Machiela and VanderKam's edition (Mohr Siebeck, 2018). For the *Hodayot*, I draw on Newsom and Schuller's study edition (SBL Press, 2012).

Unless otherwise noted, biblical quotations are from the NRSV. Translations of the Qumran biblical scrolls are from *The Dead Sea Scrolls Bible* by Martin Abegg Jr., Peter Flint, and Eugene Ulrich. English translations of the Septuagint are from *A New English Translation of the Septuagint* (NETS) edited by Albert Pietersma and Benjamin G. Wright. Hebrew and Aramaic language citations of the Hebrew Bible are from *Biblia Hebraica Stuttgartensia*. Greek citations of the New Testament come from Nestle-Aland 28.

Translations of the Apocrypha or Deuterocanon are also from the NRSV. Renderings of most pseudepigrapha texts are from *The Old Testament Pseudepigrapha* edited by James Charlesworth, save for those of 1 Enoch, which come from VanderKam and Nickelsburg's recent revised translation from the Hermeneia series.

Translations of rabbinic literature come from sefaria.org. Classical writings come primarily from the Loeb's Classical Library series. Sources for additional primary texts or translations beyond these materials are footnoted when relevant.

In all instances, I may slightly revise translations but will track closely to the excellent renderings of the above editions and sources. Full publication details on all sources are included in the bibliography.

Lastly, to extend your encounter with the Dead Sea manuscripts, scribal cultures, and artifacts referenced throughout this book, I highly recommend perusing the following online digitization projects: The Leon Levy Digital Dead Sea Scrolls Library by the Israel Antiquities Authority (www.deadseascrolls.org.il) and The Shrine of the Book at the Israel Museum (http://dss.collections.imj.org.il).

Now, let me tell you about the time I skipped class and my world changed.

Introduction

Tattered Scrolls and a Tissue Paper Time Machine

"The story of the Scrolls continues to unfold itself."
F. F. Bruce, *Second Thoughts on the Dead Sea Scrolls* (1955)

I love old stuff, always have. Maybe it was growing up in a generation that was heavily analog yet on the cusp of a digital revolution. There's just something essential to our human experience and identity that is best understood through material objects—things that can be touched, felt, and encountered. The way we understand the world around us and our beliefs are also deeply connected to, shaped by, and reflected in such items. This is why the best theology is also connected to studies on material culture: stuff made, cherished, and handed down, and the people and communities involved in those processes. Texts, contexts, and beliefs: they're all connected.

It was during my undergraduate days that my passion for analog artifacts and curiosity for exploring the Bible were connected in profound, unexpected, and even life-altering ways. At the time, I was contending with many of my own assumptions and misconceptions about how the words of the Bible came together, beginning to encounter the historical, social, and cultural worlds that shaped them, and embarking on a lifelong journey of asking hard yet authentic questions about what these sacred words and ancient worlds mean for us today.

Around midterm season, my school hosted a duo of guest speakers on the Dead Sea Scrolls (DSS). I was intrigued. So I did what juniors do: I skipped class and opted for the free lecture, coffee, and cookies. I heard about an unexpected discovery starting in 1947, the recovery of some one thousand–plus tattered ancient manuscripts and thousands more fragments, a connection with a previously overlooked archaeological site called Qumran, and the decades of drama it had taken to acquire, piece together, and eventually publish these materials.[1]

More than twenty years have passed since that lecture. I've spent most of that time encountering the DSS and being confounded, inspired, and perplexed by them. This book is a new invitation to the DSS. Even if you don't yet know what the DSS are or why they matter, chances are you've heard of them. In their short modern history, these tattered manuscripts continue to both captivate and spark controversy. Why?

On one hand, these discoveries at once challenged, changed, and confirmed what we thought we knew about the words of the Hebrew Scriptures. For Jews, we're talking about the Hebrew Bible. For Christians, it's the Old Testament. Both collections are foundational for Western Culture. The scrolls contain our earliest copies of books of the Hebrew Scriptures in their original languages, Hebrew and Aramaic, and samples of early translations into Greek. Almost right out of the gates, these discoveries and this level of detail were game changers. This was truly a discovery of biblical significance in every sense.[2]

Already by 1952, the Revised Standard Version committee was aware of the DSS Isaiah and Habakkuk texts and the need to restore Scripture to make it more ancient in light of such modern discoveries. Today almost any modern translation, the NIV, NLT, NRSV, ESV, NKJV, ABC123—just pick one—draws on the DSS to enhance the biblical texts to their best possible form.[3]

IMAGE A: 1QIsaiah^{a} from Qumran Cave 1 is the second longest manuscript from the Dead Sea Scrolls (7.34 meters; 24 feet) and dates to approximately 125 BCE. Though damaged at the lower edges, the scroll contains content from all sixty-six chapters of the book of Isaiah and attests to both the continuity and variety of the text of Isaiah when compared with other witnesses. (Image credit: John C. Trever)

On the other hand, the DSS also challenged, changed, and confirmed what we thought we knew about the *worlds* before, in, around, and beyond the Bible.

Pick up a Christian Bible—an actual printed page version. (If you don't have one, you can swipe a copy from most hotel rooms. It's not theft. They want you to take it.) Flip to the end of the Old Testament. As Malachi gives way to Matthew, a solitary tissue page separates the tandem testaments towering against each other. This gives the impression of a brief interlude between Old and New. But the time gap between the latest writings of the Hebrew

Scriptures and the times of the early Jesus movement was at least two hundred years. It's a tissue paper time machine, and one you don't even know you're in.

We all see, know, and feel how much things change in a single generation. Now imagine how much can transpire in a few centuries. Unrecorded on that flimsy intertestamental page are tales of empires toppling, cultures clashing, and generations caught in the timeless tug-of-war between staying faithful to the past while living in the present. *This* is the world of the DSS. The age is often referred to as Second Temple Judaism, with the mid– to late–Second Temple period being most relevant to the DSS (third century BCE to 70 CE).[4]

But this fresh perspective comes with growing pains. You might have picked up on those three C verbs above: *challenge*, *change*, and *confirm*.

As the nearly seventy-year-old quote at the outset of this chapter hints, the story of the DSS is not only ancient but ongoing today. The more we learn about the scrolls—what they say, what they mean, why they matter—the more we need to engage complex, better, and new questions, and not shy away from unexpected or even uncomfortable answers. This shouldn't surprise us: the DSS are quite literally a trove of *new* information. It would be surprising (even suspicious) if these discoveries didn't change what we know about the texts and contexts of biblical words and worlds. There's an opportunity here to journey into these lost words and forgotten worlds of the DSS.

How does this book fit into your journey with the scrolls?

In a word, it's an invitation. It's the type of book you read if you've heard of the DSS yet have never actually encountered them. It's not really a textbook and not exactly a popular introduction. It's designed to be the missing link between those two genres. There were many such DSS books published in the decades after their initial discovery. But, apart from a few more recent, accessible introductions, I feel this important space has become sparse. You don't need a PhD to read this book. Which brings me to my next point.

Who is this book for?

Speaking of not-really-a-textbook-pseudo-popular-invitation-type books, I'll quote a line from another early DSS volume. Millar Burrows opened his excellent 1955 book *The Dead Sea Scrolls* bluntly: "This book is not intended for the scholar."[5] I'll plus one that point and apply it here. I am a scholar of the DSS and have had the good fortune of learning from and working with an exceptional, brilliant, and diverse international community of other DSS researchers. This has been one of the great privileges of my life—to be a professional reader, thinker, teacher, and communicator about the DSS and their relevance to the Bible, theology, and culture, and to do so among great minds housed within generous people. That is a rare gift.

This book is one attempt at extending that gift to those around me. While the book isn't written for academics, it is rooted in solid research of what I take to be the best ideas about the words and worlds of the DSS today. There are periodic endnotes for those who want to delve deeper. But if not, that's fine. In the few instances I refer to something in the original biblical languages—Hebrew, Aramaic, and Greek—I'll always provide English translations and explanations so there are no barriers for readers.

Since the book's not aimed at academics, I've also tried not to write like one. Nothing kills an exciting topic like grandiosity, tergiversation, and magniloquence. Those are actual words. Translated into normal English they mean lofty style, the evasion of clear arguments, and the excessive use of ornamental words. I wrote this book in what I hope is a clear, compelling, cogent, and even conversational tone. This casual approach shouldn't be confused with a lack of seriousness—on the contrary, I take writing as seriously as research. More important than being a scholar, I'm a relatively normal guy. I work hard to write and sound like one without hiding behind the dense and confounding fog of academic-ese.

What can you expect in the pages ahead? The bulk of this book is a tour in and around the words and worlds of the DSS in nine chapters.

In chapter 1 we'll establish an outline of the DSS by looking at the first seven texts found in Qumran Cave 1. Intriguingly, this group of seven represents most of the types, categories, or genres of writings of the one thousand–plus fragmentary scrolls discovered in other caves. It's a good opener and great first impression.

Next up in chapter 2 we'll explore the story of the discovery of the scrolls. Of course, we'll cover some baseline facts, but we'll also learn a lot about what such discovery narratives tell us about the expectations and biases of the modern cultures creating and telling these tales. This won't be your usual take on the discovery of the DSS, I promise.

The big headline story in the world of DSS research lately is potential new discoveries, withheld finds, and even forgeries. In chapter 3, we'll walk the line between opportunity and risk, and see that there is big business today in trafficking antiquities and peddling multimillion-dollar souvenirs to museums, churches, academic institutions, armchair collectors, and just about anyone with a checkbook.

Chapter 4 takes us back in time. We'll rewind into the ancient world and try and determine which Jewish group is associated with the DSS and likely lived at the site of Qumran. These scrolls didn't just fall from the sky. Understanding who penned and preserved them before they became an accidental time capsule in the Judean wilderness will help us understand the DSS and Qumran, as well as their context in the broader life, thought, culture, and identities of Jewish groups in the Second Temple period.

Then in chapter 5 it's on to rocks, rubble, and remains. One of the remarkable and rare elements of the DSS is they are paired with an archaeological site of the community who lived more than two thousand years ago. In this chapter we'll take a day trip of sorts to the Dead Sea region and the site of Qumran, with the aim of recovering some aspects of the lives of the actual human beings associated with the scrolls. We'll even study an ancient toilet.

In chapter 6 we'll dive into the biblical scrolls and see how they're both remarkably similar and revolutionarily different in details from other biblical texts in Hebrew, Aramaic, and Greek. We'll restore some readings for modern Bibles and expand our understanding of the shape and scope of Scripture in antiquity. We'll also learn some new lessons from error-riddled fragments that change how we think about the formation and reconstruction of Scripture.

With the wider world of Scripture in view, chapter 7 reveals how ancient scribes not only created texts; they also crafted traditions around the authority of famous figures from the scriptural past. This exploration will include previously unknown writings that reimagine and extend the authority of Scriptures. It will also reintroduce some writings typically bundled up in other collections of so-called Pseudepigrapha or Apocrypha.

Chapter 8 brings us to my personal favorite DSS: the small but mighty collection of Aramaic writings. We'll meet dreamers and demons, hear about love affairs and lost books, crumbling empires and towering giants, and at least one instance of a divinely dispatched case of the clap. (You read that right. I'm not making this stuff up.)

In chapter 9 we'll explore the intersection of ideas between the world of the DSS and that of the early Jesus movement. Here we'll see that the scrolls help us read in between the lines to recover lost or overlooked ideas, tensions, and theologies in the Gospels and writings of Paul.

In the conclusion, we'll loop back to the opening questions above to reflect on what the DSS challenge, change, and confirm about the words of scripture and worlds before, in, and beyond the Bible. But before we get there, we'll need to press into these lost words and forgotten worlds of the DSS and be ready to ask how we make sense of them today.

The story of the DSS is still developing. This is your invitation to be part of it.

Chapter 1

First Impressions from Qumran Cave 1

I don't know how you feel about puzzles. But love them or hate them, I bet we can agree on two things: they're a whole lot more fun if you have all the pieces *and* the front of the box. Depending on your disposition to puzzling, the DSS are either the most epic or atrocious puzzle of all time. They're known as "scrolls," but in most cases they're scraps. Apart from a few nearly pristine and largely preserved texts, the collection consists of tattered and torn remains of some 930 ancient Jewish scrolls. Leave these out in the desert for two millennia, and things tend to deteriorate. So we have a lot of puzzle pieces.

Some scroll-scraps are of writings that later land in the Hebrew Bible and Old Testament. I'll refer to this shared heritage as "Hebrew Scriptures."[1] Most fragments, however, are of writings that were lost, forgotten, or unknown. We had no idea these writings existed until their recovery some seventy-five years ago in the Judean wilderness. In many such cases, we also don't know what the complete and original forms of those works would have looked like in the ancient world.

There you have it: thousands of fragments decayed through years of confinement in caves, an unknown number gone missing through accident or acquisition, and often no clue of what the overall texts are supposed to say. Great. Where do we start?

The initial DSS were recovered in 1947, but waves of discoveries continued into the mid-1950s, with local talent and professional archaeologists combing the cavernous cliffs off the northwest shores of the Dead Sea for more caves. By the mid-1950s, eleven caves—some natural, some carved out by human hands—were found to hold texts. After this initial flurry of activity, the speed of publication slowed to a turtle's pace and spanned several more decades.

As scholars and the public fumed with frustration over pauses in publication and perceived withheld secrets, in the early 1990s a clever hack by a tag team of researchers (Ben Zion Wacholder and Martin Abegg) reverse-engineered the entire library of the DSS by digitizing all the textual data of a card catalog concordance into a Macintosh computer database. The catalog had been developed by an early insider publication team working with the scrolls to aid their own work. A copy was made available to Wacholder and Abegg, whose at first controversial move made a brilliant breakthrough: the entirety of the collection was made available to all. Or so we thought.

Around the turn of the millennium, news of unseen fragments circulated. Buyers queued up, checkbooks were opened, and private institutions and museums clamored for the chance to own a piece of alleged Scripture. Not long after this, a band of archaeologists and scholars took to the Judean Desert yet again and discovered what appeared to be more caves that had once held material and textual items related to the scrolls, now lost or looted.[2]

So why throw all this on the table of already mixed and muddled puzzle fragments? Because first impressions matter. Our first impression of the scrolls must recognize that "discovery" was, and is, ongoing. These are ancient texts,

IMAGE 1.1: As discovery gave way to sorting and sifting, the early team of scholars working with DSS in the Palestinian Archaeological Museum in Jerusalem (now the Rockefeller Museum) organized fragments between glass plates. While this helped make the texts readily visible for identification, the pressure also damaged some fragments. (Image credit: Wikimedia Commons)

---

but they are bound to also be part of our modern world. Despite the many unknown variables of sifting, identifying, and deciphering the scrolls, first impressions matter. By reading the fragmentary texts strategically, and at times reading between the lines, the epic jigsaw puzzle of the DSS provides unprecedented insight into the thought, culture, belief, history, and practice of a foundational time for Western culture, formative to biblical literature and foundational for emerging Judaism and Christianity.

But which handful of puzzle pieces should we choose for our own first impression of the texts?

A Seven Scroll Sample of Cave 1

Our best bet is to wind back the clock to the very first finds of Qumran Cave 1, discovered in the winter of 1946–47. The exact nature of the discovery is, frankly, a tricky story and one I'll save for the next chapter. For our introductory interests it is significant that the initial cache from Qumran Cave 1 reflects the general types of literature of the entire DSS collection that would come to light—so it's a good place to start.

The first finds included seven fragmentary scrolls: two copies of Isaiah (1QIsaiah[a] and 1QIsaiah[b]), a commentary on Habakkuk, a rewritten Aramaic rendition of ancestral narratives known as the *Genesis Apocryphon*, a writing outlining the ideals of Qumran life and thought known as the *Community Rule*, a liturgical collection called the *Hodayot*, and an end-times playbook dubbed the *War Scroll*. Apart from the copies of Isaiah, all these texts were previously unknown. As a group, they provide a snapshot of the scope, content, and context of the DSS collection. They also help front some key insights and questions about the ideas and identity of the group that lived at Qumran.

The Fraternal Twins of 1QIsaiah[a] and 1QIsaiah[b]

Let's start our venture on some familiar turf: Isaiah. This beast of a book eventually shows up in the Hebrew Bible and the Old Testament. Well before this reception, however, Isaiah was an essential read for the group that lived at Qumran. The case of Isaiah provides some immediate and essential insights into scribes and scripture at Qumran.

First, it is significant that there are multiple copies of this book. In fact, 1QIsaiah[a] and 1QIsaiah[b] represent but a pair of some twenty-two fragmentary manuscripts of Isaiah in the Qumran collection. While counting manuscripts is not always a reliable method for determining how significant or meaningful a given book was to the Qumran community—remember, this is a damaged and fragmentary library—having a single work in these numbers

IMAGE 1.2: Unlike the pristine specimen of 1QIsaiah[a], seen in a sample image last chapter, most other DSS were found in various states of decay. For example, the Aramaic *Genesis Apocryphon* from Cave 1, was in a near mummified roll. Once dissected, much of its contents could be deciphered but several lines and column sections were lost or damaged. (Image credits: © Israel Museum, Jerusalem, Shrine of the Book; bottom two images by Ardon Bar-Hama)

is one criterion suggesting it was authoritative for the group that penned or preserved the DSS.

Second, the scribal hands of these two manuscripts date to the first century BCE (1QIsaiah[a]) and to around the turn of the Common Era (1QIsaiah[b]).[3] This means we're in a world that was centuries before the Bible and the media form of a book even existed. This is an era of scripture cultivated by scribes on scrolls.

Third, the textual profile of these two Cave 1 copies of Isaiah reveals both great similarities and many differences. Isaiah 41:11 illustrates this, with the main difference noted in italics:

> 1QIsaiah[a]: "Look! All who are incensed at you will be disgraced and put to shame. Those who contend with you *will all die*."

> 1QIsaiah[b]: "Look! All who are incensed at you will be disgraced and put to shame. Those who contend with you *will become nothing and be ashamed*."

These verses mostly parallel one another, but there is a critical variation—you might say a life-or-death situation. This difference—known as a "textual variant"—may seem slight to some, but I'd say a death sentence versus embarrassment is a big deal. Were we to track this against the Septuagint (the ancient Greek translation of the Hebrew Scriptures), we would see further diversity within this unity. But we'll save some of those comparisons for chapter 7.

What does this mean for our first impression? The world of Qumran is one where texts, including those of most books of Hebrew Scripture, are still developing. Their core content in most cases was stable, yet not static. While our initial interest in the modern day might be in mining this data for "new" readings that are actually very old, the Qumran community didn't seem to share our Western mindset that insists on fixed forms of texts. The world of Qumran is one where differences were points for conversation, traditions were bigger and better than any single manuscript, and scribes rose to the challenge of both transmitting traditions and innovating texts.

Conversing with and Critiquing Culture in *Pesher Habakkuk*

Our pair of Isaiah texts hints that scripture was not fixed and scribes were not photocopiers. The commentary (known as a *pesher*) on Habakkuk from Qumran Cave 1 reveals that the interpretation of scripture was not something that occurred *after* the Bible was formalized. Rather, scriptural interpretation occurred simultaneously with the development of scripture itself.

Ancient Jewish scribes were deeply committed and creative exegetes. They constantly delved into their scriptural heritage, yet ever explored its contemporary relevance in a world of political, religious, economic, and institutional turmoil. Sound familiar? We might not always agree on their interpretations, but the DSS provide us with the beginnings of scriptural commentary and document an ancient community asking the timeless question: What does this ancient tradition mean today?

There are many genres of interpretive texts at Qumran, but this Habakkuk text, and others like it, are based on a rather bold assumption. While God spoke to the prophets ages ago, the *real* messages of those oracles were lost on them and needed to be unlocked *later* to a righteous teacher at Qumran. Why? Because this teacher claimed a fresh, exclusive, divine revelation to understand their true meaning. We find this expressed at the outset of the scroll in 1QpHab 7:1–5.

To unlock and convey this proprietary perspective, this Habakkuk commentary alternates between quotes and notes on scripture. These hinge on phrases based on the Hebrew word *peshar* (פשר), which rather conveniently means "interpretation."[4]

Let's see this in action. Take the sweet little scriptural nugget of Habakkuk 1:5: "Look at the nations and see! Be astonished! Be astounded! For a work is being done in your days that you would not believe if you were told."

Nice little verse, right? Doesn't everybody want something radical, remarkable, and world-changing to transpire in their own days? Turns out

IMAGE 1.3: Though fragmentary in places, Pesher Habakkuk is a relatively well-preserved manuscript from Qumran Cave 1, likely created in 50–1 BCE. The sample columns shown here also include several material features relating to the making of the scroll (horizontal dry rule lines for inscribing text and vertical dry rule lines for margins) and the use of the scroll (marginal Xs and lines as well as updated text written in between some lines). (Image Credit: © Israel Museum, Jerusalem, by David Harris)

---

the Qumranites did too. After quoting this passage, the interpreter of *Pesher Habakkuk* offers his interpretation:[5]

> [This passage refers to] the traitors with the Man of the Lie, because they have not [obeyed the words of] the Teacher of Righteousness from the mouth of God. It also refers to the trai[tors to the] New [Covenant], because they did not believe in God's covenant [and desecrated] His holy name; and finally, it refers [to the trai]tors in the Last Days. (1QpHab 2:1–6)

Bet you didn't see that coming. One minute this sounds like a cozy verse we could plaster on a fridge magnet, then *wham!* Liars, traitors, abandoning the faith, desecration, and, just for good measure, the end of all things. (Now that would make for more interesting fridge deco.)

This interpretation is unexpected—to us. But it provided a way of constructing meaning and identity from scripture for the Qumran community. Within this specialized interpretation are sound bites of lost conversations and controversies between two priests who parted ways, one of whom retreated into the wilderness to found a new movement. We don't know *who* he was—though many have guessed—but we know he was foundational in the early days of the movement and the memory of him loomed large for the group that lived at Qumran. The memory and mention of this figure shows up in several DSS writings.

The scribe of *Pesher Habakkuk* was culturally conversant and aware of geopolitical events, and leveraged cryptic hints in scripture to critique current events and chart a way forward where the good guys win. When it came to a verse like Habakkuk 1:11—"Then they sweep by like the wind; they transgress and become guilty; their own might is their god!"—the interpreter perceived a message about the scandalous, oppressive, imperial power of the Romans.

> This refe[rs t]o the rulers of the Kittim (i.e., the Romans), who cross the land by the advice of a family of sinn[ers]: each before his fellow, [their] rulers come, one after the other, to devastate the la[nd. (1QpHab 4:10–13)

Again, a little unexpected, but insightful for understanding how the Qumran group saw themselves at an intersection between the scriptural past and the turbulent present.

What does *Pesher Habakkuk* add to our first impression? The Qumran group may have been geographically separated from society, but they were intellectually invested, spiritually aware, politically charged, and culturally conversant. All these qualities helped them define their identity and orientation to outsiders, be they other Jews down the road in Jerusalem or the emperor in Rome.

From our perspective, the world around the Qumran group was scarcely accounted for in both confessional and Western culture's memory of the "biblical" past. The culture and history *Pesher Habakkuk* rails against is one *later* than narratives of the Hebrew Bible or Old Testament and *earlier* than the traditions of the Mishnah or New Testament. Readers of Christian Bibles are particularly susceptible to missing this, as the history is largely unrepresented and unaccounted for due to that tissue paper time machine I mentioned last chapter. But the DSS come from this world. In this way, *Pesher Habakkuk* is a reminder that the DSS are as much about engaging with new *contexts* as they are encountering new *texts*.

Remaking the Hebrew Past in the Aramaic *Genesis Apocryphon*

Today, many associate the book of Genesis with cosmic beginnings. For many ancient and modern readers, however, it is a book of origins of a different sort: the beginning of boundless questions. You can't get far into Genesis without hitting hard questions. If nobody else was around, why was Cain paranoid about murder (Genesis 4)? Why did evil persist after its apparent eradication in the flood (Genesis 6–8)? How could Lot offer up his two young daughters for sexual abuse to save his own skin (Genesis 19)? What red stew recipe is delicious enough to sell your birthright (Genesis 25)? The list goes on.

While *pesher*-type texts commented on scripture by alternating with quotes and comments, the scribe of the Aramaic *Genesis Apocryphon* from Cave 1 did so by rewriting within the text. Something like a modern remade film, the *Genesis Apocryphon* aimed to capture the timeless qualities and authoritative aura of the original while remaking, retelling, and rewriting it so that it was edifying, instructive, and even entertaining for a new generation.

How did this play out two millennia ago in the *Genesis Apocryphon*? Quite often, the creative-interpretive flair occurred when the scribe perceived a hook, gap, or loose thread in the narratives of early ancestral figures, specifically Lamech, Noah, and Abraham. To ensure this message was mobile and intelligible to a wide audience, he penned the interpretation of the Hebrew book of Genesis in Aramaic, a common imperial language of the day. We'll regroup around the Aramaic collection among the DSS in chapter 9.

Let's look at a sample scene of this Aramaic remake and retrace the origins of the scribe's questions in Hebrew Genesis.

The *Genesis Apocryphon* often expands sordid sections of scripture. Take the preflood narratives of Genesis 5 and 6. Smack in the middle of this section of genealogies and a portrait of the righteous Noah, Genesis 6:1–4 casually references angelic beings who abandoned their heavenly posts for a one-night stand with human women, resulting in a hybrid race of giants known as the *Nephilim*. Wait, what? It's in there—go have a read. The Bible isn't boring.

Of all the interpretive questions presented by this tiny passage—and there are tons!—the scribe of the *Genesis Apocryphon* noted a potential ambiguity over Noah's genealogy. Could a reader/hearer of this story think that Noah's parentage was mixed up in this angelic paternity fiasco? That would be awkward.

Just to be sure, the scribe retells the narrative by making room for a scene between Lamech and Batenosh, Noah's birth (and earth) parents. Lamech suspects Noah may be a child of the fallen angels from Genesis 6:4 and, despite Batenosh's pleas to the contrary, travels to his all-knowing grandfather, Enoch, to find certainty on the matter.

What does this sample from the *Genesis Apocryphon* add to our first impression of the DSS via Qumran Cave 1? First, it confirms that Aramaic texts were part of this predominantly Hebrew—with a bit of Greek—collection. About 15 percent of the overall collection was written in this common, ancient Near Eastern language. Aramaic literature connects our story of the DSS to a much broader ancient Jewish intellectual culture in the context of empire.

Second, the *Genesis Apocryphon* reveals that scriptural interpretation was dynamic and was often an activity internal to texts, extending traditions. Scribes of such traditions often (re)presented the material in first-person voices of famous figures to show that the past continued to have a voice in the present. The technical term for this is "pseudepigraphy."[6] This was not trickery, but reverence. It was a way of capturing voices from the past and ensuring that they continued to speak.

Third, the *Genesis Apocryphon* reminds us that our vexing interpretive concerns or eventual explanations may not be the same as ancient ones. At times, this means we can recover insights from the ancient world, as well as correcting dominant or biased interpretations. Did you notice in the above example that Lamech's wife has both a name and a voice (neither of which she has in Genesis)? A forgotten ancient Aramaic interpretation of Genesis provides an unexpected modern departure point for opening up critical questions related to gender in and beyond scripture.

The "Way" of the *Community Rule*

The materials introduced so far have been, at most, within a degree of relation to books from the Hebrew Scriptures. The final three of the initial Cave 1 finds are not biblical texts or interpretations. This is not to say they weren't authoritative. Rather, it is a reminder that as we leave the crutch of modern cultural and canonical categories behind, we venture further into the ancient world where our ideas, concepts, and convictions are increasingly foreign or demand nuance.

This is nowhere more apparent than in reading the *Community Rule*, which from the very first line describes itself as a brand-new genre: a "rule" (*serekh*; סרך) text guiding the life and thought of a group.

While early church followers were once referred to as members of "the Way" (Acts 19:23), the *Community Rule* lays claim to the nickname for the

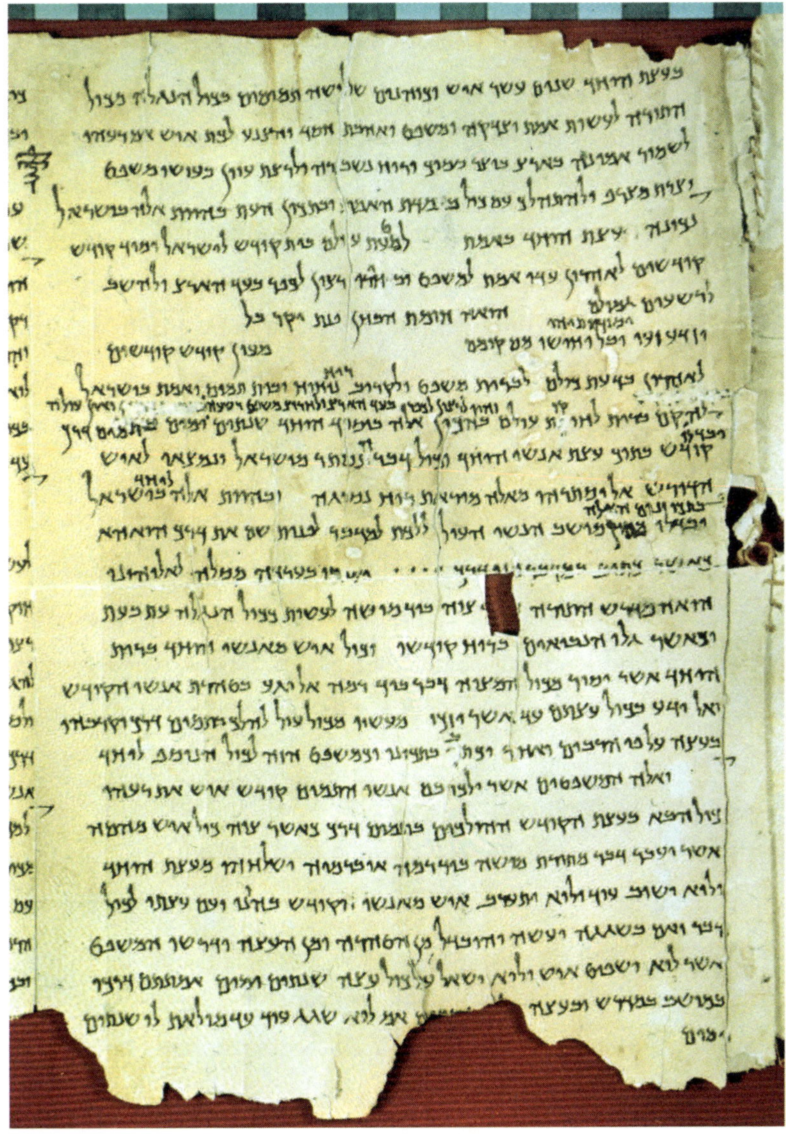

IMAGE 1.4: The Cave 1 copy of the Community Rule dates to around 100–75 BCE and includes additional rule texts appended to the main composition (1QSa and 1QSb), which provide views of community identity and practice as well as eschatological and messianic outlooks. The discovery of additional copies of Community Rule texts in Cave 4 revealed that the text developed over time, likely in multiple forms. (Image Credit: John C. Trever)

Jewish group at Qumran well before the early Jesus movement. For both groups, however, this branding was scripturally inspired. *Community Rule* 8:10–20 references the phrase "preparing the way in the desert" from Isaiah 40:3 as the directive for forging into the barren wilderness to find new life, which led to the Qumran movement's self-understanding of being "the Way" (1QS 8:21). But what did being part of the Way at Qumran entail? It meant seeing the new Way as emerging from a scriptural way. In one instance, the text asserts that any time ten or more are gathered they "must always be engaged in study of the Law," accompanied by interpretation and prayer (1QS 6:6–8). As noted already in *Pesher Habakkuk,* the interpretation was bound to the authority and inspiration of their founding Teacher. To galvanize the association between this interpretation and insider identity at Qumran, *Community Rule* 8:17 speaks of expulsion for those who speak against the secret teachings of the community. Intriguingly, then as now, scripture itself was rarely the issue—it was the interpretation of traditions that constructed ideologies and boundaries.

It meant knowing one's place *within* the Way. This works itself out both hierarchically and practically. The *Community Rule* outlines an authority structure that touches on everything from new initiates, entry requirements, and reviews for life in the *Yahad* (יחד), a Hebrew term repeatedly used as a self-designation of the unity of the insider group.

Remaining unified, apparently, was a delicate enterprise. The *Community Rule* includes a penal code of infractions and punishments for a variety of actions—drifting off to sleep in a meeting, gossiping about a fellow member, grumbling against the *Yahad*, strolling around in the nude (1QS 6:24–7:25). The development of this material provides both glimpses into the practice of the movement and insight into how group identity was constructed through legal rulings and revision.[7] (By the way, just because I know you're curious, acts of ancient exhibitionism will get you six months reduced rations. Not to mention a likely sunburn.)

It meant not being part of *another* way. The *Community Rule* routinely juxtaposes two realities, often epitomized as the "children of light" and the "children of darkness." As a covenantal community with priestly roots, the *Yahad* was naturally on the bright side, often praising God for his foreordination of their position and calling down curses on those on the dark side, which included pretty much everyone else.

For example, in a priestly blessing we read, "May He (God) bless you with every good thing and preserve you from every evil." Then in nearly the same breath, the flipside: "May you be damned without mercy in return for your dark deeds, an object of wrath licked by eternal flame, surrounded by utter darkness." To which all new initiates respond, "Amen, amen" (1QS 2:2, 7, 10). Later, we learn these two sides are ruled by corresponding angels of light and darkness (1QS 3:13–26). This way of ordering the world and orienting themselves to it is often referred to as "dualism."

How does this *serekh* text contribute to our developing first impression of the DSS? First, the *Community Rule*, like all of the DSS, is a thoroughly Jewish text, written and/or received at Qumran before the advent of Christianity. This is not to say the DSS are irrelevant to the thought and writings of the early Jesus movement—more on that in a later chapter. But it is an important element about the DSS to clarify at the outset.

Second, as with any ancient text, the *Community Rule* must be interpreted. It is not a one-way mirror providing an exact view of the happenings of the Qumran community. Rules, even in rule texts, are as much about forming and maintaining boundaries and identity as they are about laying down the law. These are not necessarily journalistic reports on day-to-day life at Qumran.

Third, the Way does not seem to have been lived out in the single location of Qumran. The *Community Rule* outlines the ideas and ideals of a community that, at many turns, implies other clusters of like-minded groups beyond the salty shores of the Dead Sea. At the outset then, we should be open to how the DSS enable us to peer into unknown social and historical worlds *beyond* Qumran. We'll come back to the identity of the group behind the DSS in chapters 5 and 6.

The *Hodayot* and the Hymnic Imagination

As seen above, the *Community Rule* emphasized the importance of prayer for the Qumranites. As more texts were discovered, it became apparent that this group was not only investing in the study of scriptural prayers but was inventing new praises and prayers through an active liturgical life. The *Hodayot* of Cave 1 offered insight into the liturgical and poetic imagination of the group.[8] As with the Isaiah or Rule texts, subsequent discoveries of *Hodayot* scrolls and fragments revealed the importance of this work at Qumran. There are at least seven fragmentary copies of the *Hodayot* known among the DSS.

The Cave 1 *Hodayot* dates to around the turn of the Common Era and includes at least thirty previously unknown Hebrew poems and prayers. They are intimate, emotional, and include a blend of materials that both praise God and cry out to him. As Eileen Schuller commented, the poems of the *Hodayot* collection "are modeled on the biblical Psalms ... but there is considerable diversity in both form and content, rather than strict imitation of the biblical form."[9]

The common English title *Hodayot* is derived from the routine Hebrew phrase "I thank you, Lord" (אודכה אדוני) that frames many individual hymns and creates a current of thanksgiving throughout the collection. Many of these hymns are deeply personal, suggesting they are associated with the experience or memory of the community's Teacher. Expressions of anguish and affliction are juxtaposed with statements of confidence rooted in special revelation.

Note, for example, the first-person reflection: "You have appointed me as an object of shame and derision to the faithless, but a foundation of truth and

IMAGE 1.5: The first Cave 1 copy of the Hodayot (1QH[a]) includes a collection of hymns from the perspective of a community as well as an individual. The latter are often called "Teacher Hymns," as they perhaps originated or are later associated with the founding figure, the Teacher of Righteousness. Not unlike Isaiah, the Community Rule, and the *War Scroll*, the Cave 4 discoveries would later reveal additional Hodayot materials. The image here is an excellent example of the complex state of some scrolls, which even in their clustered and matted state provided glimpses of relatively well preserved, or at least legible, text contained within. (Image credit: Top, Prof. Bieberkraut at work opening the Thanksgiving scroll, © Israel Museum, Jerusalem; bottom photo © Israel Museum, Jerusalem, by David Harris)

understanding for the upright" (1QH^{a} 10:10–11). Elsewhere this remembered figure is thankful for divine deliverance and predestination: "They (the figure's adversaries) [did not kn]ow that my steps are directed by You." Edifices of identity are built higher as this individual affirms his inspired interpretive authority, for "You (God) have revealed yourself to me," contrasted with the outsiders and oppressors, who are "mediators of a lie and seers of deceit" (1QH^{a} 12:7–11).

In tandem with the so-called "Teacher hymns," the *Hodayot* includes poems that are oriented around the community's collective memory and outlook. At times, these echo sentiments of the Teacher-type hymns, such as thanksgiving for the revelation of mysteries and the certainty that God has determined all things and ways "before you created them" (1QH^{a} 5:17, 25). Community hymns also tend to ratchet up the hellfire and brimstone. In one hymn, the wicked were "created for [the time of] your [w]rath, from the womb you set them apart for the day of slaughter." Naturally, it's better to be on the flipside of this split, which leads to "everlasting salvation and everlasting peace" (1QH^{a} 7:29–30). There's that underpinning dualism again.

How does the *Hodayot* enhance our first impression? First, it connects us to writers and a community in the timeless struggle between belief in a God who foreordains all things and the conviction that prayer can somehow influence the course of action. Part of this reflection is carried on in the idioms and expressions inherited from the Psalms. It also reveals that, as hinted in the *Community Rule*, this was a thoroughly apocalyptic community.

Second, it affirms the idea and importance of interpretive authority in this movement. Be it access to a fountain of truth or revelation of special mysteries, the claim was that the creators and collectors of this hymnic material held the keys to proper life, practice, and thought.[10]

Third, it underscores the creativity of ancient scribes who traversed the boundaries of genres and topics. Here we have a collection of ancient Jewish poetry with strong doses of traditional wisdom and dashes of apocalyptic fervor, dotted across hymns thanking God for topics across the spectrum of human emotion and experience. They are at once particular and timeless. Because of its diversity, brilliance, and beauty, the *Hodayot* is a wonderfully difficult text to describe in only a few words. It's worth a read on your own.

The *War Scroll*: The Final Faceoff between Good and Evil

Our final Cave 1 text also sees the dawn of an apocalyptic age breaking on the horizon. Like the *Community Rule*, the *War Scroll* describes itself as a "Rule" text,[11] only now the words do not govern life in the present. Rather, they are a manual for the inevitable final battle between the "sons of light," the "sons of darkness," and their respective angelic forces (1QM 1:1). Since nothing spells suspense like a best-of-seven series, the *War Scroll* protracts the final faceoff between good and evil in a set of seven battles. Spoiler alert: the series goes to game seven, with God coming off the bench to best the battalions of evil.

We gain a glimpse of this dramatic conclusion late in the scroll. After six engagements, the tiebreaker comes when "the Kittim shall be crushed without [remnant and survivor. So] the God of Israel shall raise his hand against the whole multitude of Belial" (1QM 18:3). We already met the Kittim (a codeword for the Romans) in *Pesher Habakkuk*. Here the cipher includes them as well as anyone else not part of the light side.

Why this unrelenting angst against Rome and all others outside of the *Yahad*? In the Hellenistic period, key institutions like the Jerusalem temple and priesthood were, in the eyes of the *Yahad*, increasingly corrupted or coopted

IMAGE 1.6: The *War Scroll* from Cave 1 gives insight into the eschatological battle against the Romans and the Qumranites' expectations of triumph. Though not an apocalypse itself, the writing has a complex apocalyptic outlook, which informed group identity, intersected with concerns for purity, and galvanized the insider/outsider dichotomy of the community's self-understanding. Additional copies of *War Scroll* texts were later found in Caves 4 and 11. (Image credit: © Israel Museum, Jerusalem, by David Harris)

---

with imperial interests. The Maccabean revolt (167–160 BCE) offered hope to some for Jewish independence. Yet as time wore on, the religious-political interests of this coup-turned-temporary-kingdom appeased some, aggravated others, and resulted in the high priestly office becoming a political pawn. By the time the Romans rolled onto the scene in Judea, they quickly grew weary of charismatic leaders and uprisings. As Romans do, Romans did, and set about squashing them. The battle forecasted at the end of the age in the *War Scroll*, then, was meant to overturn the imperial domination and undo the increasing oppression suffered by some Jewish groups.

The site of Qumran was destroyed by the Romans in 68 CE as they chased a group of Jewish brigands into the desert to quell yet another revolt. Pause on that for a moment. Imagine the heartbreak and loss of the *Yahad* covenanters. Their home was reduced to ash soaked in their own blood by the very hands of what they conceived as the utter embodiment of evil. Darkness. Abomination. Presumably they rose to the occasion, perhaps expecting the beginning of the sevenfold battle. Yet tragically, they did not see the second engagement. In the archaeological record of Qumran, there are hints of this dramatic end, such as Roman tri-barbed arrowheads and ash.

While the *War Scroll* ends with an epic battle scene, most of the composition is occupied with what seem like mundane reviews of battle preparations: detailed descriptions of standards, elaborate accounts of trumpets, outlines of the duties of priestly officers, etc. On a closer read, however, these reveal key insights into belief and practice. Take for example the following pair of excerpts from the *War Scroll.*

> On the day of their battle against the Kittim, they shall g[o forth for] carnage in battle. In three lots the Sons of Light shall stand firm so as to strike a blow at wickedness, and in three the army of Belial shall strengthen themselves so as to force the retreat of the forces [of Light. And when the] banners of the infantry cause their hearts to melt, then the might of God will strengthen the he[arts of the Sons of Light.] In the seventh lot the great hand of God shall overcome [Belial and al]l the angels of his dominion, and all the men of [his forces shall be destroyed forever.] (1QM 1:12–15)

This eschatological optimism transitions into the finer points of battle in the columns that follow, including comment on the criteria for recruits:

IMAGE 1.7: Masada was an ancient fortress atop a plateau and cliff precipice to the south of Qumran, overlooking the Dead Sea. Once a summer palace of Herod, the site became a dramatic last stand of the first Jewish rebellion against Rome in 73–74 CE. Fragments of texts at Masada such as Songs of the Sabbath Sacrifice and the Genesis Apocryphon suggest some survivors from Qumran fled with scrolls in tow. According to the Jewish historian Josephus, the siege at Masada ended in a mass suicide of the Jewish rebels, who would rather fall to their own swords than concede defeat to Rome. (Photo credit: Faithlife)

> No youth nor woman shall enter their encampments from the time they leave from Jerusalem to go to battle until their return. No one crippled, blind, or lame, nor a man who has a permanent blemish on his skin, or a man affected with ritual uncleanness of his flesh; none of these shall go with them to battle. All of them shall be volunteers for battle, pure of spirit and flesh, and prepared for the Day of Vengeance. Any man who is not ritually clean in respect to his genitals on the day of battle shall not go down with them into battle, for holy angels are present with their army. (1QM 7:3–6)

Two details from these excerpts are essential for our first glance at the DSS: angels and purity. The conceptual world of Qumran and wider Judaism was populated with benevolent and malevolent spirits (for lack of better terms, angels and demons). One of these figures is name-dropped above: Belial, an ultimate demonic bad guy in Qumran thought. But there is also a liturgical element to all this. It was not simply that angels were lofty and "up there" or that demons were lingering "out there." On the contrary, through their worship and lifestyle, the *Yahad* believed heaven could touch earth, making it possible to intermingle with the heavenly host. In this end-of-days battle, angels were expected to be among the ranks, enjoined with the sons of light. This was literally a holy war.

With this way of thinking in place, the intense, almost obsessive specifics of battle preparations and purity concerns make far more sense. Along with an inspired-by-Leviticus list of items that could impute impurity, the *War Scroll* limits participation in the ranks by age, ethnicity, gender, and disability. Remember: this "Rule" war text is not for everybody. It is an exclusive operations manual for an insider group that is emphatically committed to retaining their cultic status among the company of angels.

We don't have to agree or like this approach to forming and maintaining religious identity. In fact, it is completely fine to see the DSS as at once inspiring for what they can offer as well as offensive for some of the ideas they endorse. Yet even the underside of the DSS can help us see something differently in the Jewish worlds of antiquity.

Take purity, for example. Though the stance on inclusion in the *War Scroll* is extreme and with an eye to an idealized future, consciousness around ritual purity in ancient Judaism is too often caricatured as some sort of trite fundamentalism. But this is historically inaccurate. In ancient Judaism, ritual purity in all its forms was less about rules to follow than it was about daily opportunities to embrace and live out a worshipful lifestyle. Impurity did not equal sin. In the case of the *War Scroll*, of course, the urgency is stronger still: no longer was the call to purity about daily life, but about ensuring survival on *the* day at the end of all life.

How does the *War Scroll* round out our first impression of the DSS? First, it helps us see the connectedness of traditions from the *Yahad*'s past, religious expression in the present, and expectations for an apocalyptic future. The *War Scroll* is steeped in scriptural allusion and routinely interacts with patterns of thought formative to the *Yahad*. These are blended into imaginative expectations where the end of the age is, as always, just around the corner.

Second, it underscores the importance of accounting for the religious practice of ancient Judaism as a key marker of identity. If a description of the DSS accounts only for their theological systems or textual significance, it is incomplete. This also reminds us of the need for nuance, or even correction, as some common understandings of ancient Jewish practice are misguided.

Third, this identity establishes boundaries between insiders and outsiders, yet it does not assume complete isolation. Rather, the construction and critiques of the "others"—whether imperial foes or other non-*Yahad* Jews—suggests the group behind this text was conversant with culture and up on their current events.

Conclusion

Our flyover in this chapter aimed at fronting writings: the DSS, as their name suggests, are *textual* objects. In the chapters that follow, we'll examine cross sections of texts in the Qumran collection to explore a range of topics. The seven scrolls discovered in Cave 1 provided a convenient point of departure for the general types of literature found in the rest of the caves, and gave us something of a primer on key issues. The outlines above are far from the final word on these texts, but they do provide a compass for navigating some of this uncharted world of lost texts.

The texts of the DSS are also *material* objects. They are archaeological items created and collected by a scribal culture that was unknown, yet under our noses, for the better part of two millennia. One of the most beautiful things about manuscript studies is experiencing these artifacts and studying everything around the inscribed words. We can gain incredible insights into scribal culture by studying how the words were inscribed and corrected, what was or wasn't included around the text, how a scroll was prepared or repaired, and in many cases how the text has deteriorated. This requires a basic sense of curiosity matched with the capacity for some observation. If you have eyeballs and a brain, preferably connected in some way, you are qualified for this type of activity. In our increasingly open-access age it is now possible to view the vast majority of the DSS online, thanks to the digitization efforts of the Israel Antiquities Authority (www.deadseascrolls.org.il) and the Shrine of the Book (http://dss.collections.imj.org.il). Scroll through the scrolls, and gain an impression of their material and scribal quality. Experience them.

Texts, however, are more than words penned on a page. The DSS are most importantly *cultural* objects. The scribes who created these materials and the communities that cherished them were—not unlike us—at different intersections in life. They reflected on scriptural traditions of the past and responded to the questions, concerns, practices, and ideas of the present. They were aware of the political atmosphere of their day and sought to speak into or against it as they defined identity boundaries. They were intensely theological yet practical in their religious expression, which at times cohered or clashed with other contemporary groups. They lived in a balance of hope and pain, anticipation and uncertainty. They were human. In these ways, the DSS reveal an almost entirely forgotten world shaped by timeless questions: Who are we? Where are we going? What is good? How do past, present, and future relate?

Behind these texts were real humans, in real time. The life and literature of the Qumran community, however, became an accidental time capsule. That is, until their modern discovery—which is a fantastic tale in every sense of the word.

Chapter 2

(Re)Discoveries in the Judean Desert: Fact, Fable, and Finding the Dead Sea Scrolls

The tales of the discovery of the DSS involve a blend of fact and fable: a wandering Bedouin shepherd boy, a lost sheep in the wilderness, a stone casually tossed into a cave, the unexpected *clink* of shattered pottery, the fortuitous discovery of a hoard of manuscripts, and their eventual rescue into the hands of Western scholars. Over the years, popular imagination has elevated the thrill meter and intrigue factor of this tale, giving it a near Indiana Jones–esque appeal.

Unlike Indy, I am not an archaeologist. But I am a professional interpreter of texts. I might not be able to interpret a pile of ancient rubble on the fly, but I know a good story when I hear one. I also know that stories, ancient or modern, evolve and change. We remember, forget, embellish, conflate, recreate, reorganize, and prioritize. Each new telling creates a new tale.

The discovery narrative of the DSS, as it is often told, is a great story. But like any story, it demands interpretation. Of course we all want to set the record straight about what *really* happened (history). But our job can't end with merely sifting for facts. We need to pause on the fable for one important reason: the *way* a story is told (historiography) is as important as the story itself.

Why? Because the way we tell stories about ancient finds reveals a great deal about our modern ideological interests, the sordid colonial realities of many antiquities' acquisitions, and our attempts to romanticize dusty objects to reconcile our own broken backgrounds.[1] But before we determine the *history* and dissect the *historiography* of the DSS find stories, let's talk a little Star Wars, medieval rockets, and Muhammad 'Ali.

Exploding Kitties, Medieval Wookies, and the Cultural Curb Appeal of Manuscript Finds

Ancient and medieval manuscripts are remarkably newsworthy in our present day. Take, for example, two recent digitization announcements that came across my news feed. The first press release came from a team at the University of Pennsylvania, who boldly announced that they had discovered jetpack cats in a medieval manuscript. Researchers had recovered a sixteenth-century CE illustrated theoretical military manual that pondered the potential of strapping primitive bombs to animals set loose behind enemy lines. Ethics aside, at a logistical level this is a terrible idea: where does your cat return at the end of the day? "Welcome home, Ginger." *Kaboom!*

A second story claimed that researchers had discovered Star Wars characters in a series of medieval manuscripts. The article explained how researchers at the British Library found a series of drawings in medieval manuscripts that, on first glance, look very much like Yoda, Leia, and Chewbacca. Turns out these were artistic depictions adorning the margins a fourteenth-century CE French manuscript of the Smithfield Decretals, which includes a collection Catholic canon law of the period. Intergalactic, hardly, but insightful nonetheless.[2]

These news items demonstrate a widespread academic effort and resurgent popular interest in antiquities for uncovering something forgotten or overlooked in our cultural memory. These objects carry not only inscribed texts but the allure of a lost world.

They are also excellent examples of how, in order to capture the cultural interest of a modern audience, discoveries must be presented in a way that underscores their significance and meaning on the terms of the discovering culture. Sure, antiquities and discoveries are important, but they're really only headline-worthy if it matters to *me* on *my* terms. While the above newsy items are pretty harmless, these trends become far more problematic when it comes to the discovery narratives of the DSS—what I'll call "find stories"—and other key manuscript finds from the past few centuries.

Discoveries Obscured by Time and Legend: Calls for Caution in Vintage Textbooks

There are many detailed accounts of the circumstances that led to the discovery of the DSS. These range from impressions by the first generation of DSS scholars, found in several now-vintage introductions and in more recent and comprehensive accounts based on research, interviews, correspondence, and archival study. While few contemporary DSS introductions proceed with such candor, some of our earliest descriptions of the DSS include essential provisos about the complex and clouded nature of the circumstances leading to the finds.[3]

Before telling the tale of the discovery, Frank Moore Cross Jr. warns the reader, "The story of the first cave has been obscured by time and legend. This circumstance, it must be confessed, is due less to the faulty memories of the native discoverers than to the fervid imagination of Western writers."[4]

At the time, the content and scope of scrolls were known only to a small group of scholars, with Cross at the helm. Writing less than a decade after the original discoveries, Cross sensed the hard facts of discovery were circulating with increasingly soft edges. And those softening them came from a culture with a vested interest in both capturing the significance of the new texts and cultivating a heroic story. From early on, a Western fog lingered over these discoveries from the Near East.

IMAGE 2.1: The interest in revisiting ancient or medieval manuscripts for fresh insight cuts across disciplines. Discoveries in these cases were less about a new text and more about a fresh perspective on overlooked or unknown aspects of culture, thought, and art. The rocket cat image here is from a German artillery manual by Franz Helm (ca. 1500–67), a self-described "shooter, cannoneer and fireworker." (Image credit: Wikimedia Commons)

IMAGE 2.2: The seeming Star Wars-esque figures here—Yoda, Wookies, and an unmasked Darth Vader—are from the Smithfield Decretals (ca. 1300-1340 CE). (Image Credit: Wikimedia Commons)

Another key aspect of the DSS find stories in these throwback introductions (though increasingly less in many that followed) is that there is not one but at least two versions of the story of the discovery. After all, every great story exists in multiple forms.

Before offering his attempt at navigating the differences, R. K. Harrison flagged this duality for the reader. He wrote of the discovery of "an amazing number of manuscripts" which seem to predate other known Hebrew writings. The problem? In the next sentence, he lets on that "different accounts exist of the manner in which the original discovery was made."[5] Though not part of the insider publication team, Harrison was also writing within years of the news of the discovery. But even as a scholar at arm's length from the texts themselves, Harrison perceived the duplicity and disagreement of emerging renditions of the find story. From an early time, the tale has been complicated by a mix of fact and fiction.

Far be it from me to romanticize the past in a chapter such as this. But perhaps these were more sensible times: both Cross and Harrison's books have a cover price of $1.25. Those were the days! Yet the initial hesitancy over the "facts," and candor regarding the growing "fable," or at least fog, of the discovery narrative in these vintage textbooks provide an ideal departure point for rethinking the modern tale that has become part of the pitch that accompanies the DSS.

The "Fabulous Story" of "Ordinary Caves"

Let's look at two renditions of the discovery tale of the DSS from another set of vintage scrolls introductions. This sample captures the content and contours of the commonly taught and popularized versions of the story.[6] After sifting the problems from the prospects of these narratives, we'll circle back to a plausible timeline of events. For now, let's listen closely to *how* the story is told.

The first comes from A. Powell Davies's 1956 introduction, *The Meaning of the Dead Sea Scrolls*. Davies begins on a somewhat ironic note. The beginning of the book blurb at once promises to deliver "the true facts about one of the most amazing discoveries of our time" and then proceeds to capitalize on "the fabulous story of the Dead Sea Scrolls."[7] A few pages later, Davies provides an outline of the details of discovery.

> Early in the spring of 1947, some Bedouins of the Ta'amire tribe took a roundabout journey from Transjordan into Palestine. It is said that they wished to avoid the legal point of entry at the frontier since the merchandise they were transporting was contraband. The route that they chose took them through desolate country to the springs at 'Ain Feshka on the northwest shore of the Dead Sea. Here they replenished their supply of fresh water and lingered for a while before going on to the markets at Bethlehem.

With the scene and characters set, Davies continues to craft the action.

> While they were waiting, one or more of their number climbed the cliffs not far from the shoreline, and, either accidentally or as a result of a search, discovered a cave. The true details of the story may never be disclosed. It is known, however, that the Ta'amire Bedouins were not without previous experience in exploring caves and that they were astute vendors of whatever they happened to find.[8]

If you're familiar with the standard issue story of the scrolls, you've likely noted the absence of some common themes and characters. No shepherd boy. No lost goat. No stone. No clink. Just a cave.

Take two is from John Allegro who, like Cross, was a member of the insider scholarly group working on the scrolls. In his 1956 book *The Dead Sea Scrolls: A Reappraisal* we find more of the elements absent from Davies's sample and inch closer to the version of the tale that eventually won the day. Allegro related the drama that played out in the wilderness of Judea in 1947 this way:

> Muhammad Adh-Dhib had lost a goat. The lad was a member of the Ta'amireh tribe of semi-Bedouin who range the wilderness between Bethlehem and the Dead Sea area, and he had been out all this summer's day tending the animals entrusted to his care. Now one of them had wandered, skipping into the craggy rocks above. Muhammad pulled himself wearily up the limestone cliffs calling the animal as it went higher and higher in search of food.

With the stage, cast, and climate set, Allegro elevates the drama and builds curiosity for the leading character, Muhammad.

> The sun became hotter, and finally the lad threw himself into the shade of an overhanging crag to rest a while. His eye wandered listlessly over the glaring rocks and was suddenly arrested by a rather queerly placed hole in the cliff face, hardly larger than a man's head. It appeared to lean inwards to a cave, and yet was too high for an ordinary cave entrance, of which there were hundreds round about. Muhammad picked up a stone and threw it through the hole, listening for the sound as it struck home. What he heard brought him sharply to his feet. Instead of the expected thud against solid rock, his sharp ears had detected the metallic ring of pottery. He listened a moment, and then tried again, and again there could be no doubt that his stone had crashed among potsherds.

With the curiosity crescendo at its fullest, Allegro's telling of the story brings the reader to the moment of discovery.

> A little fearfully the Bedouin youth pulled himself up to the hole, and peered in. His eyes were hardly becoming used to the gloom when he had to let himself drop to the ground. But what he had seen in those few moments made him catch his breath in amazement. In the floor of the cave, which curved back in a natural fault in the rock, there were several large cylindrical objects standing in rows. The boy pulled himself up again to the hole, and holding on until his arms and fingers were numb, saw, more clearly this time, that they were large, wide-necked jars, with broken pieces strewn all about them. He waited no longer, but dropped to the ground and was off like a hare, his goat and flock forgotten in a frantic desire to put as much distance between himself and his jinn-ridden cave as possible. For who else but a desert spirit could be living in such a place with an entrance too small for a man?[9]

Allegro goes on to describe Muhammad relaying the discovery to his superiors. Though initially critical of Muhammad's report, they return with him to the location and find the pottery and texts as promised. Allegro then describes the herders in surprising terms. Not only are they superstitious and frightened of spirits (or "jinn") lurking in the crags, but, he says, these Bedouins "have no real home. The world is their prey and usually their enemy ... they practiced highway robbery when they could, and always found a ready market for their trading, legal or illegal, in Bethlehem."[10] Not so flattering. In addition to that, Allegro's version presents several open questions and unknowns.

These questions (arguably) all focus on facts. But what is it about the *way* these stories developed as fables that demands our interpretation? Many things. Sometimes the best place to find introspection is from a little outside perspective. For this, let's place the DSS discovery narratives alongside another famous tale of ancient text discovery that sent ripples across biblical research.

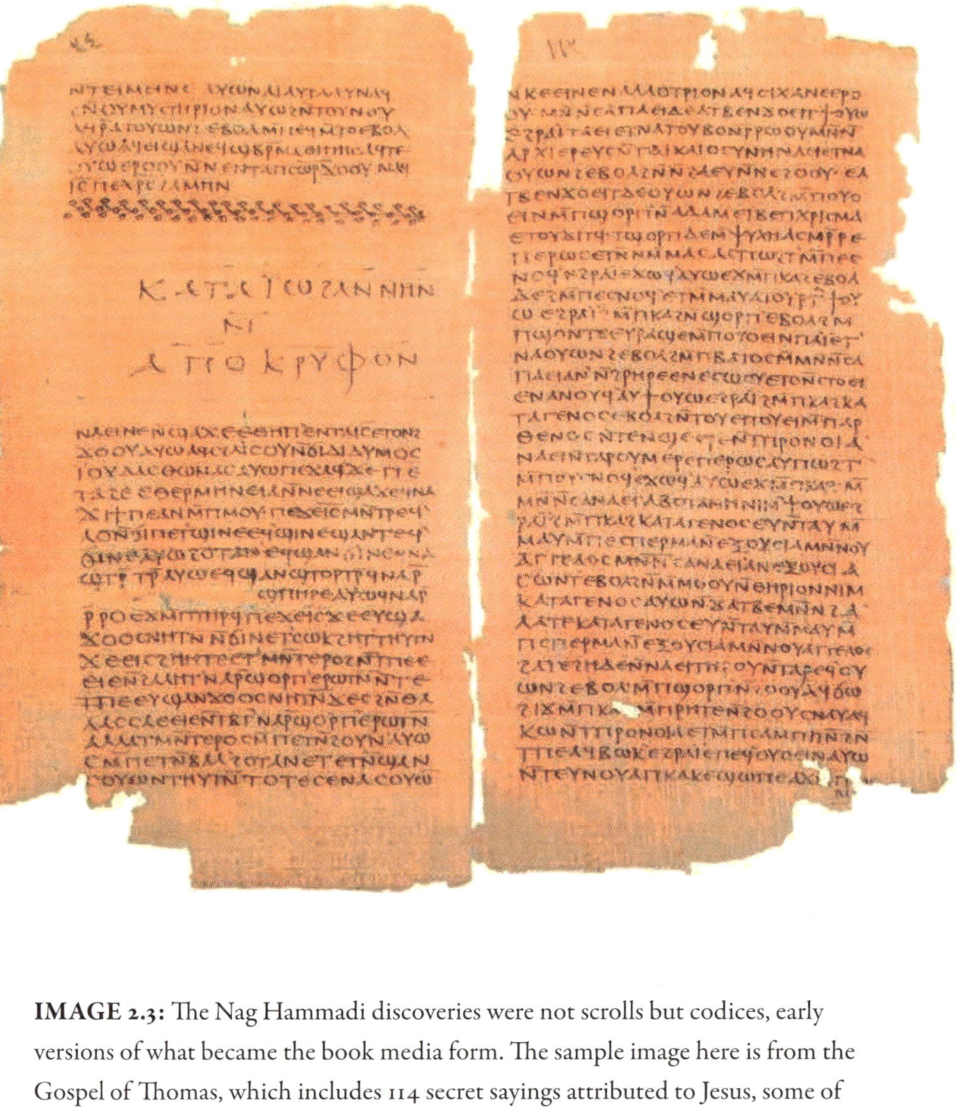

IMAGE 2.3: The Nag Hammadi discoveries were not scrolls but codices, early versions of what became the book media form. The sample image here is from the Gospel of Thomas, which includes 114 secret sayings attributed to Jesus, some of which have parallels in the New Testament gospels and are a source for assessing both similarities and sources for early gospel traditions. (Image credit: Wikimedia Commons)

Muhammad 'Ali's (Not the Boxer) Discovery of Lost Christian Texts

The Nag Hammadi collection of so-called "Gnostic" texts, from the town of Nag Hammadi in Upper Egypt, first came to light in 1945. Not unlike the discovery of the DSS, this discovery offered up new texts and contexts for exploring religious history, practice, belief, and identity in antiquity. This time, however, the materials related to an early variety of Christianity we hear but echoes of in the New Testament.[11]

The Nag Hammadi codices discovery story also exists in a variety of forms that mix fact and fable.

For our purposes, Elaine Pagels's 1979 volume *The Gnostic Gospels* provides a short version that includes many common elements of the find story of the Nag Hammadi codices. She writes:

> In December 1945 an Arab peasant made an astonishing archeological discovery in Upper Egypt. ... Thirty years later the discoverer himself, Muhammad 'Ali al-Samman, told what happened. Shortly before he and his brothers avenged their father's murder in a blood feud, they had saddled their camels and gone out to the Jabal to dig for *sabakh*, a soft soil they used to fertilize their crops.

Here too we have a simple scene set and characters introduced, only now with a notable nod to a suspenseful backstory that will come into play later. Pagels continues:

> Digging around a massive boulder, they hit a red earthenware jar, almost a meter high. Muhammad 'Ali hesitated to break the jar, considering that a *jinn*, or spirit, might live inside. But realizing that it might also contain gold, he raised his mattock, smashed the jar, and discovered inside thirteen papyrus books, bound in leather. Returning to his home in al-Qasr, Muhammad 'Ali dumped the books and loose

> papyrus leaves on the straw piled on the ground next to the oven. Muhammad's mother, 'Umm-Ahmad, admits that she burned much of the papyrus in the oven along with the straw she used to kindle the fire.[12]

If the drama of a new discovery didn't offer enough intrigue, Pagels goes on to relate how, weeks after the find, Muhammad 'Ali and his brothers avenged the death of their father by violently dismembering the accused, tearing out his heart, and feasting upon it as revenge. The resulting tale is one of danger and intrigue, enchantment and loss—but ultimately, for the eventual Western acquirers of these texts, a (relatively) happy ending.

Though unrelated to the texts and times of Qumran and the DSS, the shaping of the Nag Hammadi codices find story provides an intriguing parallel. Eva Mroczek has commented that by reflecting on these tales in tandem we can uncover how modern academic culture orients itself to "a mysterious textual past ... that always flickers uncertainly between the danger of loss and the possibility of sudden, dramatic discovery."[13] There is an allure here, a hook, that Indiana Jones–esque undertone. On the surface, the tales are about lost texts nearly compromised by *actors* within the story. Yet if we dig deeper, such find stories often say more about the lost identities that matter to the *audience*, which is both creating and relating the tale.

Qumran, Nag Hammadi, and the Modern Making of Find Stories

You probably already heard the echoes between these discovery narratives of ancient writings at two distant sites. Most of these echoes relate to plot formation, recurring motifs, and characterization. These provide insight less into the facts than the formation of the fables.

Let's start with the setting and plot. Both Goodacre and Mroczek note the "orientalizing" that is foundational for these tales. By that, they mean a romanticized view of an exotic world and time in the East that sets the scene. The plots build on the suspense and intrigue of a setting that is largely a construct of Western minds. This view did not develop out of thin air. It relates to the sort of lore popularized in *The Thousand and One Nights* (also known as *The Arabian Nights*), which entered the Western cultural imagination via translations in eighteenth-century Europe.[14] Orientalism provided a cognitive construct of what Westerners might expect or wish these worlds looked like, and within which they could craft a plot informed by their own preconceptions.

This brings us to setting and cast. In find stories, the scenes and characters are also orientalized. But these and other elements are also shaped by the realities of colonialism in Africa and the Near East, which had (and have) significant impacts on the life, economics, politics, and cultures of the regions of our find stories from the early twentieth century to today.[15]

Let's start with Egypt, the locale of the Nag Hammadi discoveries. Egypt was technically an independent state in 1922. But in the aftermath of World War II Britain still had boots on the ground in Egypt, and remained influential in directing Egyptian relations, communications, and policy until 1952. In the case of the DSS, although the 1947 United Nations partition plan established the modern state of Israel, this restructuring took place on the heels of British-controlled Mandatory Palestine in the interwar and post–World War II period. This is why so many black and white images of our discovery narratives feature Land Rovers and Brits: Empire.

These few sentences cannot do justice to the diverse, complex, and interrelated dynamics of land, identity, and conflicts in these regions. But for the purposes of interrogating find stories, it should be no surprise that the protagonists in our tales are largely the white, Western, male, elite who can read the texts, recognize their significance, and then heroically rescue them.

From whom? There is a clear juxtaposition of these protagonists with the naive, hapless natives of Arab descent. In both the DSS and Nag Hammadi find stories, the discoverers are curious yet superstitious about the lurking jinn. There is an undeniable colonial caricature of these non-Western characters that is common in find stories.

Of course, no plot or cast of characters could exist were they not bound together by a carefully crafted set of themes and motifs. Note for example, the recovery of lost texts from storage jars, which are shattered to reveal the treasure inside. These discoveries are presented as a happy accident. There is also a common theme of the near or actual destruction of some of the textual discoveries. For the Nag Hammadi texts, it some were reportedly burned in a fire. For our DSS stories, it's not uncommon to hear that the Bedouins wanted to use the leather of the scrolls to make shoes. Malevolent *jinn* spirits lurking in the desert are also a common fixture. All of these motifs add to the suspense and superstition of what was in one moment miraculously found and in the next nearly lost.

How should this comparison between the tales inform our perspective on the DSS? In a word: awareness. Yes, these texts were found. (As far as I know, there isn't a single version of the story that says they plummeted from the sky.) Yet find stories are as much a mirror for the receiving culture as they are a window into initial discovery. This mirror often reflects what the Western heroes perceive, or project onto, the foreign contexts of fortuitous finds. It also reveals how the meaning and significance of such finds are, literally, not native to the discovering culture but assigned by the Western protagonists.

While this approach to discovery narratives does not overturn the fact that the texts were indeed found, it does open some unexpected opportunities. In a broad sense, any first encounter with the DSS that starts and ends at Qumran misses the panoramic possibilities of these materials. Qumran is a tiny site, secluded in its own tiny part of the desert. When it comes to setting ancient and sacred texts in perspective, bigger is always better.

More significantly, while we might want to rush to the task of *interpretation* of the DSS to decipher what they say and mean, we would be wise to accept the invitation to *introspection* about how our own cultural perspectives, theological presuppositions, or individual interests inform our approach to the texts. We read everything through some lens or other. Even claiming no lens at all is a perspective, and generally not a very good one.

Pausing at the outset to identify the hues of our individual, cultural, or confessional lenses doesn't mean we have to go into this lost and forgotten world blind, or abandon our perspectives altogether. It simply means acknowledging that, as readers of texts or tellers of tales, we always play a role in the process of finding and organizing meaning. This awareness is foundational for any act of interpretation and contextualization. With this different take on the making of find stories, we can now establish a framework of facts for the modern discovery of the ancient DSS.

What Really Happened Out There in the Judean Desert? Lessons from the Story of the *Genesis Apocryphon*

It's tricky to arrive at an accurate account of the entire scope and stages of discovery for a manuscript find as extensive as the DSS. There are simply too many variables, unknowns, and complexities, too many storylines and subplots. Maybe part of the challenge is we're used to telling the discovery of DSS as a *group*. Perhaps we could get a better sense of the nonnegotiables and sidestep embellishments by following the trail of a *single* scroll.

Since we already know about the initial wave of finds from the last chapter, let's enlist the Aramaic *Genesis Apocryphon* as our candidate. This will give us a great example of a particular case, as well as provide elements of a larger framework for the DSS as a collection. How did this text go from an ancient cave in the Judean wilderness to a modern museum vault?[16]

Last chapter, I noted that this manuscript was discovered in Cave 1. What I didn't tell you was that it wasn't recovered by Muhammad ed-Dib, the young sheepherder of the Ta'amireh Bedouin people, in his first foray into the cave. I also didn't tell you that those seven scrolls weren't found all at once. After

IMAGE 2.4: Muhammad ed-Dib, the member of the Ta'amireh tribe associated with the modern discovery of Cave 1. (Image credit: John C. Trever)

---

discovering the cave, by accident or intent, Muhammad and his two older cousins—Khalil Musa and Jum'a Muhammad Khalil—retrieved only *three* manuscripts from Cave 1: 1QIsaiah[a], *Pesher Habakkuk*, and the *Community Rule*. This trio of scroll discoveries occurred sometime in late 1946 or early 1947.

This means that while the two older cousins, Khalil and Jum'a, were drumming up business and potential buyers in Bethlehem for the first three scrolls, the *Genesis Apocryphon* was presumably still resting in Cave 1. Nahman Avigad and Yigael Yadin reflected on the physical damage of the scroll a year later.

> The scroll under consideration here was most probably not protected by a jar; it may well have been lying for a long time on the floor of the cave, so that its lower part was constantly exposed to dampness, while its upper part was in a dry atmosphere. Since no traces of dust are visible on the scroll, it is very possible that it was wrapt in linen. Whatever the exact situation was, the scroll was very severely damaged.[17]

In slightly more descriptive terms, in 1950, *Time* Magazine described our fourth scroll as having a "cracked leather surface [that] looks like a dried cigar." While the first three scrolls were being shopped around in Bethlehem, and our cigar-like scroll still lay undiscovered, we meet our next set of key figures in the story: George Isha'ya, a merchant, and Khalil Eskander Shahin (also known as Kando), who owned an antiquities and cobbler's shop in Bethlehem.[18]

Both George and Kando were Syrian Orthodox Christians. This ecclesiastical connection links us to our next character: Archbishop Athanasius Yeshue Samuel. After several interactions and a few failed attempts, Archbishop Samuel successfully purchased the first three Cave 1 scrolls and the Aramaic *Genesis Apocryphon*. These are often referred to as the "St. Mark's scrolls," after the monastery and church Archbishop Samuel oversaw in Jerusalem.

As interest in the manuscripts grew, so did the number of the Ta'amireh Bedouin spelunking ventures in the Judean wilderness. Turns out, we lack many firm details on the comings and goings in these caves in those early months and years of discovery. Sometime in May or June 1947, Jum'a returned to Cave 1 with George in tow and recovered the remaining four scrolls, completing our group of seven from last chapter. This now included the Aramaic *Genesis Apocryphon*, then simply known as the "fourth scroll."[19]

At this point, the three other scrolls from the round two venture into Cave 1 can be treated as something of a group (1QIsaiah[b], the *Hodayot*, and

IMAGE 2.5: Khalil Eskander Shahin (Kando), Bethlehem antiquities dealer and key player in the brokering and acquisition of scrolls fragments and artifacts from members of the Ta'amireh Bedouin. (Image credit: John C. Trever)

IMAGE 2.6: Syrian Archbishop Athanasius Yeshue Samuel (Mar Samuel) and John C. Trever reviewing 1QIsaiah[a] with the *War Scroll* partially unrolled and the *Genesis Apocryphon* sealed tight. (Image credit: John C. Trever)

IMAGE 2.7: John Trever, the first scholar to receive, assess, and photograph the early discoveries from Qumran Cave 1 at the American School of Oriental Research. Here Trever is photographing the *Community Rule* (1QS). (Image credit: John C. Trever)

IMAGE 2.8: Eleazer Sukenik, Professor of Hebrew University and archaeologist, who acquired several scrolls on behalf of the Hebrew University of Jerusalem. Sukenik's son, Yigael Yadin, was an Israeli stateman, general, and archaeologist who would also play a role in early research on the DSS and the archaeology of the Qumran caves. (Image credit: Wikimedia Commons)

the *War Scroll*). Eventually these were acquired by Professor Eleazar Sukenik of Hebrew University on December 22, 1947, via several intermediaries. This cluster of texts is sometimes referred to as the "Hebrew University scrolls."

The *Genesis Apocryphon* crops up in our story again the following year. John Trever, a young scholar then working at the American School of Oriental Research in Jerusalem (now known as the Albright Institute of Archaeological Research) received two representatives from St. Mark's who had four scrolls in their possession. At the initial consultation, Trever noted that the fourth scroll was too brittle to unwrap for fear of damaging it. Turns out he was right. Trever noted how a "small leather fragment with disintegrated script" crumbled away from the scroll.[20]

Though the fragment's content was limited in itself, the damage turned out to be an accidental breakthrough. As Daniel Machiela noted, "This fragment provided the first hints that the scroll was written in Aramaic, rather than Hebrew."[21] In Trever's own account, he recalls deciphering some faint words on the fragment and exclaiming, "This is Aramaic!"[22] In hindsight, this glimpse revealed how the DSS would provide a gateway into the Aramaic scribal, intellectual, and cultural heritage of ancient Judaism (more on that in chapter 8).

Texts on Tour

Due to political unrest in Jerusalem (and the hopes of finding a buyer), the *Genesis Apocryphon* and the growing collection of St. Mark's scrolls were on the move with Archbishop Samuel in late 1948 and early 1949. Before crossing the Atlantic, this fab four toured through Homs, Syria and Beirut, Lebanon. Once stateside, the month of April turned out to be a big one in the life of the *Genesis Apocryphon*. On April 10, 1949, a large section of the scroll was separated to decipher its content, and Trever was able to deduce that the early columns retold the tale of Lamech from a first-person perspective. From this point on, the generic "fourth scroll" became known as the "Lamech Scroll."[23]

The Diggers

In the halls of Harvard's Fogg Art Museum last week, there was an expectant hush. After nine months of experimenting with bits of ancient leather, Fogg's Rutherford J. Gettens, chief of technical research, had decided to try a ticklish job: the unrolling of a brown and brittle scroll, dry with the dust of 2,000 years.

The scroll, which was brought to the U.S. by the Metropolitan of Jerusalem, was discovered in 1947 with seven others in a cave near the Dead Sea. Three of the others, which were in excellent condition and easily opened, contain a complete text of the book of *Isaiah* and other holy writings (TIME, Oct. 31). This one, whose cracked leather surface looks like a dried cigar, is believed to contain the world's oldest Old Testament text, the lost book of *Lamech* (father of Noah).

Because the leather of the scroll's outer layers has become almost completely gelatinized, Gettens plans to do the delicate job in a damp room, using sharp scalpels and other surgical instruments to separate the fused layers. The leather, said he, "breaks with a glassy fracture like glue. In fact, it is glue." But Gettens hopes that he can salvage at least the inner layers, which he thinks may be parchment. Expected time on the operating table: six months.

IMAGE 2.9: The cover image and excerpt of the reference to what is now known as the *Genesis Apocryphon* in the January 30, 1950 issue of Time. Intriguingly, the content here appears in the Science section, not the Religion section on the facing page. (Image credit: Andrew B. Perrin)

A few days later, the scroll was brought to the Fogg Museum at Harvard University to be prepared for its complete unrolling. Plans changed. Not wanting to disturb or damage the scroll until it was sold, Archbishop Samuel halted plans for the *Genesis Apocryphon*'s Harvard autopsy. If that language sounds too dramatic, the January 30, 1950 issue of *Time* cited above projected a six-month procedure.

Despite remaining rolled up like a cigar, the *Genesis Apocryphon*, along with the three other St. Mark's scrolls, stayed at Harvard until the summer of 1950. By this time Harvard had become uncomfortable about holding the text on their campus in Cambridge, Massachusetts. This connects us to the controversial issue of ownership and movement of antiquities, which we'll return to below.

After being shown the door at Harvard, the *Genesis Apocryphon*, 1QIsaiah[a], *Pesher Habakkuk*, and the *Community Rule* were featured briefly at exhibitions at the Art Museum in Worcester, Massachusetts (October 1–3, 1950) and the University of Chicago (November 1950). Meanwhile, while this batch of Cave 1 scrolls was away from the main action, back in Israel the discovery of the DSS increased at a rapid rate.

The two lead archaeologists of the Qumran site, Father Roland de Vaux of the École Biblique et Archéologique Française de Jérusalem, and G. Lankester Harding, a British archaeologist, then Director of the Department of Antiquities of Jordan, took to the desert. The volume and rate of texts pouring into Jerusalem from the Ta'amireh Bedouin suggested there were more manuscripts to be found. By studying the distinct pottery style of sherds found in Cave 1 and the Qumran site, the two archaeologists confirmed that there was indeed a connection between the archaeological site of the ancient community and at least some of the texts found in the caves. Caves plural? Yes.

More Caves, Multitudes of Texts, and Multiplying Price Tags

Leaving the *Genesis Apocryphon* aside for a moment, between 1952 and 1955 an additional ten caves were found in the region that offered up texts and artifacts.[24] Of these, Qumran Cave 4 is the most significant. Discovered in August or September 1952, it was hand-hewn from the marl terrace a stone's throw from the Qumran settlement. It included archaeological items (for example, pottery wares, phylactery cases, textiles, tags, and leather ties) and offered up some fifteen thousand fragments related to up to six hundred different compositions in Hebrew, Greek, and Aramaic. As Sidnie White Crawford commented, "Since the archeologists interrupted the Bedouin in their clandestine digging of Cave 4, only about 25 percent of the manuscripts fragments from the cave were properly excavated."[25]

News of a rising wave of textual discoveries and numerous caves meant increased intrigue, as well as increased potential digits on the price tag of the St. Mark's scrolls. All the while, our Aramaic *Genesis Apocryphon* remained unrolled. But would someone really buy it with its content still unseen? Make no mistake, Archbishop Samuel's international show-and-tell of these manuscripts was for a single reason: to sell them and turn a profit.

How much of a profit? On June 1, 1954, the Archbishop ran the now-famous classified ad in the *Wall Street Journal* advertising the items for sale. Though the asking price is not specified, the ad caught the attention of Yigael Yadin. Within a month, and through channels to retain some distance between the buyer and seller, Yadin purchased the four scrolls for Israel for $250,000 USD.

Let's put this purchase in context with some other numbers. When the first three Cave 1 items were acquired by the Archbishop—1QIsaiah[a], *Pesher Habakkuk*, and the *Community Rule*—they came at a bargain price of £16 Palestinian pounds, or the equivalent of $97.20 USD.[26] The price of our *Genesis Apocryphon* is unknown, but presumably it was equally economical.

For the math minds among us, that is a profit margin just shy of a quarter of a million dollars, and an appreciation in value of 2,572 percent. Not a bad investment—if you can call it that. As we'll see in the next chapter, the gray market of antiquities trading always favors the pocketbooks of the dealers. It is very much part of the ongoing history of the DSS today.

The Pathway to Publication and Politics of Ownership

The spring of 1955 saw the publication of the first editions of the DSS fragments. These include both volume one of the *Discoveries in the Judean Desert of Jordan*, as well as *The Dead Sea Scrolls of the Hebrew University*.[27] The latter, however, did not include our *Genesis Apocryphon*.

With its passport punched internationally, appearances at three American exhibitions, and purchases through at least four intermediaries, the *Genesis Apocryphon* was still closed up tight, its contents still a mystery. But this changed on February 7, 1956, when the scroll was painstakingly unrolled in Jerusalem by James Bieberkraut, who "had expertly opened the first three scrolls acquired for the Hebrew University."[28]

With the scroll now readable for the first time in at least two thousand years, the task of publication lay ahead. We may use this final part of the tale to connect yet another larger issue associated with the DSS: namely, the evolving modern cartography in the region due to politics and war.

Already by 1955, a handful of eight fragments of the *Genesis Apocryphon*, either recovered by the Ta'amireh Bedouin or held by Kando after damage to the main scroll, were set for publication. These were included in volume one of the official publication series *Discoveries in the Judean Desert*.[29] But what happened to the *of Jordan* bit of the series title, you ask?

On November 29, 1947, not long before the initial discovery of Cave 1, the United Nations General Assembly passed Resolution 181. This resolution supported the partition of then–British ruled Palestine into tandem states: one Jewish, the other Arab. With this, Britain declared that its mandate in the region would end. Shortly after this, May 15, 1948 marked the start of Israel's War of Independence. In both the proposed borders of the partition in 1947 and the boundaries implemented in 1948, the caves of the Dead Sea region were on *modern Jordanian* turf—yet they are *ancient Jewish* documents. These texts are also unequivocally objects of *common cultural heritage* that at once extends beyond these borders.[30]

This issue was complicated further by another event twenty years later. Apart from the Hebrew University scrolls and a few other items, the Palestinian Archaeological Museum (PAM for short) in east Jerusalem was where the scrolls were kept and studied. I say *east* Jerusalem because in 1948 the city was also partitioned, with Arab communities located predominantly

IMAGE 2.10: Cave 4 near the Qumran archaeological site was the richest in terms of scroll fragments—it has also become one of the most iconic images associated with the scrolls and Qumran archaeology. Not discovered until August 1952, the cave is hand-hewn in the marl terrace within plain sight of the settlement. (Image credit: Andrew B. Perrin)

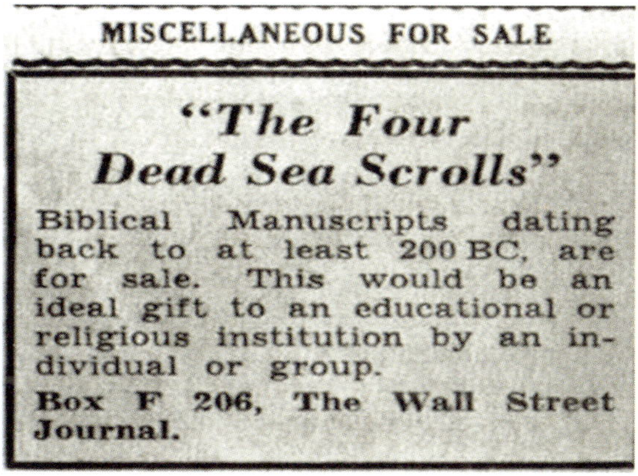

MISCELLANEOUS FOR SALE

"The Four Dead Sea Scrolls"

Biblical Manuscripts dating back to at least 200 BC, are for sale. This would be an ideal gift to an educational or religious institution by an individual or group.

Box F 206, The Wall Street Journal.

IMAGE 2.11: After unsuccessfully networking a buyer for the four St. Mark's scrolls while travelling to the United States, Archbishop Samuel ran this anonymous ad in the June 1, 1954 issue of the Wall Street Journal. (Image credit: Wall Street Journal) in the east and Jewish communities largely in the west. When battle broke out between these two sides during the Six Day War (June 5–10, 1967), the PAM became a stronghold for Israeli paratroopers. As the dust settled from this regional war, the PAM and surrounding areas fell within the new territorial bounds won by Israel—and that meant its collections too. The institution, today called the Rockefeller Museum, and its holdings fell into the custody and care of what is now known as the Israel Antiquities Authority.

Conclusion

Framing the discovery of the DSS by first rethinking the problems of find stories and then retracing the steps of a single Dead Sea Scroll has connected us with critical issues and bigger questions, both ancient and modern. They involve a web of complex questions related to politics, identity, economics, and many more issues, which will be played out for decades to come.

The DSS are archaeological artifacts. Yet the fact is that most of them—like the *Genesis Apocryphon*—were not found and recovered in a supervised dig. This means that, technically speaking, our first Cave 1 DSS texts, and many others brokered through back channels, lack clear provenience (a confirmed actual location or findspot) and provenance (a clear and verifiable postexcavation history). Archaeologists were most often trailing the original discoveries and discoverers. Many of the earliest discoveries happened in waves of undocumented, clandestine excursions to caves for the purpose of acquiring antiquities from the landscape for material gain. Nowadays we have a term for this too: looting.

The case study of the *Genesis Apocryphon* highlights questions of how we understand the ownership and mobility of antiquities. Ownership must mean more than mere purchasing power or political muscle. And the movement of cultural objects is always questionable. While Archbishop Samuel wasn't technically breaking the law by jet-setting with the *Genesis Apocryphon* and other texts as carry-ons (more on this in the next chapter), it does raise

IMAGE 2.12: The *Genesis Apocryphon* was eventually unrolled by James Bieberkraut in Jerusalem. The images here provide a view of the scroll in its unrolled state, as well as an early fragment with a glimpse of the Aramaic content tucked away within. (Image credit: James C. Trever)

the question of how we assign or assume custody of objects of cultural heritage. This is particularly so in regions where the years around discoveries are defined by a heritage of colonial boots on the ground, regional wars between domestic people groups, and, frankly, too many unknown or undisclosed variables about the chain of custody and transactions of individual objects for firm answers.

No find story or ordering of the "facts" is bias free. While ancient texts and artifacts are just that—ancient—when they are brought out of their resting places in muck, mire, dust, rubble, or in our case, caves, they also become much more than that. They are curated and acclimated. They are ancient artifacts now approached and experienced in a modern world that was not their own. They come to mean something to those who encounter or appreciate them in our day. Yet the meaning, or better, meanings, attached to them are shaped by what a given space in culture values. Some combination of political, economic, ethnic, and religious interests often shapes these values. When it comes to textual or archaeological discoveries, recovery of items *in situ*, in their original place, matters. Yet we are also all beings of our own places and contexts. Our individual or collective cultural locations inform what we think of the past and how we think of its potential to shape the present.

So where do we go from here? As we will see next, the inherent intrigue of the DSS has not gone unnoticed by today's gray market of antiquities trading and the illicit activities of forgers. If you thought the profit margin of authentic Qumran finds from Cave 1 was massive, how would you feel about an eight-figure price tag for what might be a *faux* fragment?

Chapter 3

Eight-Figure Souvenirs? Modern Forgeries of Ancient Scripture

The field of biblical studies is no stranger to forged manuscripts and artifacts. Such items are often heralded for their "groundbreaking" insights that will turn the world upside down. Take, for example, the provocatively titled *Gospel of Jesus's Wife* made public by Karen King of Harvard Divinity School in 2012. You might have guessed it from the title, but this tiny rectangular bit of inscribed papyrus purported to reveal that Jesus may not have been a bachelor till the rapture—he was in fact happily married to Mary Magdalene. If true, this 4x8 centimeter artefact could overturn two millennia of belief and practice. *If.* That is the key word here.

Close analysis, however, revealed what some had suspected all along: the item was a fake. The papyrus was indeed old, but the style of writing and material quality of the ink were suspicious. The forger also seems to have stayed too close to his source of inspiration, the *Gospel of Thomas* from Nag Hammadi, by including several suggestive words and phrases from a 1997 edition of that ancient text.[1]

The reality is that forgeries are much more common than you'd think. Unfortunately, the adrenaline rush of a potentially world-changing "new discovery" is often accompanied by brash and premature conclusions about the item's significance. While no two cases are alike, before we rewrite the

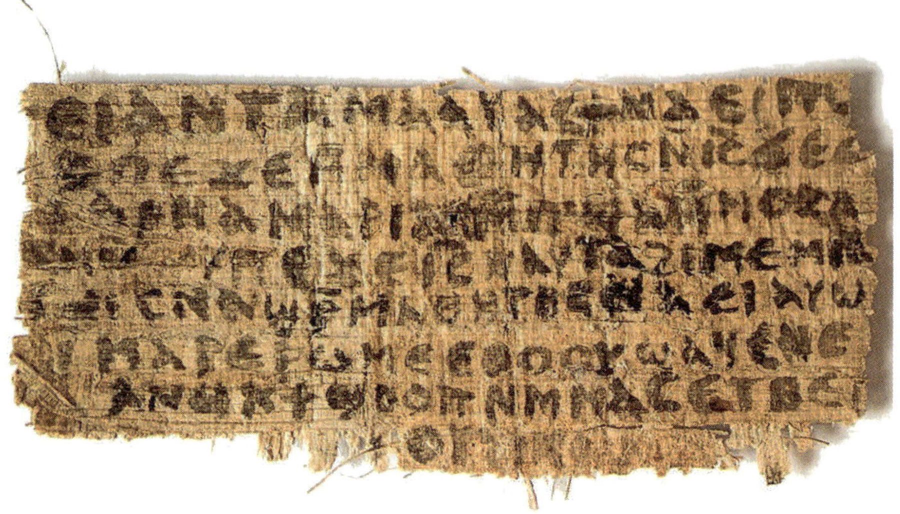

IMAGE 3.1: The so-called *Gospel of Jesus's Wife* papyrus fragment sparked excitement and controversy when it was publicized in 2012 by Harvard Divinity School professor Karen King. Close analysis, however, revealed the item is a fake. Journalist Ariel Sabar broke the story of the suspicious nature of the fragment and has now tracked the unusual backstory of the fragment and its connection to Walter Fritz, a resident of Florida who had formerly been an Egyptology student at Freie Universität Berlin. (Image credit: Wikimedia Commons)

---

history of the universe on account of an alleged ancient fragment smaller than a business card, there are three issues that need close and critical consideration.

Provenience. Where did it come from, and can we verify the object's claimed origins with certainty? I'm not talking about convenient and official-looking documentation accompanying the item at the time of sale. Those are even easier to forge. The only sure way to green light provenience is when something is found *in situ*, that is, in its original place, at a supervised archaeological dig. Rarely if ever do "new" and "newsy" finds meet that criterion.

Authenticity. Can the item stand up to a battery of scientific tests and scholarly analyses about its material, scribal, and textual quality? It's not enough to rely on the Carbon-14 dating of the fragment. Many forgeries are inscribed on blank bits of ancient leather or papyrus as a canvas. The material might date to the ancient world, or at the very least be old, but the written text is from closer to our own day. Like testing for the existence of many security features on counterfeit cash, authenticity must consider a variety of issues, methods, and tests.[2]

Chain of custody. Are there reliable materials and supporting documentation to determine the "who, what, when, where, and how (much money)" of all stages of discovery through acquisition? Another word for this I'll use is *provenance*. We need to interrogate the evidence, as several narratives develop with common features to skirt international law. For example, items are typically claimed to have spent some time in a Swiss bank vault (things are conveniently neutral there) and are reported as leaving their country of discovery *before* 1970 (incidentally, this was the year of the UNESCO convention that prohibited the illicit movement and export of items of cultural heritage across borders).[3] In most cases the details are few, out of reach, regularly censored, or in some cases shackled by non-disclosure agreements.

So how does this all relate to the DSS if they were all found seventy-five years ago? Well, let's just call it an ongoing history. This chapter contributes to that ongoing history by cataloging and contextualizing the so-called "Dead Sea Scroll fragments" bought and sold in recent years by private collectors, and critically exploring the red flags that mark the majority of these as forgeries or suspicious. It closes with a cautiously optimistic approach to two tiny Daniel fragments in a private collection, which are authentic and which add new perspectives to the early days of discovery.

Casting a Line for Fishy Fragments in Modern Collections

One of the most sensational and controversial issues in scrolls research today is how to move on in an era marked by the increasing reality of forged fragments. At present, there are at least five private or institutional collections around the world that have purchased fragments that only came to light in the late 1990s and early 2000s. The majority of the fragments in such collections are now known to be fake. A few await detailed analysis but are suspicious. All these materials—especially the few authentic items—exist under a cloud of complex questions about why and how they became available when they did.

These main collections include: the Museum of the Bible (Washington DC), Azusa Pacific University (Los Angeles, California), Southwestern Baptist Theological Seminary (Fort Worth, Texas), Lanier Theological Library (Houston, Texas), and The Schøyen Collection (Norway).[4] In addition to these known fragments bought and sold in recent times, there are also rumors of several more floating around until the price is right.[5]

Of course, institutions are not independent or unanimated entities—they are actioned, directed, and resourced by both groups and individuals. This is true of any organization but corporate entities in particular.[6] This means we can't solely focus on artifacts (authentic or otherwise) without acknowledging both the priorities of the people seeking, acquiring, and mobilizing them through organizations, whether they are private entities, museums, sponsored academic initiatives, or higher education institutions. Later in the chapter we will hear from one such individual behind a collection of his namesake (Martin Schøyen of The Schøyen Collection) as well as some scholarly voices technically adjacent to, but clearly involved in, advancing the aims of private collectors.

In the American context, the public discourse over the Green family has regularly been front page news. Well known for their arts and crafts chain Hobby Lobby, the Green family established the Museum of the Bible as a not-for-profit in 2010. The Greens and the Museum are acclaimed by some but intensely critiqued by many due to scandals and lawsuits regarding their processes of acquisition of both artifacts and forgeries, and the complex intersection of cultural heritage, religion, and public life.

The more prominent headlines concerned several illegally imported cuneiform tablets labelled as "spare tiles" on a shipping record and sent to Hobby Lobby stores between 2010 and 2011. The tablets (not tiles) were authentic, part of a lot of thousands of artifacts smuggled from Iraq via the United Arab Emirates and Israel. The Greens were required to pay $3 million in fines by the United States government and to forfeit the artifacts in question. One such item in this lot was a 3,500-year-old tablet of the *Epic of Gilgamesh*. The artefact was originally looted from the Iraqi Museum in 1991 during the Gulf War, after which it went through a series of buyers and sellers and was ultimately acquired by the Greens in 2014 for $1.67 million. In September 2019, the tablet was seized by federal agents and its forfeiture was approved by a New York judge in 2021. The recovered item, and thousands of other items with it from among the Green collection, have now been returned to Iraq. A similarly high-profile lawsuit involves the Greens' acquisition of papyrus fragments (including texts of the Gospels) that were allegedly stolen by Oxford scholar Dirk Obbink and sold to the Greens for $7.1 million between 2010 and 2013.

Over the last several years, reams of stories and op-eds have flooded the press and web regarding such cases, as well as how they relate to the intersection of religion and public life in America.[7] While I am not a proponent

IMAGE 3.2: This Hebrew fragment of Genesis 31:23–25(?) and 32:3–6 is among the suspicious and forged fragments now among the Museum of the Bible collection in Washington DC. The images here are in full spectrum color and infrared, with the latter technology being routinely used to gain a better view of text on fragments (Image credit: Museum of the Bible)

of cancel culture, these actions and cases are rightly critiqued and cannot be condoned for any arts, culture, or heritage institution.

But this book is about scrolls, not tablets or "spare tiles." Whether you look to the scrolls as an academic source or as items of significance for faith and culture, there are big problems associated with the tiny fragments in private institutions. Like it or not, modern forgeries of so-called DSS fragments have become part of the tale. So before we delve further into the authentic artifacts and texts, let's separate the wheat from the chaff.

Ongoing research both within and outside of the institutions holding them has confirmed a shocking concentration of fakes across modern collections. For this reason, the entire lot of fragments in these collections, and any others that come to light in the years ahead, must be treated with instant suspicion rather than as sensations.

In fact, in March 2020 the Museum of the Bible announced formally what most suspected: their whole lot of alleged DSS fragments were fakes. A month later, in April 2020, Southwestern Baptist Theological Seminary issued a press release indicating their lack of confidence over the authenticity of their items. These recent realizations and releases come on the heels of scholarly critique that has increasingly identified forgeries in these and other modern collections, not least in The Schøyen Collection.

While most of the items in question are forgeries, presenting an inventory of these knockoffs is essential for charting a way forward. The staggering list is as follows. Many marked as "to be determined" are viewed as highly suspicious.[8]

Before looking at a few fragments themselves, let's stand back and make some observations on the nature of this inventory.

Table: State and Scope of Dead Sea Scrolls Fragment Forgeries in Modern Collections

Legend

⃠	Confirmed forgery
✓	Authentic fragment
?	To be determined

Museum of the Bible	
⃠	Genesis 31:23–25(?); 32:3–6
⃠	Exodus 17:4–7
⃠	Leviticus 23:4(?)
⃠	Leviticus 23:24–28
⃠	Numbers 8:3–5
⃠	Jeremiah 23:6–9
⃠	Ezekiel 28:22
⃠	Jonah 4:2–5
⃠	Micah 1:4–6
⃠	Psalm 11:1–4
⃠	Daniel 10:18–20
⃠	Nehemiah 2:13–16
⃠	Fragment of Instruction
The Schøyen Collection	
⃠	Genesis 36:7–16
?	Genesis 37:8
⃠	Exodus 3:13–15
⃠	Exodus 5:9–14
⃠	Exodus 16:10
⃠	Numbers 16:2–5
⃠	Deuteronomy 6:1–2
⃠	Deuteronomy 32:5–9
?	Judges 4:5–6
⃠	Ruth 2:1–2
⃠	1 Samuel 2:11–14

⦸	1 Samuel 5:10–11
⦸	2 Samuel 20:22–24
⦸	1 Kings 16:23–26
⦸	Nehemiah 3:14–15
⦸	Psalms 9:10, 12–13
⦸	Proverbs 4:23–5:1
⦸	Jeremiah 3:15–19
✓	Daniel 2:4–5
✓	Daniel 3:26–27
⦸	Tobit 14:3-4
⦸	1 Enoch 7:1–5
⦸	1 Enoch 8:4–9:3
⦸	1 Enoch 106:19–107:1
?	Commentary on Genesis A
?	Unidentified Fragment
Azusa Pacific University	
?	Exodus 18:6–8
?	Leviticus 10:4–7
⦸	Deuteronomy 8:2–5
⦸	Deuteronomy 27:4–6
?	Daniel 5:13–16
Southwestern Baptist Theological Seminary	
?	Exodus 23:8–10
?	Leviticus 20:24, 18:28–30
?	Deuteronomy 9:25–10:1
?	Deuteronomy 12:11–14
?	1 Kings 13:20–22
?	Psalms 22:4, 6-9, 11–13
?	Daniel 6:22–24
?	Daniel 7:18–19
?	Unidentified Fragment
Lanier Theological Library	
?	Amos 7:17–8:1

IMAGE 3.3: The fragment with content from Amos 7:17–8:1 among the collection of Lanier Theological Library in Houston, Texas. (Image credit: Lanier Theological Library)

Five Red Flags about Fragments Bought and Sold Since the Mid-1990s

There are several red flags that raise caution over the materials in the list above. These relate to the features and nature of the fragments in private collections as well as the narratives developed around them in the process of their acquisition and publication. Remember, our default position from here on out should be *suspicion* not *sensationalism*. There are at least five trends we can observe about new/old fragments when studied across multiple collections. Getting a general sense of these will provide a framework for the more detailed homework on some case studies on Daniel fragments below.

Red Flag #1: Too Much Bible

When we compare the above textual data set with that of the larger DSS collection from the waves of discovery in the 1940s to 1950s, there is a disproportionate representation of biblical texts among these new/old finds. According to James VanderKam's recent tally, "among the more than 900 manuscripts identified by editors of the scrolls, approximately 200–210 qualify as copies of one or more scriptural books."[9] That means about 22–23 percent of the overall DSS collection are from biblical books. Let's check this math against the stats of the private collections.

Emanuel Tov observed that our private collections exhibit a much stronger concentration of materials related to biblical books. Reflecting on this trend, Tov concluded "it is remarkable that in all instances where there is legible text, virtually every fragment in private collections has been identified with a previously known composition" and in most cases with books of the Hebrew Bible or Old Testament.[10] These new collections, therefore, have an unmistakable orbit around *biblical* content that is entirely out whack with the stats of the larger, authentic collection that came to light seventy-five years ago.

Red Flag #2: A Curious Concentration of Theologically Loaded Passages

It is not only the number of fragments with content of biblical writings that's suspicious, it is the representation of several passages that could be seen as particularly relevant to (in all cases but Schøyen) North American evangelical audiences.

Take, for example, the fragmentary phrases of Psalm 22:4–13 in the Southwestern Baptist Theological Seminary collection. Few ears would perk up with the words of the midpoint of the psalm. But they might recognize these from Psalm 22:1: "My God, my God, why have you forsaken me?" Quoted by Jesus himself in Matthew 27:46 and Mark 15:34, the final utterances of the crucified Christ were a citation of the opening lines of this lament psalm. Imagine the prospect of owning the oldest known copy of this pivotal passage. Now, is that a thought that would motivate a buyer? Seller? Forger? All of the above?

Another curious case in the Southwestern Baptist Theological Seminary collection includes content from Leviticus 18:28–30 and 20:24. These passages come in the immediate context of a key passage in the Hebrew Scriptures that are read by some as part of the biblical case against homosexuality. The partial glimpse we get in the fragment is from the promised judgment: "For whoever commits any of these abominations shall be cut off from their people" (Leviticus 18:29).

Is it *too* serendipitous that the "ancient" items in question intersect with either pivotal passages for Christian theology or interests of current debate among the constituencies of the purchasers? Intriguing. Unsettling. And certainly worth a pause.

Red Flag #3: Too Many Groundbreaking New Readings

Several of the fragments are applauded for their new readings that could revolutionize how we understand, and even restore the earliest words of, the Hebrew Bible and Old Testament. As we'll see in chapter 6, the DSS *do* enhance modern Bibles by making them look more like ancient Scriptures. But how much should we expect these new/old fragments to drive this change?

Arguably the smokiest smoking gun textual variant—that term simply refers to a difference in wording or phrasing between manuscripts—is in a Deuteronomy fragment in the Azusa Pacific collection. This fragment makes a remarkable mention of Mount Gerizim in Deuteronomy 27:4. Why does this location matter? For centuries, Samaritan Judaism has looked to Mount Gerizim as the true place of worship of the God of Israel. All other known versions of this passage reference the familiar Mount Ebal. The potential impact of these two tiny words no doubt contributed handsomely to the reported $1.38 million price tag of the Azusa Pacific lot.

The problem is that not everyone adopted a posture of suspicion before rushing to conclusions about this fragment's possible impact on the text of Scripture. In a 2009 article in the *Los Angeles Times*, James Charlesworth of Princeton Theological Seminary proclaimed, "We finally found the original text of Deuteronomy. ... This is sensationally important."[11] Sensational indeed—but not in the way Charlesworth means. We would be wise to gear down the applause to a slow clap before rewriting the social, cultural, historical, textual, and theological histories of ancient Judaism on account of a fragment that is fishy at best, and likely a fake.

Red Flag #4: Blind Spots in Origins and Purchase History

The players in the market are often unknown, unnamed, or simply withheld from scholars and the public, making it impossible to hop the hurdles of establishing origins (provenience) and chain of custody (provenance). Let's illustrate this point with an overseas example, from the private collection of Martin Schøyen.

In the opening pages of the publication of select texts from The Schøyen Collection, Schøyen provides a rare glimpse into the passion, drive, and efforts of a private collector of antiquities and manuscripts. While he relates his quest to several other narratives of acquisition, in key places we find a redacted disclosure and the acceptance of a signed guarantor.

In one instance, Schøyen mentions receiving a "signed statement [by] William Kando," the son of the elder Kando who brokered sales from the Bedouin decades ago, "about the provenance of these artefacts."[12] The statement "hereby confirm[s]" the acquisition of fragments from a series of sources, some of which were acquired before the most recent wave of purchases in other private collections. These include fragments of Joshua and Judges, brokered through James Charlesworth, as well fragments of Joel and Leviticus, said to be direct purchases by Kando Sr. from the Bedouin in 1952–53. Save for the Judges materials, all of these were sold "to our old customer of the Kando family in Zurich in 1956." Schøyen's description continues with regular ambiguity over the origins of many other items, including his fragments of Samuel, Psalms, and Deuteronomy. Note here how the narrative nods to both a contemporary academic and early connection to Kando.

Equally routine are the nameless figures of intermediaries. The identity of the gent in Zurich from 1956 is withheld: "The name of the collector is not revealed here, as the heirs of this collector still had more fragments."

Some of the fragments were allegedly sold by Kando to an "American priest in 1972, who later served in Switzerland." The motif of an American priest is a feature of several of the origins and acquisitions stories of several modern collections. These, we are told, were then sold to Schøyen on the promise of anonymity.

The remaining texts of the collection were bought from a "distinguished family ... based in Lebanon *c.*1954–69." These were also said to have been moved to Europe as early as 1969 and kept in Zurich from 1993. These purchases too were made on good faith and confidentiality. Schøyen remarks that these "were also believed to come from Cave 4. I know the identity of the owners of this family collection, but the family asked me to be so kind as not to reveal it." Despite many questionable elements in the introduction to the Schøyen collection, it is admittedly far more information than we have for all other collections at this point. The Museum of the Bible volume of old/new fragments, for example, included only a bullet-point list of manuscript numbers and dates of acquisition, totaling just half a page!

Regardless of whether we have a dearth of information on the circumstances of acquisition or a deluge of information mixed with apologetic, these narratives need to be critically evaluated for fact and fable, sifting reality from rhetoric. When interrogated as modern tales, such acquisition stories are not merely introductions to collections—they are often legitimating narratives in support of the collector.[13]

Red Flag #5: Forging a Supply to Meet a Frenzied Demand

The surge of fragments that flooded the market around the turn of the millennium suggests that the supply was created (literally) by a spike in demand. While there were inklings of additional fragments beyond those of the main collections as early as the mid-1990s, the fervor to own a piece of holy writ ramped up with the new millennium. By 2002 the market was flooded, with reports of almost "made to order" service in some corners.

The most egregious call for cash came from Weston Fields, once head of the Dead Sea Scrolls Foundation, delivering a lecture at Lanier Theological Library on April 16, 2011.[14] Fields's opening remarks seem causal and appropriate enough. He promises to bring the audience "up to date on the Dead Sea Scrolls, which have happened fairly recently and, in fact, are happening as we sit here tonight." The focus of this news is the recent purchases of claimed scroll fragments in private collections.

But that's not all. Fields apparently has insider knowledge. He continues, "In Zurich, Switzerland, there are an unknown number of Dead Sea Scrolls fragments locked in a safe. ... You have to ask, how has all this happened?" I agree. That is precisely the question scrolls scholars are asking. A partial answer, or at least a contributing factor, is that demand is driving supply. By lecture's end, Fields reiterates his knowledge and access to this gray market.

> It all started in 2002. As a matter of fact, I know exactly the date that it all started because, out of the blue, about six weeks ago, somebody sent me scans—I know who sent them to me but I have no idea where he got them—of all kinds of faxes from 2002-2003 that went between the Kando family and antiquities dealers in California. Just out of the blue, all these private faxes about fragments and prices and where the exchange could be made and all these things.

The "prominent and respected academic contacted out of the blue" element of such stories is fairly common. This is also how Karen King became aware of the so-called *Gospel of Jesus's Wife* fragment. Shortly after Fields's recollection of a phone call and fax barrage, the tale turns into a pitch.

> If you want William Kando's telephone number, I'd be glad to give it to you. If you want his cell, his home, or his office, I've got it. And if you're in the market for Dead Sea Scrolls, I guarantee you, you can call him up tonight ... and you can offer him, say a million dollars for whatever

> he might have for a million dollars, and you can make a purchase of Dead Sea Scrolls tonight, if you want. That's how immediate it is.

The intrigue continues as Fields connects fragments unknown with a shadowy meeting under a bridge in Beirut between Frank Moore Cross and Kando, where the latter showed the former a box of fragments that, apparently, did not make their way into the lot published by Cross and others.[15] If the find stories in the last chapter capitalized on the Arabian Nights–esque appeal of the imagined early-modern Middle East, this tale leverages the more recent cultural appeal of a spy thriller.

What would Fields have the audience do about these withheld fragments?

> Talk to your friends. We need to buy these. I'm talking to some of my friends, but that's the situation we have now. And we know how it came about that that big piece of Genesis is still there, we know how it happened and we also know that it'll take forty-two million dollars to buy it.

This is a bold close to the lecture, and a clear example of the frenzy generated around the prospect of "new" fragments promising remarkable insights into the biblical past. Among the countless problems with this scene is how scholarly authority is leveraged not only to authenticate and legitimize the items for sale, but also to grant approval to a questionable procurement process for objects of cultural heritage. Provenience? It's assigned. Provenance? It's assured. Authenticity? As certain as the signature on your check book. Just make the call!

These are just five of the larger question marks that have clouded over these new/old fragments in private collections. Getting a sense of the complexities of the whole is a helpful way of providing context for case studies. Rather than try to untangle the web of *all* the fragments in question, let's now zero in on a few samples from the book of Daniel that illumine the range of problems and prospects of a very select few post-2002 fragments.

Daniel Traditions in the Dead Sea Scrolls, Then and Now

The book of Daniel was important to the Qumran community. The DSS collection includes at least eight manuscripts with content from the book of Daniel (1QDaniel^{a-b}, 4QDaniel^{a-e}, and 6QpapDaniel). The emergence of Daniel fragments in the early years of discovery might have tallied more, but the details are scant or obscured by myth.[16] What's intriguing is that four out of the five private collections (all but Lanier) include fragments with content from the book of Daniel. Curious.

This representation of new/old Daniel fragments has the potential to either expand our data exponentially—in effect it could nearly double the number of Daniel copies known at Qumran—or corrupt the data set significantly. It all depends on whether the fragments are authentic or simply too good to be true. A pair of brief case studies on Daniel materials in the Museum of the Bible and The Schøyen Collection will demonstrate the potential and peril of these new/old fragments.

A Faux Fragment: The Museum of the Bible Daniel Material

Among the Museum of the Bible collection is a small leather fragment inscribed with the Hebrew text of Daniel 10:18–20. Where did this fragment come from, how was it acquired, and should we integrate it into our Danielic data? There is a mix of caution and curiosity over the item's origins in the published edition of the Museum of the Bible fragments. In the beginning of the volume, this Daniel fragment is said to have been purchased in May 2010 alongside six other biblical fragments. We are told neither from whom nor for how much.[17]

Robert Duke, Daniel Holt, and Skyler Russell, the editors of the fragment, add that "According to the seller, the fragment was purchased from the Taʿamirah Bedouin and its provenance was Qumran Cave 4. While this is not an unreasonable identification since many fragments were recovered by the Bedouin from Cave 4, its connection to this specific cave and to Qumran cannot be made with any surety."[18] In sum, the backstory of the Museum of the Bible Daniel fragment is simply unstated and indeterminate. There is no story to tell or, more likely, the collectors are simply not telling us the story.

What about the features of the item itself? These do tell a story, and not a good one. There are several textual, scribal, and material oddities that point toward its fraudulent nature—a conclusion now also recognized by the Museum of the Bible. Even before the fragment was subjected to scientific material analysis, there are five fishy features visible to the naked eye.

First, the script exhibits oddities in character formation. Script styles (paleography) are an important gauge for dating a manuscript, and Ada Yardeni determined that the scribal hand of the fragment aligns with those of the "first half to the mid–first century B.C.E."[19] Within this description, however, she also noted that the letters throughout exhibit "unequal tilt." Some lean forward, others stand up straight, and a few recline backward. This observation of inconsistency and apparent "rudimentary [scribal] skills" is echoed by Kipp Davis in his summary of the overall material qualities of the Museum of the Bible fragments.[20] But how can we tell if this feature is due to an amateur ancient scribe or an untrained modern forger? On its own, this observation could cut both ways. This is why multiple perspectives on several features matter.

Second, the fragment has irregular word spacing and inconsistent orientation to imagined horizontal lines. While not all DSS manuscripts have drawn or cut-in ruling lines, we would expect trained scribes to write in reasonably consistent form and generally to leave spaces between words. Yet in addition to the tilt noted above, if we extrapolate the trajectory of individual lines of this Daniel fragment, it is clear they would intersect with each other or extend off in a direction of their own.

Similarly, note the awkwardly mashed together forms at the end of line two: עמי הת֯[חזקתי ("in my presence, I be[came strong"). And check out

IMAGE 3.4: The Daniel fragment of the Museum of the Bible collection includes content from the latter Hebrew section of the book (Daniel 10:18–20). It measures 2.5 x 1.9 centimeters and the scribal hand appears to be modeled after a formal script, with passing resemblance to those of the mid–first century BCE. (Image credit: Museum of the Bible)

---

the similarly economical placement of consecutive words beginning line three: ה̇ידעת למה ("Do you know why I came t[o you?"). Word spaces may vary, but crunched text at the edges of fragments is suspicious. Ever run out of room at the edge of a Post-It note? Suddenly your penmanship is diminished: words are squished and lines are less linear. That is effectively what's happening here.

Third, the placement of a complete medial *mem* (מ) in the peninsula-like extension at the very top of the fragment is a little too convenient. In the museum's published edition of the fragment, the editors reconstruct this form as כ̇מר̊[א]ה̊ ("the one with the appe[a]rance[of"). In this instance and several others among the private collections, it is *almost* as though the physical size, shape, and orientation of the fragment has dictated the amount and positioning of the text.

Fourth, the relation of ink to surface damage is instructive. See that partial form הת̊]חזקתי ("I be[came strong") at the left edge of the second line? The editors commented, "Its position is possibly problematic because it appears in a space where the surface is better preserved at the edge of the fragment and above lighter colored sections of damage where the line would be expected. This could suggest a secondary hand sometime in history, including the modern era."[21] While the DSS are certainly damaged fragments in many cases, we should not expect to find text written *on top* of damage to the surfaces of fragments.

In this same line, Kipp Davis observed "bleeding letters" in the form עמי ("with me") in line 2.[22] This is the effect of ink strokes seeping outside their frame due to being penned on poor quality or significantly aged surfaces. Imagine using a new fountain pen on a fifty-year-old newspaper. Fresh ink + porous paper = bleeding characters. We have something similar happening on this fragment.

Fifth, while the actual words of the fragment *mostly* reflect what we know from other Hebrew manuscripts of Daniel, they depart from it in a single variant reading found in the partial text of Daniel 10:19, in the second line. To illustrate this we'll need to wade into some technical details of the comparison of biblical witnesses across different manuscript families. This is known as textual criticism, which we'll unpack in greater detail in chapter 6.

In this verse, the Masoretic Text—a primary medieval manuscript family for the Hebrew Bible—reads a pair of verbs offering a command and encouragement: חֲזַק וַחֲזָק (literally "be strong and strengthen yourself"). The corresponding phrase in the Septuagint—the ancient Greek translation of the Hebrew Scriptures—reads slightly differently: ἀνδρίζου καὶ ἴσχυε ("be courageous and strong"). Since deviations in the ancient Greek translation generally reflect a different underlying Hebrew text, Duke, Holt, and Russell infer

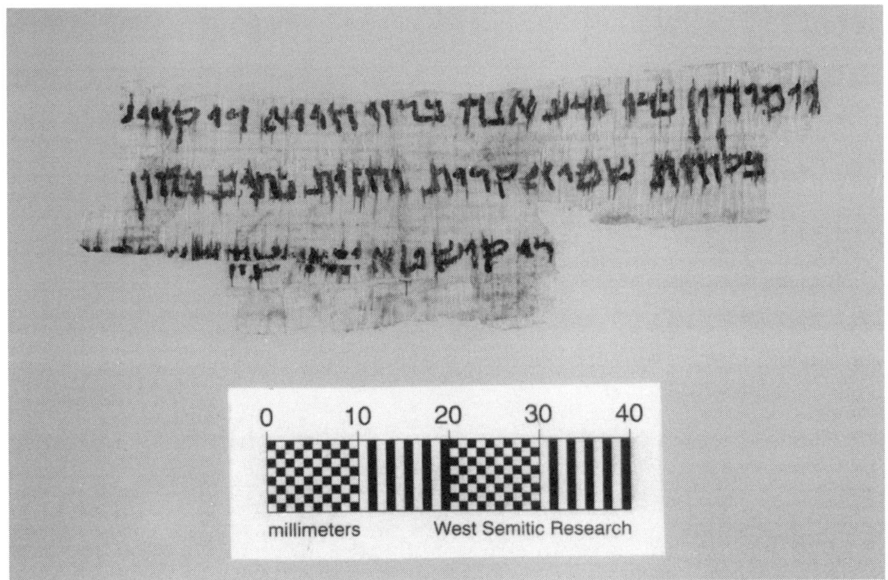

IMAGE 3.5: The phenomenon of "ink bleed" is pronounced in several of the modern fragments, such as this papyrus fragment of 1 Enoch 106:19–107:1 from The Schøyen Collection. This is the result of inscribing new ink on a porous and aged fragment. The images here are in full spectrum and infrared, and the bleed is evident in both views. (Image credit: Courtesy of The Schøyen Collection)

that the Greek translation in the Septuagint was likely based on a Hebrew base text with two verbs. This puts their Hebrew reconstruction of the phrase חזק [וֹהתחזק ("Be strong] and strengthen yourself") in fresh perspective. If accepted, it *may* suggest that the Museum of the Bible fragment includes incredible new information about the lost Hebrew text behind the ancient Greek translation. This would mean we have one of the oldest known forms of Daniel 10:19.

The problem is, we've seen this reading before—but not in a manuscript from ancient Israel. Remarkably, the same Hebrew variant reading from the Museum of the Bible fragment was already proposed on a hunch in the footnotes of the standard Hebrew edition *Biblia Hebraica Stuttgartensia* (BHS), and before this in a German commentary on Daniel by Karl Marti in 1901.[23] It's not that the DSS never reveal new readings, or provide Hebrew texts that help us reverse engineer the Greek. It's the surprising regularity of such occurrences on many of the new/old, privately owned fragments that's suspicious.[24]

On their own, the features described in the Museum of the Bible Daniel fragment may not tip the scales of authenticity. It is the concentration of peculiar features on a single, tiny fragment that flags it as *faux*. These observations have now also been confirmed by scientific analysis.

A Silver Lining on the Fool's Gold? Daniel Fragments in The Schøyen Collection

Notwithstanding the larger questions about the purchases of many items in Martin Schøyen's collection, parts of it are on firmer footing because of their acquisition before the supply and demand market that defined the post-2002 purchases. In the case of the Schøyen Daniel fragments, we may have the makings of a "best case scenario" for a set of recently acquired fragments that are in fact very old. As we'll see, these too add something to our understanding of Daniel in the DSS, yet their impact comes in a rather unexpected way.

Spoiler alert: these fragments don't reveal remarkable or revolutionary new readings. What they do offer is a fresh perspective on the presence of at least two Daniel manuscripts in the earliest waves of discoveries. Sensational? Not particularly. Significant? Absolutely. The fragments in question include Aramaic text from Daniel 2:4–5 and Daniel 3:26–27. These fragments are hardly the stuff of show-and-tell. They're small, unassuming, and, to the naked eye, uninscribed.

Unlike many other fragments in private collections, it is possible to reconstruct a reasonable history of the Schøyen Daniel fragments' acquisition and potential origins in the early waves of discovery, most likely from Cave 1. Among the many figures we met in the last chapter was the American scholar, John Trever. Trever is what we might call a first generation scrolls scholar. He wrote some of our most important early academic articles on the Cave 1 finds, as well as some of the first popular introductions to the DSS.[25] Trever was also an amateur photographer. Part of the early scholarly interaction with the St. Mark's DSS involved their imaging by Trever.[26]

But Trever is not relevant for our story because of his photos *per se*, nor because of this role as an early academic consultant. Rather, his activities provide secure dates of *when* he imaged select Cave 1 scrolls, and insight into *what* he received in exchange for his work. As we'll see, Trever's involvement with the scrolls in Israel in the late 1940s intersects with the story of Martin Schøyen in Norway in the mid-1990s.

The interactions of a scholar and a collector demand we pause to untangle some of the key issues of new/old fragments of Daniel that are now in play. Remember our rule: suspicion before sensation. Remember, too, our three areas of concern: authenticity, origins, and chain of custody. There are at least three aspects of these Daniel fragments that make it likely that they are original to the Qumran caves—more specifically, Cave 1.[27]

First, the condition and configuration of the fragments in a matted cluster associates them with two other Daniel scrolls later recovered from the

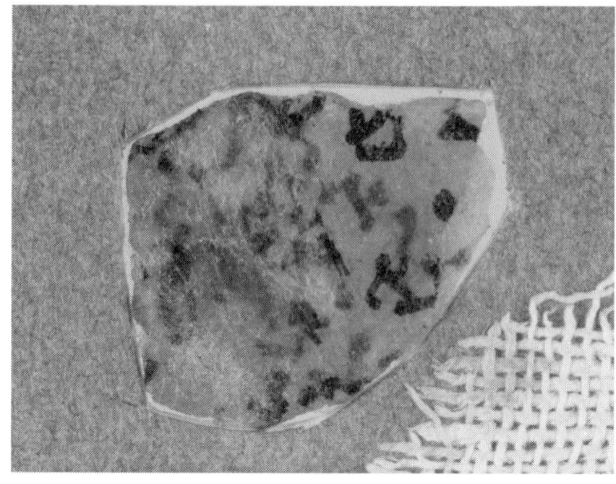

IMAGE 3.6: The pair of Daniel fragments among The Schøyen Collection are a rare case in the post-2002 fragments, as they have a likely relationship with two Cave 1 Daniel manuscripts (1QDaniel[a–b]). The sample images here are of (1) the small fragment of 1QDaniel[a] in The Schøyen Collection and (2) the same fragment set in context with the larger known fragments of that Cave 1 manuscript, in the care of the Archdiocese of the Syriac Orthodox Church for the Eastern USA. (Image credits: 1QDaniel[a] photograph by Bruce and Kenneth Zuckerman and Marilyn Lundberg, West Semitic Research. Courtesy of the Archdiocese of the Syriac Orthodox Church for the Eastern USA and its Archbishop, His Eminence Mor Dionysius John Kawak. Schøyen MS 1926-4 photograph by Bruce and Kenneth Zuckerman and Marilyn Lundberg, West Semitic Research. Courtesy The Schøyen Collection. Reconstruction by Bruce Zuckerman and Marilyn Lundberg, West Semitic Research, in cooperation with Torleif Elgvin, NLA University College, Oslo.)

---

cave, 1QDaniel[a] and 1QDaniel[b]. What exactly is a "matted cluster"? In popular imagination, we might think *all* the DSS were found in scroll jars, but this is incorrect. Only a very few items, such as likely the Great Isaiah Scroll (1QIsaiah[a]), were found in jars. Most of the DSS scrolls and fragments were found on the floors of caves in scattered piles and deteriorated stacks, or were acquired after their initial retrieval from the cave. Toss in two millennia of desert dust and bat feces, and you get a less romantic but more accurate picture (and smell) of the nature of the discoveries.

Because of this, some scrolls or fragments bonded together due to pressure, the elements, and time. When Trever wrote about the then-new discoveries of two Daniel scrolls (1QDaniel[a] and 1Qdaniel[b]), he remarked on and even depicted their material arrangement. He observed that when these materials made their way to scholars for study they were squashed and stuck together with another Cave 1 text, a Hebrew writing known as 1QLiturgical Prayers[b].[29] Trever's early observation and documentation is important for one reason: the set of Schøyen Daniel fragments were also received in a matted cluster arrangement. This time, however, the set of fragments squished together included only the Daniel texts. This configuration would be incredibly difficult to fake, and suggests that Schøyen's old/new fragments are within a degree of relation to another, confirmed, Cave 1 text.

Second, as far as we can tell from the limited available text, the scribal hand of Schøyen's Daniel fragments is remarkably close to that of the known and authentic materials from 1QDaniel[a] and 1QDaniel[b].[30] Though a good forger would presumably be up to snuff on their paleography—think of practicing your parent's signature to sign off on a bad report card—the similarity is instructive. In addition, it is also clear that there are "ghosted" letters impressed on the Schøyen Daniel fragments from other fragments in the matted cluster. This too would be a surprising feature to find on a modern forgery.

Third, in the case of the Schøyen Daniel 3:26–27 fragment, there is a small yet important textual overlap with the available text of 1QDaniel[b]. Kipp Davis and Torleif Elgvin, the editors of the fragment, observed that the Aramaic word מלכא ("the king") in Daniel 3:27 is partially preserved on 1QDaniel[b] 1–2:9 *and* the Schøyen fragment.[31] This is a little like two puzzle pieces joining together to make a complete word. Part of the word is found on a fragment of the known text of Daniel from Trever's day, while the other part is found on the Schøyen fragment.

At this point, it's reasonably certain that we can green light Schøyen's Daniel fragments as authentic. But where did this set of fragments come from (provenience)? And how did Schøyen obtain them (provenance)? Here's where Trever and his camera come in to play. Schøyen states that he acquired what were thought to be blank scroll fragments from the Trever family in 1994.[32] Before the purchase, the fragments were reportedly mounted in a frame in Trever's private collection with the inscription, "Dead Sea Scroll Fragments from Qumran Cave I."[33]

In a letter to Schøyen dated February 11, 1995, Trever indicates receiving the fragments as a reward from the Syrian Archbishop for his assistance in working with and photographing the scrolls. Though questionable in hindsight, it's not uncommon to find that blank—or what were thought to be blank—fragments were gifted to various individuals in those early days.[34] Schøyen also claims the lot came with an inscription by Trever that indicated

IMAGE 3.7 and 3.8: Only some DSS texts were found in jars. At times, damage and decay patterns on manuscripts provide clues to the orientation of a manuscript before its discovery. For example, the lower portions of 1QIsaiah[a] are discolored and show signs of rot, suggesting its vertical storage, perhaps in a jar. The sample image here includes a view of such lower damage due to decay as well as an ancient repair to a tear in the scroll (columns 12–13, with content of Isaiah 14:1–16:14). The use of scrolls jars for at least some items at Qumran opens up a broader cultural question of media storage in antiquity. Cylindrical jars with closing mechanisms on the lid for the storage of written documents is also known from Egyptian locations, such as Elephantine and Deir el-Medina in the Hellenistic period.[28] (Scroll jar image credit: Faithlife. 1QIsaiah[a]; Facsimile image credit: Andrew B. Perrin)

the original receipt of the gift on February 21, 1948. This is where things get interesting, and where Trever's academic *and* photographic consulting matter.

That date (February 21, 1948) does not coincide with the date Trever imaged the then-known fragments of 1QDaniel[a] and 1QDaniel[b]. We know that that photo shoot took place stateside, when Trever was at Yale University on April 7–9, 1949.[35] Rather, it coincides with his historic photographing of 1QIsaiah[a] and the *Community Rule* manuscript 1QS from Cave 1. This occurred in the basement of the American School of Oriental Research building in Jerusalem, just months after the initial DSS finds.

In March of 1995, Bruce Zuckerman and Marilyn Lundberg of West Semitic Research—an academic research unit at the University of Southern California specializing in advanced manuscript and artefact imaging—identified text of Aramaic Daniel in Schøyen's cluster of what were thought to be uninscribed fragments. Zuckerman even identified the presence of the Daniel cluster in "early photos by Trever, not used in his 1965 publication, showing the front and back of MS 1926/4 [the Schøyen Daniel fragments]."[36] So they had been there all along, unnoticed and unnoted.

Why does all this matter to our study of the new/old DSS fragments? We started off our first impression of the DSS with a count of seven scrolls from Cave 1. Then we learned these weren't all found at once. But the count of seven was what has become a staple "fact" of the DSS find stories, particularly as it relates to the earliest items recovered in 1947–48. However, these two tiny sets of Daniel fragments from the Schøyen collection suggest we should rethink that detail of the discovery of the DSS. While neither Archbishop Samuel nor Trever knew it at the time, when they were poring over the very first manuscripts of the DSS from Cave 1 in the basement of the American School of Oriental Research, fragments of two *more* scrolls were in the room, and both included text of Daniel. While this insight from the Schøyen Daniel fragments does not radically change what we know about the text of the book of Daniel, it does, in a small yet significant way, change how we understand the tale of the discovery of the DSS.

Conclusion

News of potential new fragments has meant that the modern story of the DSS is indeed ongoing—but just *how* new is precisely the question. This chapter of the story will continue to unfold in the years to come, yet the above exploration and case studies do permit some observations of insights, lessons learned, ongoing concerns, and open questions.

Newly available fragments are exciting but also intensely problematic. It is likely that some, but very few, of the new/old fragments in private collections are authentic. In general, all items acquired after 2002 are fake. We should recall that none of these, however, are "new" discoveries, in the sense that we cracked open a fresh cave and fragments came pouring out. These privately held fragments came from other, mostly unknown, channels. We can't get around that, yet we do need to acknowledge it. This also means the fragments were strategically withheld. By whom is not always clear, though we met some of the usual suspects in this and the last chapter.

The question of *who* is responsible or complicit is a legal matter, and one beyond my treatment here. Yet if there ever was a question that *is* in the wheelhouse of a humanities scholar, it is simply *why*? And the answer to the question, "Why were these items withheld until recently?" is evident.

$$$. £££. €€€. ¥¥¥. ฿฿฿. Pick your currency. There is also a secondary currency at play here: fame and recognition. The brokering (or better, trafficking) of such fragments is not motivated by a desire for delving deeper into the backstory of the Bible, but by profit, potential, and profile. Many of these items were either literally made or made available at the right time, when the right buyer came along who was willing to pay the right price. Make no mistake, there is *big* money to be made in this shadowy realm.

The antiquities and art trafficking market is also not black and white—it operates in shades of gray for authentic yet illicit artifacts.[37] These problems are complicated, and they're compounded when the objects in question are fake. The big issues here, then, are more than legal and economic—they are also ethical and political. While the new/old fragments of the DSS are small in size, the issues converging on them are large for buyers, sellers, and any other party involved in the procurement, promotion, and production of such fragments.

Newly created fragments carry all the baggage of the above, as well as a host of other problems related to their creation. In a way, for items that turn out to be fakes, ascertaining their chain of custody is even more important. We still don't know who is at the source, but whoever they are—and it need not be only a single source—they have advanced proficiencies on a number of fronts. Making even a decent forgery means having both advanced knowledge and technical skills in textual, material, scribal, linguistic, palaeographic, and papyrological aspects of the DSS.

The creation of faux fragments also brings up the question of what is driving the contemporary interest to own a piece of Scripture. Is it experiential? Some want to be able to touch and connect with a scriptural past. Is it pedagogical? Some want to be able to teach from a potentially one of a kind "hands on" experience. Is it theological? Some want to recover anything that will bring them nearer to an "original" text of the Bible. Is it cultural? Some are in pursuit of any items that help us understand human experiences and expressions of times and places now past. Is it political? For some, biblical artifacts and texts are part of larger identity constructs that both define and divide.

Regardless of the answer, this modern take on new/old fragments reminds us that the DSS have become part of a modern culture. Yet the story of the authentic fragments is truly ancient, and can be contextualized by exploring both the identities of ancient Judaism and archaeology of Qumran.

Chapter 4

Essene-ish: Classical and Qumran Sources on Ancient Jewish Identities and Movements

A few years ago I was in the Old City of Jerusalem with my family. My daughter, then two years old, was perched on my shoulders as we wound our way through the corners of cobblestone streets with a beautiful mix of people, culture, shops, and eats. As we meandered the afternoon away, we found ourselves in an Old City version of a corner store. The kid up top needed a cold drink, and I needed a pause from my dad-duty of lugging her around in the heat. I stood near the till with a few Coca-Colas in hand, spinning a carousel of postcards and other items begging for a last-minute purchase. Then something caught my eye near the kitschy postcards of Petra and Masada—a vintage map.

I unfurled the map from its tattered package and found it was a vintage "Pilgrim's Map of the Holy Land," decked out in mid-century modern color schemes and smattered with biblical references. For a few more shekels I purchased the map, and we enjoyed our cold Cokes as we made our way back to our home base at the Albright Institute. I tucked the map into my suitcase and forgot about it until I was unpacking my bags in Canada a few months later.

While the map started as a souvenir splurge, it captivated my academic attention when spread out on the kitchen table at home. The geography wasn't bad. The biblical references were okay, even if they were a creative push to drive theologically motivated tourists. Then I noticed something curious: almost exactly where the Qumran archaeological site and caves are today, the cartographers had placed the label "Essenes." The fine print at the lower edge of the map said the copyright year was 1942, but the DSS weren't discovered until *after* that, in 1947. Without the scrolls, how or why would a map locate the Essenes there?

The other question you may be asking is, Who are the Essenes anyway? These are key questions for my little souvenir, but more importantly for understanding the origins of the DSS in the Second Temple period, as well as identifying the group that likely lived at Qumran and penned or preserved the scrolls. They are also questions that demand we read *around* the DSS for insight as well as *within* them for information.

This chapter does double duty. First, it sketches out portraits of the main ancient Jewish groups relevant to the study of the DSS—Pharisees, Sadducees, and Essenes—with a little help from classical sources that became all the more important after the Qumran finds. We'll see that these *outsider* perspectives are essential for understanding the contours of Jewish identity in antiquity.

Then we'll add some detail to this sketch by exploring the *insider* perspective of so-called sectarian DSS that reveal some signature elements of identity, practices, and beliefs of the Qumran group and movement. This will help round out the portrait of the Essene or Essene-like movement, of which we find one expression at Qumran. As with most topics, we'll need to be selective. This is a sketch, not a detailed masterpiece.

This twofold approach will allow us to triangulate what the sources say about various groups and then compare and contrast what the scrolls reveal about the makeup of the group behind them. This will help us determine the most likely candidate for the ancient group that called Qumran home and copied or collected the DSS. In the process, we'll also gain a sense of the complexity of Jewish identities in the Second Temple period, as well as discover what is really going on in my map.

But first, a bit of who's who in the classical sources.

A Crash Course on Classic Sources Commenting on Ancient Jewish Groups

The first item on our agenda involves a bit of a meet and greet with the relevant classical authors—Josephus, Philo, and Pliny the Elder—as well as some touchpoints in key sources like the New Testament and the Mishnah. Before we can ask "What do (or don't) these writings say about the Essenes?" we need to know where they sit in the literary landscape of the ancient world.[1]

Let's begin with a brief bio of Josephus (37/38–100 CE). Josephus was a well-educated member of the Jerusalem aristocracy. Before he took up the pen, however, he wielded a sword. Josephus led Jewish troops against the Romans in Galilee in the first Jewish revolt (66–70 CE). Eventually, Josephus and his men were driven back to a fortification in Jotapata. After a siege lasting several weeks, he surrendered in early July of 67 CE. Somewhat controversially, as a captive to the Romans he aided them in translation and negotiations with Jewish soldiers.

After the revolt was quelled, Josephus became a Roman citizen and spent his days reflecting on Jewish history and interpreting the traditional Hebrew Scriptures as a member of the Flavian house (hence the name Flavius Josephus). Josephus's works come in handy for Qumran research because he comments in numerous places on the Jewish groups of his day: Pharisees, Sadducees, Essenes, and the unnamed "fourth philosophy." Both in his political and military experience in the Jewish revolt as well as his intellectual and literary contributions, Josephus is an essential source for studying thought, life, and identity in ancient Judaism.

Next up: Philo of Alexandria (15/10 BCE–45/50 CE). Like Josephus, Philo was a prolific Jewish writer from a well-established family. However, his perspective and works are penned from the Jewish community of Alexandria in Egypt—an entirely different hub of Jewish culture than Josephus in his Judean homeland.

Philo's volumes include philosophical treatises as well as several scriptural commentaries. Perhaps more than any other Jewish writer of this period, Philo was immersed in and interacting with both ancestral traditions and Hellenistic forms of thought. Many of Philo's writings reflect what Alexandria became known for later in the early Christian tradition: allegorical biblical interpretation. For our purposes, his writings also include comments on Jewish groups and demographics. Along the way, he references the Essenes as well as an ascetic Egyptian group known as the "Therapeutae," which may be related to (or at least parallels) Philo's depiction of the Essenes elsewhere in his writings.

Our next classical writer who needs a short introduction is Pliny the Elder (23–79 CE). Pliny came to the topic of Judea from a different angle and for a different purpose than Josephus or Philo. He was a Roman author, administrator, and military official. As such, when it came to Judea, he was interested in both the lay of the land and who lived in it. As we'll see, Pliny's remarks on the Essenes and Dead Sea region are striking.

There is one final major Greek source that is highly relevant here: the New Testament. While we often use other sources to contextualize the New Testament, for the present topic, it is select writings of the Greek New Testament itself that are sources for the study of Jewish groups and identities in ancient Judaism.[2]

IMAGE 4.1: Bust of Jewish historian and patron of the Roman Flavian house, Flavius Josephus (37/38–100 CE) in the New Carlsberg Museum collection. (Image credit: Wikimedia Commons)

Essenes are not mentioned in the New Testament, but Pharisees and Sadducees are regularly on the scene in the Gospels. and of course the apostle Paul was a Pharisee prior to becoming a Jesus follower. While these groups are sometimes represented in a less than favorable and often rhetorical light in the New Testament, their portrayals regularly hinge on key items of belief or practices. This information can be read critically alongside other sources, like Josephus or Philo, to add to the portrait of the Jewish groups of the day.

Early rabbinic literature—particularly the catalog of rabbinic conversations and thought in the Mishnah (second century CE)—is also an important source for reflecting on Jewish identity, practice, and belief in antiquity.[3] While it is not always clear which groups are in view in rabbinic debates, it is often possible to recover some likely associations with groups known from earlier times, particularly the Pharisees and Sadducees.

With profiles of the main sources that figure in the conversation for assessing Qumran identity in place, now comes the "whodunit" question of which group is most likely behind the DSS. Along the way, we'll observe how these *outside* sources align (or not) with the *inside* materials of the DSS that portray group identity, practice, and belief. We'll also weigh a few pros and cons using examples for each of the main Jewish groups.

The Pharisees and Qumran? Hopes for Resurrection, Marrying Your Niece, and Godfather-Like Vengeance Plots

Spoiler alert: most would agree that the Pharisees, or a Pharisee-like group, were not likely behind the DSS. Why? Many reasons. Let's look at a few.

On one hand, there are some similarities in belief between the Pharisees and this group at Qumran. For example, their hopes for an afterlife and even resurrection are similar. The New Testament captures this belief and some intergroup tensions in Acts 23:6–8:

> When Paul noticed that some were Sadducees and others were Pharisees, he called out in the council, "Brothers, I am a Pharisee, a son of Pharisees. I am on trial concerning the hope of the resurrection of the dead." When he said this, a dissension began between the Pharisees and the Sadducees, and the assembly was divided. (The Sadducees say that there is no resurrection or angel or spirit; but the Pharisees acknowledge all three.)

The Qumran group also embraced a robust view of fates beyond the grave, including an expectation of resurrection. There are several places and passages that touch on this in the DSS collection. Arguably the clearest image of this is found in a Hebrew text from Qumran Cave 4, dubbed *Pseudo-Ezekiel*.[4] This will probably sound familiar, but with a twist:

> Son of man, prophesy over these bones, and say, "Come together, bone to its bone and joint [to its joint.'" And it wa]s s[o.] And he said a second time, "Prophesy, and let sinews come upon them and let skin cover [them." And it was so.] And he s[ai]d, "Again prophesy to the four winds of the heavens, and let them blow [upon the slain." And it was so.] And a great many people [revi]ved (Ezekiel 37:4–10). And they blessed the Lord of hosts wh[o had revived them. And] I said, "O Lord, when will [th]ese things come to pass?" And the Lord said to [me, "Until] [... and after many] days a tree shall bend, and it shall stand up. (4Q385 2:5–10)

The citation of Ezekiel 37:10 ends with a symbolic vision of rattling bones reviving with the winds of heaven. Our scribe, however, seamlessly extends this with the statement, "And they blessed the Lord of hosts wh[o had revived them" (4Q385 2:8–9). This changes everything: the bones are no longer bound to a metaphor promising new life. Rather, they have become embodied actors in the vision promising the hope of bodily resurrection. There are other images and references to resurrection in the DSS, too, that indicate the group there was at the very least aware of, if not advocates of, this expectation.[5]

On the other hand, we find some major tensions in religious practices between the Qumran group and the Pharisees. This is where we need to remind ourselves that, while belief (theology) is a defining feature of group identity, in ancient Judaism the expression of those beliefs in practice was what truly distinguished groups and identities. One great example is the different perspectives on appropriate configurations of marriage within a kinship group.

Some Hebrew texts in the Qumran library prohibit marriage to one's niece in explicit terms:

> No man is to marry his brother's daughter or his sister's daughter; that is abhorrent. (*Temple Scroll*, 11Q19 66:16–17)

> Let no man take the w[ife of his father, let him not uncover the skirt of his father. Let no one take] his brother's daughter or the daughter of [his] si[ster ... Let no] man [uncover]. (*Messianic Apocalypse*, 4Q251 17:2–3)

The *Damascus Document* (CD 5:7–11) also speaks to this issue, indicating that the practice of marrying one's niece was one of many infractions that resulted in the defilement of the Jerusalem temple by the Qumranite's opponents. Collectively, these three sample texts indicate a strong and clear stance on the matter.

However, one Aramaic text found at Qumran, the *Visions of Amram*, portrays a scene of uncle-niece marriage in a reimagined story of a woman named Miriam's wedding to her uncle Uzziel.[6] This reminds us that the Qumran library isn't always uniform—few libraries are—so we should expect some diversity of thought and expression. Not all these texts will reflect the beliefs of the Qumran group.

So where do Pharisaic views come into play? In later Rabbinic literature in the Babylonian Talmud, we learn that the rabbis permitted niece marriage (B. Talmud Yebamot 62b; Gittin 83a; Sanhedrin 76b.). It seems likely that in this case (and many others) rabbinic thought has a heritage in earlier Pharisaic Judaism. Therefore, this would be a key difference from what appears to be the majority view expressed in the Hebrew DSS above.

IMAGE 4.2: The Temple Scroll (11Q19) is a remarkable item the DSS for several reasons. Measuring in at 8.146 meters (26.7 feet) in length, it is the longest scroll among the DSS finds. It is a bold interpretive text that rewrites material from Exodus and Deuteronomy in the first-person voice of none other than God himself. (Image credit: Wikimedia Commons)

If we drill deeper, however, we can recover a shared interest. The Qumran texts and rabbinic sources listed above, though they disagree about practice, are all interpreting Leviticus 18:7-20. That passage in the Hebrew Scriptures outlines the parameters of acceptable marriage practices in the community, but leaves the uncle-niece variety ambiguous. What we have here, then, is a shared substructure of approaches to forming and maintaining identity through engagement with the Hebrew Scriptures and extending them into key issues. The conclusions differ, but the basis and approach are similar.

There are also several Hebrew DSS that level not-so-subtle critiques against opponents of the Qumran group, using ciphered names for outsiders. The *Damascus Document*, for example, talks about how Qumran's founding figure, the Teacher of Righteousness, fell out with the "seekers of smooth things" over disputes about Torah interpretation (CD 1:14–2.1).

The *pesher* text on the prophecies of Nahum is even more telling. After a citation of a passage in Nahum 2:11, which references "where the lion goes, and the lion's cubs, with no one to disturb them," the Qumran commentator describes the following:

> [This refers to Deme]trius, king of Greece, who sought to enter Jerusalem through the counsel of the ones who look for smooth things; [but it never fell into the] power of the kings of Greece from Antiochus until the appearance of the rulers of the Kittim (i.e., the Romans); but afterwards it will be trampled [by the Gentiles]. (*Pesher Nahum*, 4Q169 3–4 1.2–4)

Pesher Nahum continues with other references to "the seekers" and their involvement in the geopolitical events of the period, particularly the invitation of the Seleucid King Demetrius III Eukerus to invade Judea by opponents of the Hasmonean ruler, Alexander Jannaeus. With a little help from Josephus (*War* 1.92–114; *Ant.* 13.376–418), we're able to piece together the crisis that ensued and how the Pharisees were caught up in the turmoil.

Though Demetrius defeated Jannaeus, Jewish infighting ensued upon Alexander's withdrawal. Jannaeus reportedly captured some six thousand opponents and crucified eight hundred of them in front of their wives and children (*Ant.* 13.380). Josephus indicates that in Alexander's dying moments he adjured his wife Alexandra to deal well with the Pharisees—to concede a degree of power to them, lest chaos crescendo after his death (*Ant.* 13.401). As James VanderKam notes, this is "a hint that the individuals he had executed so cruelly were Pharisees."[7] Following his death, the Pharisees reportedly approached Alexandra to seek out vengeance by killing those who had advised Alexander to crucify the eight hundred men.

IMAGE 4.3: Antiochus IV Epiphanes (215–164 BCE) was among the more notorious of Greek rulers in the centuries leading up to the Common Era. His intense Hellenization policies included imposing emperor worship and sponsoring the desecration of the Jerusalem temple (see Daniel 12:11). These actions sparked the Maccabean revolt against his Seleucid rule. The coin depicting Antiochus here reads, "King Antiochus, God manifest, bearer of victory." (Image credit: Wikimedia Commons)

The references in the DSS Nahum commentary are a bit cryptic, and retracing the history of Pharisaic involvement in this Seleucid-Hasmonean crisis is tricky. Be that as it may, it seems that this text is speaking against the "Lion of Wrath" and those Jewish groups sympathetic to him, making it nearly impossible that there is a Pharisaic connection to Qumran.

While the Pharisees are off the list of candidates for the group behind the DSS, the exploration reveals insights into thought and practice, recovers some common approaches to forming and maintaining identity through scriptural interpretation, and surfaces contentious group dynamics and politics of the Second Temple period.

The Sadducees and Qumran? (Im)Purity, Angels, Afterlife, and Code Names

Not unlike the compare and contrast with the Pharisees above, there are a blend of points and counterpoints for considering the Sadducees or a Sadducee-like group in relation to Qumran and the DSS. Here too there are illuminating correlations with Sadducean thought and practice, but also some deal-breaking distinctions that make this association unlikely.

One of the biggest areas of similarity and dissimilarity between the Sadducees and the Qumran community regards views of purity and impurity. Many ancient Jewish groups and writers had an acute awareness of the ways one could become ritually impure. This meant the state of being unfit for involvement in aspects of community life and or participation in religious practice. Impurity was not about a list of religious rules, and impurity was not sin—a common misconception today. For ancient Jews, each day was full of opportunities to exhibit one's devotion and commitment to God. Becoming impure was part of a regular rhythm of life. Take for example menstrual impurity (it isn't sinful or unnatural to menstruate) or contacting a corpse (it isn't sinful or irreverent to tend to the dead). But understanding how, when, and where to engage in practices for recovering purity was of great importance. The traditions that emerge around impurity in ancient through rabbinic Judaism are referred to as "Halakhah."

One area of halakhic tradition explores how impurity could be transferred through liquids. Does a liquid form a barrier between the pure and impure, or is it a conduit through which impurity could transfer from one item to another?

The letter known as 4QMMT—which we'll return to in greater detail in chapter 9—outlines key points of religious practice that the Qumranites disagreed on with their external opponents.[8] One portion of the text reads:

> [Co]ncerning streams of liquid, we have determined that they are not intrinsically [p]ure. Indeed, streams of liquid do not form a barrier

> between the impure and the pure. For the liquid of the stream and that in its receptacle become as one liquid. (4Q394 8iv:5; see also 4Q397 6–13:1)

Intriguingly, the Mishnah indicates that the Sadducees adopted this same position:

> The Sadducees say: "We complain against you, Pharisees, that you declare an uninterrupted flow of a liquid to be clean." (m. Yadayim 4:7)

On this point of Halakhah, the legal ruling of the Qumranite group seems to square with the Sadducean position.

While the example of liquid purity and impurity is a remarkable point of continuity, there are several large obstacles to identifying the Qumranites as a Sadducean group. One key area relates to beliefs in an afterlife and angelic beings.

The New Testament says that "The Sadducees say that there is no resurrection or angel or spirit; but the Pharisees acknowledge all three" (Acts 23:8; cf. Mark 12:18; Luke 20:27). We saw above that the belief in resurrection was explicit at Qumran and present in writings like *Pseudo-Ezekiel*. And we saw in chapter 2 that belief in angels was a core component of the apocalyptic battle scenario of the *War Scroll*. In a few pages, we'll see that interaction with angels was also a signature element of Qumran liturgical life. In this instance, then, we have clear alignment with the thought and expectations of two groups (Qumranites and Pharisees) against another (Sadducees).

Elsewhere in the DSS we find ciphers and code names abound for Sadducee-like group. One common term we find is "Manasseh," a term used in the Hebrew Scriptures for the errant northern kingdom, associated with the sin of King Manasseh (ca. 687–642; see 2 Chronicles 33:18–19). Apparently bad nicknames are tough to shake. The Qumranites picked up this moniker

IMAGE 4.4: The work known as 4QMMT shed new light on the identity of the Qumran group and their self-differentiation from other Jewish groups. The writing also caused a reorientation in DSS studies to pay greater attention to religious practices as a hallmark of identity. The work is attested in six copies at Qumran, ranging in dates from 75 BCE–50 CE. The sample here is from the manuscript 4Q396. (Image credit: Courtesy of the Leon Levy Dead Sea Scrolls Digital Library; Israel Antiquities Authority, photo: Shai Halevi)

---

and applied it to an outsider group who they saw as wayward and not aligned with the true way of the community.

Pesher Nahum (discussed above) includes this cipher to speak against a group with some posterity and position in Jerusalem.

> The meaning of the passage: they are the wicked of […] a divisive group who ally themselves to Manasseh. "She, too, w[ent] into exile [a captive,] her infants were smashed at the head of every street. They throw lots for her respectable citizens, all her nobles [have been bound] with chains" (Nah 3:10). This refers to Manasseh in the Last Days, for his kingdom shall be brought low in Is[rael …] his women, his infants, and his children shall go into captivity; his warriors and his nobles [shall be killed] with the sword. (4Q169 3–4 iv:1–4)

Admittedly, this sample from *Pesher Nahum* is less explicit than the rhetoric against the "seekers of smooth things," or the Pharisees, which we tracked above. Yet, taken along with other clues that indicate the Qumranites were critical of the priestly establishment in Jerusalem, and given the proximity of the Sadducees to that strata of society and religious institution, it seems we may have here a coded jab at the Sadducees.

In the quest for the identity of the Qumranites, then, we have another negative conclusion. While the Sadducees are an unlikely fit, the samples above reveal that the diversity and discord between these groups often stems from shared concerns over key matters of expressions of identity and institutions.

The Essenes and Qumran? First Impressions, a Hypothesis, and a Movement

We now come to our next and most likely candidate: the Essenes. It didn't take long for this connection to present itself following the initial discovery of the scrolls. More recent studies have nuanced the association in view of the now fully published collection.

Already in February of 1948, a brother of Archbishop Samuel's assistant told John Trever that he was aware the Essenes once lived near the Dead Sea, and suggested the Qumran scrolls and site were their legacy and home.[9] The connection was also made publicly in early press releases, first by Yale University (April 1948), in which Millar Burrows suggested that the *Community Rule* was likely a rule text of the Essenes. Shortly after this, a Hebrew newspaper article on the upcoming release of Eliezer Sukenik's book on the scrolls also included a similar statement connecting that text to the Essenes.[10]

Within a decade of discovery, the certainty over the association is found throughout first-generation scrolls scholars' writings. Frank Moore Cross, for example, stated, "There is now sufficient evidence, to be supplemented as publication of the scrolls and reports of excavations in the vicinity of Qumran continue, to identify the people of the scrolls definitively with the Essenes."[11]

What led to this connection? Why was it made so promptly? And why has it had such a lasting impact on DSS scholarship? Here is where our classical sources come into play. Let's start by thinking about geography; then we'll turn to questions of demographics and ways of life.

According to Pliny, the Essenes were at home just off the shores of the Dead Sea. Pliny's words on this point in *Natural History* are worth quoting in full:

> On the west side of the Dead Sea, but out of range of the noxious exhalations of the coast, is the solitary tribe of the Essenes, which is remarkable beyond all the other tribes in the whole world, as it has no women and has renounced all sexual desire, has no money, and has only palm-trees for company. Day by day the throng of refugees is recruited to an equal number by numerous accessions of persons tired of life and driven thither by the waves of fortune to adopt their manners. Thus, through thousands of ages (incredible to relate) a race in which no one is born lives on forever: so prolific for their advantage is other men's weariness of life! Lying below the Essenes was formerly the town of Engedi, second only to Jerusalem in the fertility of its land and in its groves of palm-trees, but now like Jerusalem a heap of ashes. Next comes Masada, a fortress on a rock, itself also not far from the Dead Sea. This is the limit of Judea. (*Nat. Hist.* 5.15.70)

While there is much more going on in this quote than a point on a map, Pliny's identification is incredible. Apparently, his homework on the terrain and geography of Judea located an Essene community remarkably close to the site that we now know as Qumran. At the very least, by the first century CE, there is an attestation of Essene life on the western shores of the Dead Sea.[12] (This is how the folks behind my souvenir map made the Essene connection—apparently they had an eye on Pliny, as well as the Bible).

What about demographics? According to Pliny, the Essenes were a celibate and cashless cadre of men in the desert whose numbers self-perpetuated in the shade of palms. Some of these elements—except for the palm tree bit—resonate with aspects of Josephus and Philo's descriptions, although in Josephus and Philo we find more complete and complex characterizations of Essene life, location, and lifestyle.

Josephus says that not all Essenes were ascetic. Some preferred to live in towns but, regardless of location, they all led a simple existence (*War* 2.151; 5.145). When traveling, he notes, they bore arms for safety (*War* 2.125). Some Essenes married, mostly for procreation, while others remained celibate but adopted children to grow their ranks (*War* 2.120–121; 2.160; *Ant* 18.21). All told, Josephus tallies a total of about four thousand Essenes (*Ant.* 18.20). Josephus references some individual Essenes, such as one "John the Essene" (*War* 2.567; 3.11). This specific mention is one of a few times Josephus shows a clear affection for a few Essenes he knew. In terms of outlook, Josephus underscores that the Essenes were big on determinism. The Essenes at once declared "fate is the mistress of all things" and left "everything in the hands of God" (*Ant.* 13.172; 18.18). We'll see shortly that this squares well with the determinism and dualism embedded in key sectarian writings.

Philo remarks on similar issues of Essene identity, but also has his own signature elements. He indicates that some Essenes fled the cities but may live in villages or in large groups (*Every Good Man* 76; *Apol.* 1–2). He too underscores that their lifestyle required only the essentials (*Every Good Man* 76). Remarkably, Philo's population count of around four thousand is the same as Josephus's (*Every Good Man* 75). Unlike Josephus, though, Philo claims the Essenes banned marriage flat out and practiced sexual self-control (*Apol.* 14–17).[13] Finally, Philo says that no weapons were found among the group and that they were apparently pacifists, which is also different from what we saw in Josephus.

There are also shared elements and differences in Josephus and Philo's comments regarding Essene community structures and core practices of Essene life. Josephus underscores that the Essenes were intensely hierarchical and had a three-year admission process (*War* 2.137–142). In this process, all newcomers submitted their finances and property to the common purse of the group (*War* 2.122–123). The rhythm of daily life was set by a schedule of prayer, meals, and work on repeat (*War* 2.128–132). Meals were open to Essene initiates only and prepared by a priest according to purity laws (*War* 2.131). The Essenes maintained purity through a practice of twice-daily immersions in water (*Ant.* 18.22; *War* 2.129–32; 243). Josephus also notes that the Essenes sent offerings to the Jerusalem temple, yet he also makes a foggy reference to some Essenes performing sacrifices according to a different custom among themselves (*Ant.* 18.19). When we dig into archaeology in the next chapter, we'll consider the curious case of dismembered and charred animal bones at Qumran.

Philo also highlights that Essene property, goods, finances, and clothes were all communal (*Every Good Man* 76–77, 85–86; *Apol.* 12). He seems to have a network of Essenes in view, remarking that houses of Essenes are open to members "of the sect arriving from elsewhere" (*Every Good Man* 86). Like Josephus, Philo too notes the importance of communal meals (*Apol.* 5, 11–12). Philo famously ends on a high note, writing that, "The life of the Essenes is indeed so enviable that not only individuals but even great kings are seized with admiration before such men, and are glad to pay homage to their honourable character by heaping favours and honours upon them" (*Apol.* 18). One can't help but get the feeling that Philo has let his affection for the lifestyle of these desert intellects run away with him here.

So where does this land us in terms of a plausible association between the DSS and known Jewish groups of the Second Temple period? The internal and external evidence makes a link with the Pharisees or Sadducees tough to maintain. When the classical sources are brought into the mix, the Essenes become a compelling candidate from the perspective of external sources.

Qumran Identity from the Inside Out: Realities and Idealized Views from the Dead Sea Scrolls

We can now add some detail to our outlines of Jewish group identities with more insights from the DSS themselves. Admittedly, a full portrait is beyond the scope of this book; rather, the aim here is to complement the above comparisons and contrasts with a selective sample of the distinct features of life, belief, and practice in the arid, ancient Judean wilderness—this Qumran "Way" we heard about back in chapter 1. The areas we'll detail below include principles and ideals of community organization, imaginative and innovative liturgies, apocalyptic outlooks and writings, and conceptions of time.

An Ordered Community with a Clear Orientation to Others and Otherworlds

The DSS that describe or depict the life of the community are not necessarily a direct lens into its functions or formations. Sometimes—even often—they contain what are likely real glimpses of this reality, but they also include idealized elements of how the community understood its own identity.

Take the *Community Rule*, for example, which opens with a long section of a covenant ceremony expressing how the life lived by the elect is one of utter devotion to the ways of God, rooted in scriptural precepts, governed by hierarchical leadership, and lived in the "light" (1QS 1:1–15). This sets up future sections that elaborate on the elect as the true Israel, in language laden with covenantal precepts inspired by Deuteronomy 28–31.

From here priestly references and liturgical language abound, which are also core to a description of annual ceremonies for the ranks and order of the members (1QS 2:19–25). But even this order gives way to otherworldly considerations. This is nowhere clearer than in a famous section called the "Treatise on the Two Spirits" (1QS 3:13–4:26). This subsection establishes the stark dichotomy of light versus darkness as two appositional forces at work in the cosmos and in the human heart.

Much of this is arguably heavily idealized, or at least creatively stylized. The sections thereafter are perhaps more descriptive of how the community actually ordered itself in view of their priestly (Zadokite) lineage and authority structure. Here too reality rests in revelation: all that the community says and does derives from their all-important, inspired, insider interpretation of Torah.

This Way was one of togetherness (recall their affinity for referring to themselves as the *Yahad*). The *Community Rule* speaks of settlements of groups and a charter of sorts for founding a community. The basic start-up includes a chapter of at least ten men plus a presiding priest, who share common meals, continually engage in study of the law, read scripture, and pray together (1QS 6:2–8).[14] The Cave 1 *Community Rule* then features a section known as the prayer of the Maskil (1QS 9:26–11:22). This material reveals that prayer was central to the group as well as indicates how the community's identity and practice were informed by their religious calendar. We'll return to that point below.

Then, just when you think it's all over, there is an appendix of sorts: the *Rule of the Congregation* (1QSa) and the *Rule of the Blessing* (1QSb). These materials reveal the ongoing development of *Rule* traditions and, in this case, the inclusion of the *Yahad*'s expectation for the end of time, including a messianic banquet.

We also find different glimpses of the shape and size of communities that were part of this way: for example, in the *Damascus Document*.[15] This text includes a section that is a "rule for those who live in camps," including the requirement of a priestly leader with deep knowledge of the "Book of Meditation" (CD 12:22–13:7), a "rule for the Overseer of the camp" (CD 13:7–12), and subsequent ranks within the group (CD 14:3–6).

Whether idealized, stylized, or realized, works such as the *Community Rule* and the *Damascus Document* provide context, new insight, and information into the complex dynamics of Jewish life and sectarian identity at Qumran and beyond.

Liturgy Reimagined and Religious Life without the (Earthly) Temple

The *Community Rule* touched on the importance of liturgy for the Qumranites: that is, a rhythm of life and worship inspired by tradition, affected in the present, and encompassing movement, thought, practice, and performance in religious experience.[16] Arguably the biggest liturgical innovation revealed by the DSS is that the Qumranites were devout and deeply liturgical *but* disapproved and distanced themselves from the Temple in Jerusalem.

How was this possible? Enter the liturgical imagination.

Take, for example, the writing *Songs of the Sabbath Sacrifice*, known by up to eight manuscripts at Qumran and some fragmentary materials found atop Masada. This tradition describes the angelic liturgy of select Jewish festivals on the paradigm of the sectarian calendar (more on that in a minute). This cycle of liturgy included the movement, even elevation, of the community into a celestial temple among the angels. We see this in a sound bite from 4Q400 1:1–6:

> [A text belonging to the Instructor. The song accompanying the sacrifice on the] first [Sabbath,] sung on the fourth of the first month: Praise [the God of ...] you godlike beings of utter holiness; [rejoice in his divine kingdom. For he has established] utter holiness among the eternally holy, that they might become for Him priests [of their inner sanctum in His royal temple,] ministers of the Presence in his glorious innermost chamber. In the congregation of all the [wise] godlike beings, [and in the councils of all the] divine [spirits,] He has engraved His precepts to govern all spiritual works, and His [glorious] laws [for all the] wise [divine beings,] that safe congregation honored by God, those who draw near to knowledge.

IMAGE 4.5: The liturgical work *Songs of the Sabbath Sacrifice* includes a series of hymnic compositions that both ordered and oriented the community's liturgical life. A signature element of these hymns is their expectation of elevation through worship to join the angels in a celestial temple. The image sample here is from 4Q400. (Image credit: Courtesy of The Leon Levy Dead Sea Scrolls Digital Library; Israel Antiquities Authority, photo: Shai Halevi)

One critical item expressed here is the close connection between the worshipful actions of the community's liturgy and the heavenly liturgy of the angels in the heavenly temple. This is both a bold move and a clever innovation. The claim is that Qumran's liturgical cycle was not limited to this world; rather, they believed their worship joined them with angelic worship ongoing in the heavenly temple.

This hallmark of Qumran religious thought is truly innovative. Remember, this group was estranged from the temple establishment, yet had a deep commitment to maintaining proper temple worship. By reimagining and reorienting their liturgical life in this way, the Qumranites extended their liturgical trajectory to the *celestial* temple. This meant they retained the central place of temple worship in their liturgical practice while maintaining their disdain for the present, *earthly* temple. Not only did this outlook emphasize the unification of earthly and heavenly worship, it also made the not-so-subtle critique that earthly temple worship is but a pale shadow of the true and full liturgy that is open and active to the Qumran sectarians.

An Apocalyptic Community That Read (and Wrote?) Apocalypses

In later chapters on the Aramaic texts at Qumran, the DSS, and Christian origins, we'll see just how formative the DSS are for overhauling what we thought we knew about apocalyptic theologies and literature. For now, we'll see that these discoveries revealed how a community could be so steeped in apocalyptic outlooks that they could be considered an "apocalyptic community."

We saw glimpses of this already in the *Community Rule*. For example, there is an openness to special revelation as well as time and space divided into light and darkness. Taking 1QSa and 1QSb into account (those bonus texts included at the end of the scroll) we see a community that was expectant, looking to the horizon in messianic hope. Similarly, there were glimpses of this in the *Songs of the Sabbath Sacrifice*: heaven and earth could collapse together as the community was elevated into other realities among the angelic host. Already these elements point to a community rooted in the past but reaching beyond their present reality and experience with the help of signature elements of apocalyptic thought.

For all this apocalyptic inspiration, the Qumran community has not been traditionally associated with writing formal apocalypses themselves. But this assumption is challenged by the complex and rich apocalyptic literature penned in Aramaic among the discoveries. Those writings too dealt in time and space, angels and demons, dualities and destinies, revelation and revolution—and scholars agree that many of these texts are among our earliest known examples of the apocalyptic genre. At the very least, the Qumranites were avid readers of this literature. It is perhaps not surprising that apocalyptic thought informed their self-understanding and view of the world around them. Even if we are unsure *if* the Qumranites wrote formal apocalypses, we have still discovered something arguably as important: an apocalyptic community.

Keeping Time and Contesting Calendars

The topic of organizing time relates both to Qumran's liturgical innovations and apocalyptic imaginations—only now we're not focused on patterns of prayer (as in liturgy), or ages, eras, or endgames (as in apocalypticism), but in conceptions of calendar related to legal matters. Not in the modern, judicial sense of the word *legal*, but in the interpretation and application of the social, religious, and communal codes of the Hebrew Scriptures in ancient Jewish life.

This brings us into the context of another major and defining feature of Qumran identity. Here too, we'll only scratch the surface of calendrical estimations and thought. We'll see that like the other topics above, time and calendar loom large in the DSS, and hint at tensions with other outsider Jewish groups of the day.

In ancient Judaism there seem to have been a few competing calendar systems. The predominant calendar of choice at Qumran was reckoned on a

364-day system. Lawrence Schiffman described the situation like this: "The calendar consisted of three hundred sixty-four days, divided into twelve months of thirty days each. The months were calibrated according to the cycle of the sun. At the equinoxes and solstices at the end of each three-month cycle, a thirty-first day was added to that month."[17] This summary provides an explanation of the general mechanics of this calendar. But how did this 364-day calendar manifest itself in the DSS writings?

We see some of this in the *Damascus Document*. The *Damascus Document* says it is essential "to keep the Sabbath day according to specification and the holidays and the fast day according to the commandments of those entering the new covenant in the land of Damascus" (CD 6:18–19). We have hints here of the importance of calendar observance according to the interpretation of the "new covenant," which reminds us of how interpretation and identity are enmeshed in the world of the DSS. Once again, it was that all-important insider interpretation of Torah that defined the group, and now ordered their calendar of religious practice.

We get another glimpse of this in 4QMMT. This text concludes with the all-important statement: "[On the twenty-eighth of the month] is a Sabbath. (The month) continues (with the day) after [the] S[abbath, the second day (Monday),] [and an addition]al [day.] The year is complete: three hundred s[ixty-four] days." (4Q394 3–7 1:1–3). This reflection provides the community perspective on the scope and structure of the approved calendar. As far as they were concerned, the calendar was 364 days. End of story.

But why did time and calendar matter so much to this group? First, it set them apart from what many (or most) Jewish groups of the day followed: their 364-day calendar was reckoned based on the sun's journey through the cosmos, with a secondary interest in lunar phases and movements. Second, the Qumran calendar seems to have been based in Enochic literature, which goes to great lengths to demonstrate that the calendar is woven into the fabric of the universe (for example, 1 Enoch 80:2–4). Third, despite the many uncertainties of community origins and the historic Teacher of Righteousness, *Pesher Habakkuk* 11:4–8 seems to describe how the historic falling out between the Teacher and the Wicked Priest came down to a difference about the calendar.[18]

Talking about time and calendar in the DSS connects us with a concept that is likely foreign to many modern readers, yet was integral to several facets of ancient Jewish life. The Qumran community's calendar was distinct, ordered their experience, positioned them with or against other groups, was inspired by a deeper tradition of Enochic thought, and even had a crucial role to play in their memory of the founding of their community.

Conclusion

Our tour of Jewish literary antiquity has cut across classical sources, biblical writings, rabbinic literature, and samples of the DSS. The combination of outsider perspectives and insider insights helped us make a plausible geographic association between the site of Qumran and a known group, the Essenes, and it contextualized the finds in the broader social and ideological landscape of ancient Judaism. We'll build on this further in the next chapter on archaeology.

Like all writings—ancient or modern—the DSS neither originated nor existed in a vacuum. We are used to thinking of the scrolls as *texts* and *artifacts*. And they are. But every text has a context and every inscribed artefact originated in human hands—in our case, within a known ancient community at a specific archaeological site. Part of the task of this chapter was to begin appreciating the scrolls in the broader social context of Second Temple Judaism and to recall that they can't be approached or understood without this context. We saw that the scrolls reveal both continuity and tensions with other groups. While Qumran was geographically *apart from* the main scene of ancient Jewish culture in Jerusalem, the Qumranites were still *a part of* the social fabric of that era.

IMAGE 4.6: In ancient Jewish scribal imagination, the brief reference to Enoch "walking with God" before "God took him" in Genesis 5:24 gave rise to an expansive apocalyptic tradition of Enoch's otherworldly journeys and dream-visions. Among the knowledge Enoch is granted via these revelations is deep knowledge of the workings of the cosmos and the cadence of times and seasons determined by the divinely set order of the sun, moon, and stars. The image here is from Figures de la Bible by the Dutch engraver Gerard Hoet (1648–1733). (Image credit: Wikimedia Commons)

Judging from the classical sources, the group portraits, and the process of elimination also landed us on the group that is the best match for the Qumran site and the DSS: the Essenes. But we'll never be 100 percent sure. Why not? The complexity of social groups in ancient Judaism is likely greater than any of our sources relate. We can't assume that the sources available to us provide a comprehensive account of *every* Jewish group identity or individual inclination of Jews in the Second Temple period. Based on what we do know, however, the Essenes or an Essene-like group fit with the geographical, social, ideological, and practical elements of life reflected at Qumran and in the DSS. As far as we know, they were Essenes or Essene-ish.

We can add additional nuance to our findings by embracing what has emerged as a growing recognition among DSS scholars. While our focus often falls on *the* group that lived at *the* site of Qumran, it is likely that what we encounter there and observe in the DSS is just one instance of an Essene way of life that was part of a broader movement. Logically, this makes sense. Even modern movements—political, national, religious, etc.—have degrees of diversity in their unity, as well as location-based expressions. The ancient evidence also points in this direction. Philo and Josephus, for example, had remarkably similar outlines of Essene demographics, belief, and practice, but they also differed in the details. When we looked into the scrolls themselves, we saw some additional hallmarks of this group's identity and orientation to the world around them. We also saw some glimpses of varied models for communities even within the expressions of identity in the DSS. Either way, things like a deep priestly DNA, inspired interpretation of Torah, orderly rhythms of life and liturgy, expressions of time, heightened commitment to purity, and apocalyptic thinking were all formative to the identity of this particular Essene-ish group and the movement of which they were part.

What we see in writings like the *Community Rule* or the *Damascus Document*, then, are pictures of a movement with some variety to its patterns of life, organizational structures, and locations. John Collins suggests that the sectarian movement described in the DSS was "never confined to Qumran."[19]

I started this chapter with an anecdote about a vintage map that pinpointed the Essenes off the northwest shore of the Dead Sea. Now we'll return to that landscape with an eye to archaeology and to explore the rocks, rubble, caves, and artifacts that are essential to these discoveries.

Chapter 5

Tour de Qumran: Death, Toilets, and Other Archaeological Highlights

A friend of mine studies burial practices and prehistoric human remains. We met as doctoral students. If you've ever met a doctoral student, you know they have a rather limited repertoire of conversation starters. The go-to question is inevitably, "So ... what are you working on?"

At our first encounter, we both played our stereotyped role and swapped research interests along this script. He told me how his groundbreaking work on the world's oldest burial sites shed new light on human history millennia ago. As he spoke, I leaned forward, nodded at a nice 6/8 tempo, and uttered "interesting" at intervals. (Those habits are also part of the PhD candidate starter kit.)

Then it was my turn. "How about you?" he asked.

"I study the DSS." After leaving a pause for dramatic effect, I added, "They're our oldest known texts for reconstructing lost aspects of ancient Jewish life and literature." *Nice, Perrin*, I thought. *Nuanced, concise, a tad alliterated, and with enough loose ends to guarantee a follow-up question*. But his response threw me.

"The scrolls? That's not history, that's journalism!"

Ouch! Fine, on the grand clock of the cosmos, my two-thousand-year-old texts weren't as old as his Neanderthals.

This momentary deflation helped me realize there is a simple yet profound complexity to DSS studies: we have both textual finds and archaeological remains. While not prehistoric, this combo is truly remarkable and rare—in ancient studies in general, and in biblical studies in particular. Yet having more sources and more recent material doesn't make the historical homework any easier. In fact, the multiplication of sources increases questions and compounds unknowns.

Since archaeology is all about attempting to recover lived experiences of past peoples and lost cultures, there are many approaches one might take to the Qumran archaeological record—too many, in fact, for a single chapter. So let's take a casual stroll, as if we were on a day trip to see the highlights of sites around Qumran. As day trips do, we'll move through key items and pause for conversation and context, but we'll have to keep a good pace to get along to the next artefact or location.[1]

Our tour de Qumran will include insights into death and gender, takes on toilet practices, a bit of spelunking, chasing water in the wilderness, thousands of dishes, hoards of coins and animal bones, and at least two inkwells—and these are just the highlights. But before all that, let's get started with a bit of geography and create a mental image of the lowest place on earth: the Dead Sea region in the Judean wilderness.

Setting the Scene: Welcome to the Lowest Point on Earth

You can see many of the sights in the Dead Sea region in a day trip. If you leave Jerusalem early, you can make it to Qumran ahead of much of the heat, and mostly ahead of the crowds that will come to float in the saline waters of the Dead Sea and mud-bathe in its world-famous therapeutic sludge. By car it's about a forty-five-minute drive from Jerusalem. The 45-kilometer (28-mile) trip takes you out of Jerusalem into the rugged and desert shrub–laden

IMAGE 5.1: A selfie opportunity that's a common feature in the convenience store parking lot, the last stop before winding down to the lowest point on earth in the Dead Sea region. (Image credit: Andrew B. Perrin)

---

wilderness. As the road winds its way southeast, your car will curve between cliffs that loom increasingly higher, with occasional pauses at military check spots, before you make it to a last outpost of modern civilization near the northwest corner of the Dead Sea: a convenience stop and restaurant, complete with a guy and a camel posing in the parking lot for tourist photo-ops for a few Israeli shekels.

Welcome to the lowest point on earth.

By now the temperature is rising and the traffic is increasing. What I want to focus on here—or ask you to imagine—is the landscape of the place, without the obstructions of contemporary life. No cars, no people, no cameo camels or check stops, no mudslingers or throngs of overly buoyant humans. The landscape here is the backdrop of Qumran archaeology, and it's an experience and sight in and of itself.

The Dead Sea basin is 50 kilometers (31 miles) long and 15 kilometers (9.3 miles) across at its widest point. It is 306 meters (1004 feet) deep, but you'd be hard pressed to get down there given its high salinity levels.

The first thing you'll notice is the color. This is among the saltiest bodies of water on earth and it's rich in minerals, giving it an unforgettable, almost electric, turquoise glow reflecting the regularly cloudless sky above. This striking color is complemented by the beige shades of the desert cliffs that encase it. These stark and looming limestone and marl cliff edifices make what is already a deep point in earth's geography feel lower still.

The mix of salt and sun make for rapid evaporation. The shores around the edges of the Dead Sea are a mix of rocks and sporadic salt deposits that are sought and sent the world over for their remarkable purity and regional specificity. What keeps the Dead Sea from evaporating into oblivion? Seasonal rains help, as does the waterflow from the mouth of the Jordan River at the northern tip, which carries fresh water down from the Sea of Galilee in the north.

The archaeological site of Qumran itself is near the northwest corner of the Dead Sea, set off its saline shores about 1.5 kilometers (0.9 miles). As you look further south, the Dead Sea stretches into what at times feels like a heat-wave hallucination, where sea, sand, and sky converge. But squint a little and you'll see the cliffs and landscape shift near the curving southern shores of the Dead Sea.

IMAGE 5.2: The salt deposits and mud of the Dead Sea shoreline are world-famous for spa products and health uses. The view here is from atop Masada, and it gives a sense of the scale and juxtaposition of the landscape. The cliffs in the region include many natural and some hand-hewn caves. A small number of scroll fragments were also found at the fortress of Masada, from the Jewish Revolt.
(Image credit: Andrew B. Perrin)

Dotted along the way, south from Qumran, are a few other sites of note, including Muraabba'at, Ein Gedi, Nahal Hever, Ein el-Ghuweir, and the towering walls of Masada. These areas are part of the DSS story too, as several of the sites also included textual discoveries and artifacts from the Second Temple period. Perhaps most dramatic and tragic is the site of Masada, which was the last stand of the Jewish revolt against the Romans in the first century CE.

This backdrop was home to the ancient community at Qumran, and housed thousands of scrolls and fragments in caves until their modern discovery.

Caves, Contents, and Connections with the Qumran Site

While they may look empty, those imposing cliffs I told you about are not devoid of life. The wildlife that lives or has lived there includes Nubian ibexes, rock rabbits, and foxes.[2] By day, you'll see small black birds with orange feathers, called Tristram's Starlings, fluttering and perching around the cliffs. By night, you might see other dark-colored creatures take flight: bats. In the story of the DSS, the bats are perhaps most notorious for the damaging effect of centuries of guano in some of the caves, which damaged and decayed the scrolls. But we shouldn't be too hard on the bats. When a bat's gotta poop, a bat's gotta poop.

The cliffs and low crags of the region are dotted with natural pockets, and with some caves carved long ago by human hands. For our story of the discovery of the DSS and Qumran archaeology, there are at least eleven caves that we'll note. I say *at least* because, while most of the modern story of the scrolls has centered on eleven caves identified in the late 1940s to mid-1950s, additional caves have been discovered in waves, some very recently. There have been various attempts to comb and recomb the desert for new caves to get ahead of antiquities hunters and artefact traffickers. In 2017, news of at least one new cave discovery (Cave 53) upped the count of caves with scroll fragments or evidence of scrolls to twelve.

The following list outlines the discovery dates and nature of the finds in the twelve caves.[3]

- Cave 1 (February to March 1949): The initial wave of seven scroll discoveries plus approximately six hundred more scroll fragments (seventy-nine fragmentary manuscripts in total), as well as the remains of at least fifty jars, other pottery (bowls, a pot, a pitcher), four lamps, three phylactery cases, a wooden comb, and some fifty linens.

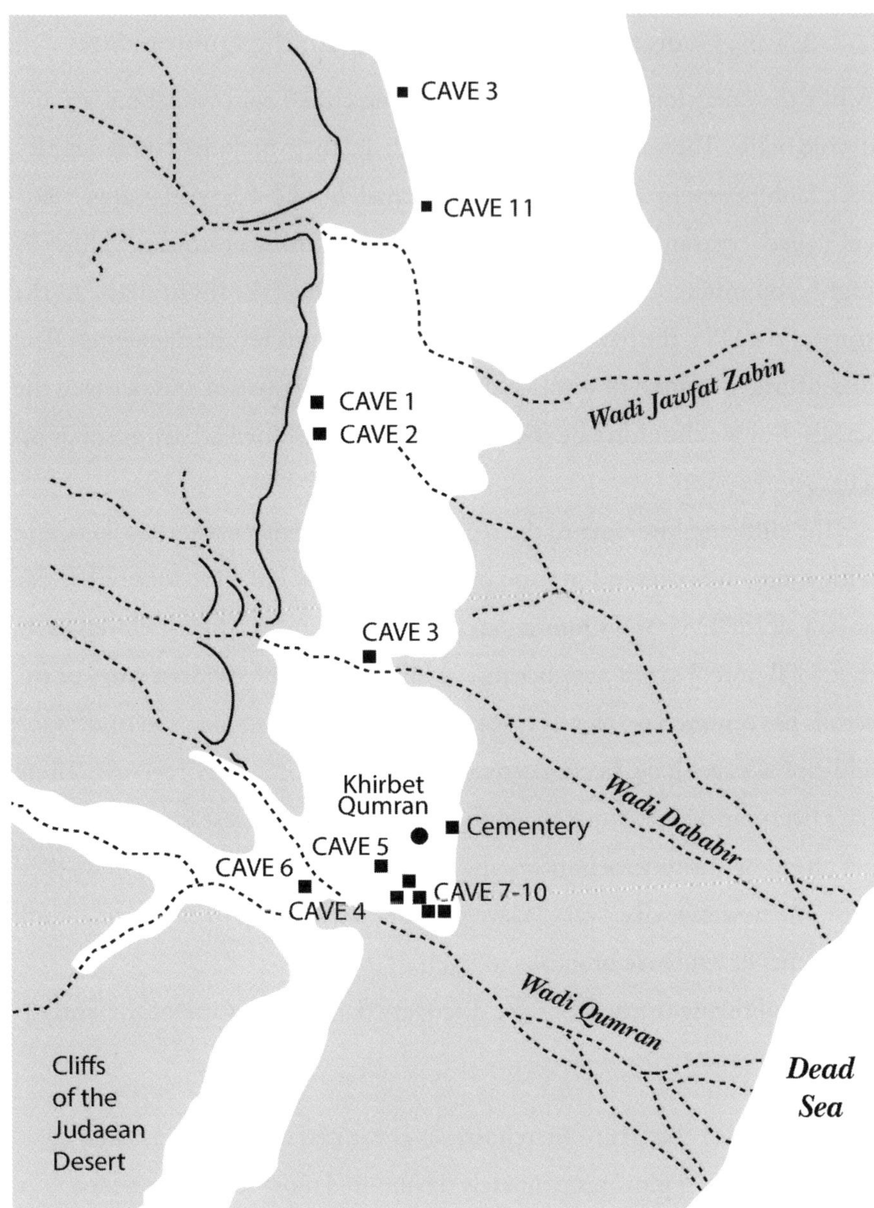

IMAGE 5.3: Location map of the first eleven caves in the Dead Sea region where the scrolls were discovered. (Image credit: Faithlife)

- Cave 2 (February 1952): Remains of approximately thirty-three fragmentary manuscripts, two whole jars and one lid, and remains of six other cylindrical jars.
- Cave 3 (March 14, 1952): Remains of at least thirteen fragmentary scrolls, including the *Copper Scroll*, and cylindrical jars. This is the northern-most cave of the initial wave of discoveries.
- Cave 4 (August 1952): The largest of cache of artifacts recovered, including fifteen thousand fragments and many pottery items or remains of various wares (lids, plates, bowls, cups, jugs, and a lamp) as well as phylactery cases, textiles, tags, and ties. This is the most iconic example of a hand-hewn cave from the marl terrace, which is in fact two adjacent caves (4a and 4b).
- Cave 5 (September 1952): Fragmentary remains of some twenty-five fragmentary manuscripts, a single potsherd, and animal bones. This cave is offset but within the same terrace as Cave 4.
- Cave 6 (September 1952): Fragmentary remains of at least thirty-one scrolls and a small number of wares (one inscribed sherd, one jar, and one bowl).
- Cave 7 (February to April 1955): Fragmentary remains of nineteen manuscripts, all of them in Greek and inscribed on papyrus. The discovery also included three cylindrical jars, one bowl-shaped lid, two bowls, one inscribed jar fragment, and one inscribed ostracon. Caves 7–9 are accessed by stairs carved into the marl terrace.
- Cave 8 (February to April 1955): Fragments of between three and five manuscripts, one inscription, and three phylactery cases, as well as a small collection of material artifacts (one jar, four

bowl-shaped lids, one plate, one lamp, leather straps and ties, one sandal sole, and date and olive pits).

- Cave 9 (February to April 1955): Only one inscribed papyrus fragment was found, alongside one inscribed ostracon, some rope and cord, and date and olive pits.
- Cave 10 (February to April 1955): A single inscribed potsherd, a woven mat, and some date pits were discovered in this almost entirely collapsed cave.
- Cave 11 (January 1956): This cave contained fragmentary remains of some thirty scrolls, including the *Temple Scroll*, reportedly found wrapped in linen and encased in a scroll jar. Cave 11 also included an abundance of material artifacts: one bowl-shaped lid and jug, one iron blade, one iron chisel, one pickax, one iron rod, one iron key, one copper buckle, one bead, leather fragments, and many pieces of cloth, basketry, and rope. This is the largest of the natural caves in the limestone cliffs.[4]
- Cave 53 (2017): This cave included storage jars and lids, inscribed remnants of a scroll, possible cloth of a scroll wrapping, and a pickax. It's debated whether the ax is ancient or was left behind by looters decades ago.[5]

Caves 1, 2, 3, and 11 range from between 1.2 kilometers (0.75 miles) and 2.4 kilometers (1.5 miles) north of Qumran. Caves 4–10 are much closer, all within strolling distance of the site. Cave 4 is the most famous, and the closest of the caves to Qumran. This cave was rich in textual discoveries. It contained more manuscripts and fragments than any other of the caves associated with the discoveries in the Judean wilderness. It is also special for a few other reasons.

It is, quite literally, within a stone's throw of the Qumran site. It is a hand-hewn and human-made cave carved out of the marl and rock for a purpose: storing stuff. It has two access points to drop in from up top, and an almost eye-like hole peering out from the crag across to the Qumran settlement. Despite its proximity to Qumran, and what now feels like its obvious and disruptive presence in the natural landscape, Cave 4 sat there undiscovered until 1952, while teams of archaeologists excavated for multiple seasons nearby, and while bands of people lived, explored, and passed through the region for countless generations before them.

Among the many other noteworthy features of Cave 4 are small inset holes or niches in the wall. It is possible that these once held pegs for shelves to hold items or hang lamps. Like several of the other caves, Cave 4 included many artifacts and evidence that suggest human lives were lived within or nearby. Were these items brought and stored from Qumran? Were the caves not only for storage but also habitation? Good questions. Open questions. Either way, the connection between the caves and the site of Qumran seems clear enough to associate the material, textual, and archaeological discoveries.

Iconic in their own right are the so-called cylindrical "scroll jars" recovered in both fragmentary and complete specimens in some of the caves. These jars are approximately 62 centimeters (24.4 inches) high and 27.9 centimeters (10.9 inches) wide. They also have a distinctive lid to keep the contents encased and protected, either for storage or travel. Research on the material composition of these jars indicates that they were made from clay in the Qumran and Hebron regions.[6] The pottery remains and styles are, therefore, some of the clearest material evidence confirming a connection between the caves and the site of Qumran.[7]

The shape of these lids has inspired the modern design and architecture of the Shrine of the Book at the Israel Museum, with an exterior roof above the main exhibit shaped as a glistening white scroll jar lid, in stark contrast

IMAGE 5.4: In addition to the famous scroll jars, the caves near the Qumran site itself offered up several other types of pottery and wares of various uses. (Image credit: Israel Museum, Jerusalem)

to a black wall meant to symbolize the light/dark dualism that is threaded throughout the Qumran sectarian writings.

A Rough and Ready Timeline of the Qumran Settlement

Now that we know where we are in the natural space of the Judean wilderness, we should pause to think about time. Like ancient texts, artifacts at archaeological sites don't interpret themselves. Recovering a likely portrait of life in ancient times requires thoughtful and cautious reconstruction and revision of timelines in light of new discoveries, ongoing research, fresh perspectives, or emerging methods.

While there is still much we don't know about the life and times of Qumran, and thus about the timelines associated with the site, the most compelling timeline is what is now known as the "revised chronology." This chronology was advanced by archaeologist Jodi Magness but is based on the earlier work of Roland de Vaux (hence the "revised" descriptor). While de Vaux was among the first scrolls scholars and the lead archaeologist at Qumran starting in the late 1940s, the official reports of his work are still in process by his successors and are ever forthcoming.[8]

What are the key elements of Magness's revised chronology? It is based on a simple yet profound archaeological principle: the solution that accounts for the most evidence while creating the fewest problems is preferred. (In fact, this principle could be applied to life with great success!) Armed with this aphorism and a career's worth of archaeological experience at Qumran, Magness's chronology is rooted in two key critiques of de Vaux's proposal and new contributions.

First, we know that the Qumran site has evidence of earlier infrastructure and human habitation, such as a water cistern dating to the Iron Age (the eighth and seventh centuries BCE).[9] But the Jewish group that lived there in the Second Temple period settled in and developed the site around 100 BCE. De Vaux argued that the collection of 561 Tyrian silver coins found in three pots at Qumran, the latest internal dates of which are 9/8 BCE, are the *start* of a new period of occupation after a lengthy hiatus following the earthquake of 31 BCE. Magness, however, reasoned that these coins were evidence of mostly continuous occupation extending into the last decade of the Common Era. In short, Magness's revision to the Jewish settlement of the site was later than de Vaux's estimation, and allows for a more consistent occupation of Qumran.

Why did de Vaux place the sectarian occupation of Qumran earlier? He pushed the Jewish occupation back into the second century BCE to make the archaeological materials fit with the following detail in the *Damascus Document*:

> But when he (God) called to mind the covenant he made with their forefathers, he left a remnant for Israel and did not allow them to be exterminated. In the era of wrath—three hundred and ninety years at the time He handed them over to the power of Nebuchadnezzar king of Babylon—he took care of them and caused to grow from Israel and from Aaron a root of planting to inherit his land and to grow fat on the good produce of his soil. They considered their iniquity and they knew that they were guilty men, and had been like the blind and like those groping for the way twenty years. But God considered their deeds, that they had sought him with a whole heart. So he raised up for them a teacher of righteousness to guide them in the way of his heart. He taught to later generations what God did to the generation deserving wrath, a company of traitors. They are the ones who depart from the proper way. (CD 1:4–13)

Unfortunately, this is neither a journalistic report of sectarian origins nor a simple math equation for crunching timelines from the Babylonian exile to Qumran beginnings. Rather, it is a memory serving the group's identity, which likely uses symbolic figures.[10] Magness's revision, then, is a helpful correction to the chronology and a reminder that a text like this can't dictate our understanding of archaeological remains on the ground.

Second, the Qumran site was more or less continually inhabited by a group of Jews from the early– to mid–first century BCE until 68 CE. We know the hard stop at 68 CE due to evidence of destruction by the Romans in hot pursuit of Jewish rebels en route to Masada.[11] The archaeological evidence of a known earthquake in 31 BCE (more on that in a minute) suggests we could speak of a pre- and post-quake time frame. On Magness's reading there was at best a five-year interlude in the site's occupation. De Vaux's theory, however, saw this quake and coinciding fire as a major disruption to the habitation of Qumran, resulting in decades of abandonment before the same group returned and renovated the site. In short, Magness's revision is for a more plausible minor hiatus from the site in what is then a relatively consistent sectarian habitation at Qumran.

The world of Qumran archaeological theories and timelines is more complex than this quick take. But for the purpose of setting the context for our day trip, the basic contours of the "revised chronology" help us locate key aspects and artifacts of the Qumran archeological site in space and time as well as within the broader world of Second Temple Judaism.

Death and Demographics via the Qumran Cemetery

The first major element of archaeology we will encounter on our tour down the Dead Sea coast is actually Qumran-adjacent. On a plateau some 30 meters (98 feet) east of the settlement is a relatively large cemetery that, despite being a literal place of the dead, is essential to our understanding of Qumran life. It is also among the most confounding archaeological features of the Dead Sea region.

The cemetery holds between eleven hundred and twelve hundred plots. Most are identified by heaps of rocks with a larger stone at the head. In the early modern archaeology of the site, de Vaux excavated around forty-three of these. As you can imagine, excavating a burial ground is not without its ethical and political complexities, particularly in a region with deep ties to land and life by many groups. So the sample data set here is relatively small.

Then there is the problem of the walking dead. The whereabouts of these remains today is a bit unclear. Twenty-two are in Munich, nine are in Jerusalem, and eight are in Paris. The quick math here indicates there are four Qumran corpses unaccounted for. Public service announcement: if you happen to encounter one, please ask them to report to the nearest archaeologist or museum technologist for assistance.

But what do we know—or what do we wish we could know—about life and death from this sample? Judging from burial goods found in some plots and the orientation of many graves, it is evident that not all the graves are ancient and are likely associated with different groups. The north-south orientation of many of the plots suggests that they are not Muslim burials, since "Muslim burials in Palestine are usually oriented east-west, with the head laid to the east and the face turned south toward Mecca."[12] It is also evident that many of the graves are Bedouin, a general observation that also requires much more nuance and detail.

The cemetery near Qumran also reveals intriguing insights into demographics. There appears to be a higher proportion of males buried in the western sector. This area included remains of only two adult females. Alternatively, remains of women and children seem to predominate in the southern extension of the cemetery. This is also where there are more recent Bedouin burial plots.

Unfortunately, there isn't a lot in the way of gendered artifacts in the excavated plots (that is, items buried with the dead that might indicate whether the remains are male or female). This is an area where we wish we knew more, for two reasons. On one hand, we saw in a previous chapter that the classical sources and many Qumran texts comment on issues related to women, marriage, and family. On the other hand, other sites nearby, such as Masada and the Bar Kokbha caves, include epigraphic, literary, and archaeological evidence suggesting the presence of women and children. But, in view of the evidence presently available (or lack thereof), Magness is correct in noting that "the archaeological evidence suggests only minimal female presence at Qumran."[13]

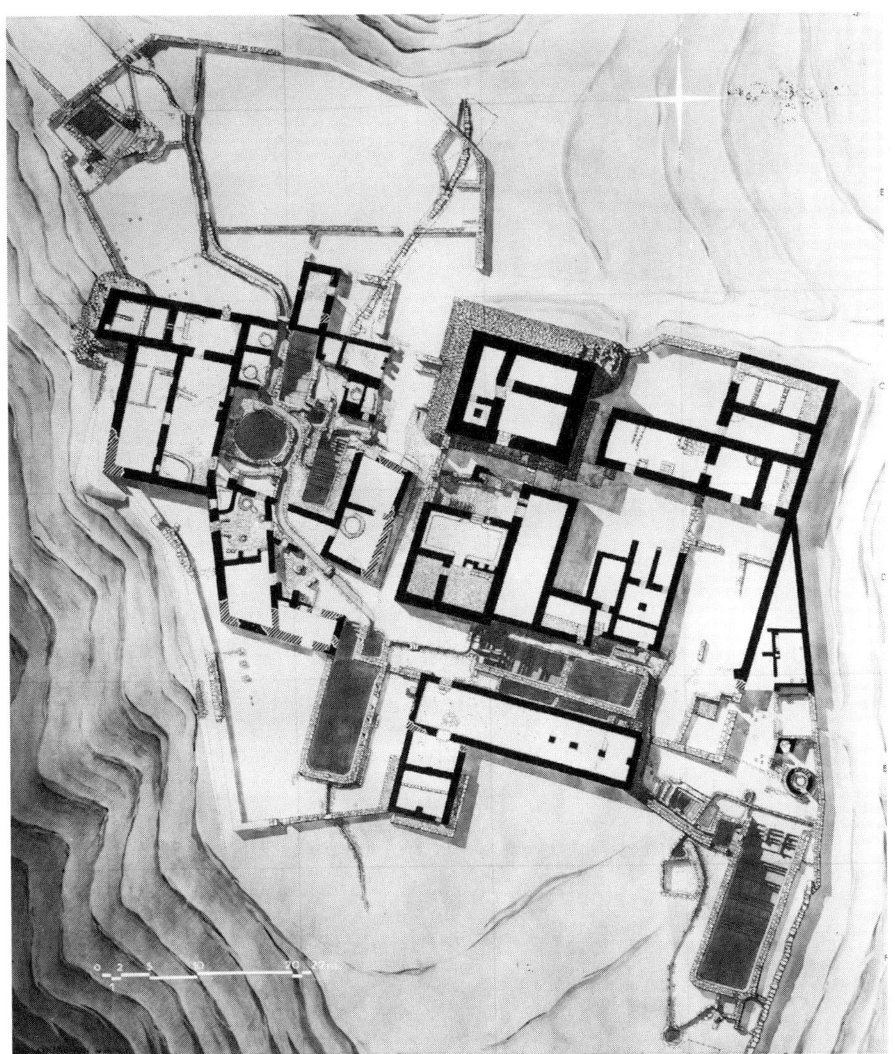

IMAGE 5.5: Roland de Vaux's plans of the archaeological site of Qumran were established through his early seasons of digs there and eventually published in his volume, Archaeology and the Dead Sea Scrolls. The renditions here are earlier and based on the work of the architect Fr. Charles Coüasnon, with whom de Vaux worked on the representation in view of the remains.
(Image credit: École biblique et archéologique française de Jérusalem)

A Watch Tower, Walls, and Waterways

The actual complex of the Qumran site is approximately 79.2 by 100.5 meters (260 by 330 feet). It includes the remains of dozens of rooms and areas that served various functions for the ancient Jewish community that lived at Qumran. The question of how many people lived in this community in the Second Temple period is debated. White Crawford's proposal that "a safe estimate would be that the site accommodated 25–75 inhabitants at any given time" seems likely.[14]

Let's tour around the exterior walls and then through the site via waterways that were essential for both community infrastructure and identity. The most visible exterior element of the outer walls at Qumran is the watchtower on the northern edge. In its day, this tower was likely up to three levels high and provided a view of the surrounding landscape. Archaeologist Hanan Eshel commented that this building may have also served as a hub for the administrative functions of the community.[15]

But if you pause and look more closely, you'll see the remains of a more impressive and perhaps more important element of Qumran architecture not far from this once-imposing watchtower. The rubble and remains of an ancient waterway winds out of the settlement and up toward the nearby cliffs. Freshwater access is essential in any desert, but particularly this one, where the only natural body of water nearby is saline beyond belief. The Dead Sea region,

IMAGE 5.6, 5.7, and 5.8: Images of the Qumran archaeological site. (1) The Qumran watchtower and possible administrative hub, (2) a view of interior rooms and remains of walls inside the site, and (3) the Iron Age cistern that became a part of the later water system of the Second Temple period habitation. (Image credits: Faithlife)

however, is subject to seasonal rains and flash floods, which can create torrents of water rushing through riverbeds, or wadis. The Qumran waterway was designed to capture and channel some of this fresh water toward the settlement and through a system of pools and courses networked within and around the site.

No doubt the Qumranites continued to use this naturally occurring source of water for hydration. In fact, decantation basins are set where the aqueduct entered the community, as well as ahead of other functional pools to settle and filter silt out of the incoming water.

But is there more to these pools than hydration? Yes. The sheer number of plaster stepped pools at the site suggests that water was integral to the community for ritual purity practices. There are several ritual immersion pools (in Hebrew, *miqveh*, or *miqva'ot* in the plural) at Qumran. While stepped pools like this are known from other sites, the sheer number of *miqva'ot* at a single site from this period is noteworthy.[16] In light of the heightened concern and consideration for purity we've already seen in the DSS, this element of the archaeological record is important for understanding ritual purity through water immersion at Qumran.

Perhaps the most telling of the pools is the one found in locus 48/49. Like others at Qumran, this *miqveh* has steps that would have allowed a person to descend into the waters. This one, however, also includes small plaster partitions running down the stairs, creating lanes within the wider staircase. These partitions, it seems, were meant to provide pathways for purity. Presumably one would enter the waters via one avenue, immerse, and arise ritually clean up another lane. Of note in this *miqveh* is also a distinctive scar across the stairway, which reveals the damage to the site from the earthquake of 31 BCE.[17]

Finally, in addition to meeting the needs of sustenance and purity, the watercourses of Qumran flowed into other areas and served other functions of community life. For example, the site includes what appears to have been a small potter's workshop, complete with a basin for washing clay connected to the main water channel, and remains of other tools and infrastructure to support the craft, such as two kilns, a furnace, and an iron hook.

IMAGE 5.9: Sample *miqveh* (ritual pool) from Qumran, with plaster partitions for entry for the impure and exits for emerging in a pure state. The pool here also bears the marks of damage from an earthquake in the region in 31 BCE. (Image credit: Andrew B. Perrin)

After winding its way through the community, any excess water was spilled out at the southern end. The organization and flow of the system, with its purification basins, cisterns, and sequenced flow, qualified the *miqva'ot* as "ritual baths from the standpoint of Jewish law" while ensuring that other functions and needs could be met as well.[18] Our quick tour of the architecture of waterways at Qumran demonstrates the essential importance of water for human life, group identity, ritual practice, and community craft.

A Dining Room, Dishware, and Animal Bone Deposits

The largest room at Qumran seems to have been used for community assemblies or related functions (locus 77). This is suggested both by the size—approximately 22 meters (72.2 feet) long by 4.5 meters (14.8 feet) wide—and a platform on the western end. That the space was designed with cleanup in mind is evident from the sloped floor and the water channel at the doorway.

Adjacent to this room is a pantry that included a sizable hoard, not of coins, but of more than one thousand stacked pottery items. The discovery of so many plates, bowls, cups, cooking vessels, and pots here and elsewhere at Qumran is significant. Presumably these were for preparing and partaking in communal meals.

If you're going to eat, you have to cook. The Qumran ruins also include what seems to have been a kitchen. This area, on the northern side of a main courtyard, included at least three ovens. Not unlike the *miqva'ot*, the remains of staircases at the kitchen include a pair of passages, which may have also been designed with purity in mind.

What did the Qumranites eat? Good question. While it is important to interpret the archaeology in its own right, recall the descriptions of communal ceremonies and references to common meals from the DSS, as well as comparative comments in the classical sources. To this we could add references to "pure" or "sacred" food and meals in the *Community Rule* (see 1QS 6:16, 25; 8:17).

In terms of material remains, however, the best indication of what may have been on the menu at Qumran are a number of pottery vessels that held hundreds of animal bones within. These were found primarily in spaces outside of main buildings and in proximity to spaces used for food preparation (the kitchen) or eating (the dining hall). Some are charred and separated, indicating they were separated as they were being prepared. In total, there are 492 bones in ten deposits, which represent the remains of a minimum of forty-six sheep and goats and ten cattle.[19]

The more interesting question is whether or not these deposits were for eating only, or for consumption following animal sacrifices. The species found in the jar deposits—the bones of many of which are also charred—reflect the predominant species acceptable for sacrifice in the Hebrew Scriptures (Leviticus 1:3, 10). Josephus noted that some Essenes practiced animal

IMAGE 5.10: The traditional image of the presentation of the stacked bowls and pottery features archaeologist Roland de Vaux, who oversaw the early seasons of the dig and established key insights into the history and artifacts of the site. This photo is a rarity, and depicts a similar scene of the hoard of stacked bowls in the Qumran pantry with an unknown worker at the site. (Image credit: École biblique et archéologique française de Jérusalem)

---

sacrifices as a sort of private rite (*Ant.* 18.19). We now know that there were other Jewish settlements, not least the Egyptian site of Elephantine, which included a temple and a site for sacrifice well afield from the Jerusalem establishment. We also saw a few chapters back that the Qumranites innovated a life of worship apart from the Jerusalem temple, which they viewed as defiled. Scholars also debate whether there are the remains of an altar at Qumran. So where does this leave us? I would suggest we're in the domain of intriguing potential, but not certainty regarding whether sacrifice preceded sacred meals at Qumran.

A Scriptorium at Qumran?

Another area of contention in the Qumran archaeological remains is what was initially described by de Vaux as a second floor scriptorium (locus 30). Was the group that lived at Qumran a scribal community that not only collected but also copied and created the scrolls found in the caves nearby?

At least three inkwells were discovered at the site of Qumran, one of which still contains traces of ink. The presence of inkwells clearly indicates writing activity and some level of scribal craft at Qumran.[20] Where things get less certain is in de Vaux's reconstructed narrow and low-lying table and associated low seats running along the walls of the so-called scriptorium. On de Vaux's read, these tables and benches were for writing scrolls.[21] This is possible, but far from certain.

On one hand, the image of a scriptorium was clearly imagined under the influence of the texts found in the caves. While we cannot divorce these finds from the interpretation of Qumran—as noted above there is reason to connect the sites—we also can't impose the scrolls on the interpretation of the site in this way. In addition, several scholars have noted that "ancient scribes generally did not write at tables."[22] On the other hand, it would be quite surprising if the community at Qumran were *not* involved in the creation or preservation of at least some of the DSS in their collection. The inkwell evidence cannot be underestimated and the proximity of scrolls to the settlement should not be forgotten.

Once again, the most likely conclusion is in the realm of possibility. While the mental image of a scriptorium complete with tables and benches pushes the evidence too far, the likelihood of some scribal activity at Qumran is confirmed by the inkwells and strongly suggested by the proximity of the site and texts found in the caves.

IMAGE 5.11: This is the location of the so-called "scriptorium" at Qumran, where the remains of long tables or benches and an inkwell were recovered. (Image credit: École biblique et archéologique française de Jérusalem)

IMAGE 5.12: One of the challenges to the scriptorium theory is that the mental image of scribes seated on benches working at long tables reflects modern postures of authors and academics seated at desks. But there is limited evidence for this posture in antiquity. See, for example, this statue of a seated scribe from ancient Egypt. Whether or not this posture would be possible or appropriate for Jewish scribes creating long manuscripts out of flexible materials is a point of debate. (Image credit: Rijksmuseum van Oudheden via Wikimedia Commons)

Toilet Talk and Connecting the Dots between Bodily Functions, Identity, and Expectations

Our day trip at Qumran started with death and cemeteries, and it ends in the toilet—literally. Let's round out our tour with another find at Qumran that connects a few threads woven throughout the previous chapters regarding purity and identity.

One of the remarkable things about archaeology is that it grounds our understanding of ancient cultures and peoples in real time and real human lives—and nothing makes the past more real than the fact that every person throughout human history has had to relieve themselves. So where did this happen at Qumran?

Among the ruins of the Qumran site are the remains of up to two toilets. De Vaux first identified the remains of a toilet in a room at the northeastern end of the main building. This unit is known only by a clay pipe embedded within a conical, mud-lined pit in the floor. It is possible that a block found in locus 44 was the stone seat for this toilet fixture.

While many occupants of Roman cities went outdoors or tossed refuse into the streets, a few Roman houses included facilities not unlike those at Qumran. The design is also paralleled by finds of eight toilets in the City of David in Jerusalem (dated approximately to the eighth to sixth centuries BCE).[23] As far as we can tell, this Qumran loo went out of use and service after the earthquake of 31 BCE.

More recently, Joe Zias and James Tabor argued for the identification of a second toilet to the northwest of the complex.[24] This one is intriguingly out of sight and outside the community settlement. Soil samples of this find have also been analyzed, revealing parasitic worms common in human waste. These finds ground our study of Qumran in daily life, and connect some dots from earlier chapters. We saw that texts like the *War Scroll* and the *Temple Scroll* underscored in different ways the necessity of purity in the

IMAGE 5.13: A view of the remains of the ancient toilet at Qumran. (Image credit: Wikimedia Commons)

---

eschatological war (the former even going as far as to locate the end-of-days latrine well outside the camp).[25] Suddenly a simple one-seater in the rubble of Qumran links into larger issues of identity, purity, belief, and practice.

Conclusion

Archaeology attains insights by giving us hints into human lives, often from partial remains that must be recovered, reconstructed, contextualized, and interpreted. At Qumran, we have the challenge and opportunity of deciphering the site on one hand, and decoding DSS on the other. They need to speak for themselves, yet they are also both part of the story. So where does this leave us?

In some cases (like death and demographics) we might have more questions than answers. How populous was the settlement? Were women and children well represented? Were there survivors after the arrival of the Romans? In other cases (like toilets and purity pools) we found unexpected avenues into a diversity of topics that relate to everyday experience and practice. At times these insights also connected into a larger complex of identity markers or even exegetical interests and eschatological expectations.

In chapter 4, we roughed out an understanding of the Qumranites likely being part of an Essene or Essene-like movement. In this chapter, our archaeological day trip provided some grounding—literally—in what daily life in this community expression of that movement might have looked like. There is much more we might like to know about the archaeology of Qumran. Yet items like inkwell discoveries and textual finds in nearby caves prepares us well for exploring what is for many an essential insight and opportunity of the DSS: the development, transmission, and shape of scriptures at Qumran.

Chapter 6

The Vitality of Ancient Scriptures and the Making of Modern Bibles

By 1952, the DSS were poised to revolutionize modern Bibles. As scroll fragments poured into Jerusalem, the Revised Standard Version (RSV) went to press in its second edition. Though the full scope of the DSS was still unknown, the translation committee made special mention of the Qumran discoveries in the preface, saying:

> The problem of establishing the correct Hebrew and Aramaic text of the Old Testament is very different from the corresponding problem of the New Testament. For the New Testament we have a large number of Greek manuscripts, preserving many variant forms of the text. Some of them were made only two or three centuries later than the original composition of the books. For the Old Testament only late manuscripts survive, all (with the exception of the Dead Sea texts of Isaiah and Habakkuk and some fragments of other books) based on a standardized form of the text established many centuries after the books were written.[1]

That was just beginning. Today, *any* modern Hebrew Bible or Old Testament worth the paper it's printed on (or screen it's displayed on) meaningfully integrates the DSS. Why? Whether you realize it or not, most modern Bible translations are a convergence and synthesis of *many* manuscripts. These come from a variety of cultural settings, time periods, and corpora of writings. Whether you read the Jewish or Christian Bible as a remarkable piece of ancient cultural literature or a reliable anthology of sacred Scripture, don't you think we should ask where it came from?

The DSS present both problems and prospects when it comes to the Hebrew Scriptures—the common heritage of the Hebrew Bible and Old Testament.[2] They come from a time that was at once *formative* to, yet *before*, the Bible. How is it, then, that we have "biblical scrolls?" Exactly.

Before we explore the impact and implications of the DSS on modern scriptures, let's talk terminology. When you hear the word *Bible*, what image comes to mind? I bet it's a book. Perhaps black leather bound. Maybe with gold letters on the cover. Probably with hundreds of thin tissue pages, printed in parallel columns, in that impossibly tiny font.

These associations are reasonable. They are also modern. The English word *Bible* comes from the Greek βίβλος, which literally means "book." Yet culturally and confessionally, the term has come to signify more than just any old book. We're talking about *the* Book.

Here's the problem: this mental image works for us, but it doesn't work in the ancient world of the DSS. Their world is one of scribes and scrolls.

The media culture of early books (the codex) didn't exist until around the second century CE.[3] The canon of scripture (an agreed-upon list of uniquely authoritative writings) didn't emerge until as early as the second or as late as the fourth century CE.[4] To speak of "biblical scrolls," then, is a double misnomer. As Eva Mroczek remarked, "The study of early Jewish texts continues to be constrained by two kinds of anachronism: a religious one—'Bible'—and a bibliographic one—'book.'"[5] No single document containing all the scriptures existed at the turn of the era. Even if such a unicorn of an item had existed, the communities of the day would have no doubt still debated which writings were authoritative.

But even though "biblical scrolls" didn't exist in this technical sense, the reality is that about 23 percent of the Qumran library are writings that later Jewish and Christian communities would receive as biblical.[6] Therefore, the DSS invite us to see scripture as it was *then* before exploring what it has come to be *now*. The big question, then, is: How do these ancient scrolls impact our understanding of the Hebrew Scriptures?

In many ways. In fact, too many for a single chapter, so we'll break it into two chapters. This chapter is all about finer points: the *content* of scripture. Words and details. The next chapter is more about the big picture: the *scope* of scripture. Worlds and dimensions.

For this first leg of the journey, we'll track toward three waypoints:

Traditions: What are the main biblical manuscripts from past communities that relate to the formation of the Bible?

Transformations: How have the DSS impacted Bibles in our present day?

Text criticism: How do the DSS challenge us to think differently about scripture in the future?

Along the way, we'll see that the DSS provide new data about the backstory of the Hebrew Scriptures. When they are integrated into Bibles today, modern scriptures are, in fact, more ancient than ever.

Manuscripts Behind Modern Bibles *before* the Dead Sea Scrolls

The Hebrew Scriptures at Qumran revealed both remarkable continuity with other known biblical manuscripts and remarkable differences. To appreciate this insight and account for its implications, we need to know a little bit about *text criticism* and *textual traditions*.

Text criticism is the art and science of comparing and critiquing differences between manuscripts—called "textual variants" or "variant readings." Scholars and translators do this work for you to provide the best, earliest, and most authentic text of scripture (and not everyone agrees on the outcomes or aims of this process). Textual traditions are the families of manuscripts that text critics consult in the process of text criticism.

Before we capture the present impact and projected implications of the DSS for Bibles today, let's establish a profile of three main textual traditions that enable the text criticism of the Hebrew Scriptures. These are the Masoretic Text (MT), the Septuagint (LXX), and the Samaritan Pentateuch (SP).

The Masoretic Text: The Foundation of Modern Hebrew Scripture

When scholars and translators work up a new edition or translation of the Hebrew Scriptures, the MT is almost always their departure point. The MT family of manuscripts provides our most complete copies of the entire Hebrew Scriptures.

In the late first millennium of the Common Era, a group of Jewish scribes in Tiberias penned and preserved copies of the Jewish Scriptures, the Hebrew Bible. The most important MT witnesses are the Aleppo Codex (930 CE) and the Leningrad Codex (1008/1009 CE), though the Masoretic tradition is certainly older than these key codices. Today, the Leningrad Codex is most often used in the form of *Biblia Hebraica Stuttgartensia* (BHS), published by the German Bible Society. This edition of the Hebrew Bible is the basis of most modern Bibles.[7]

One critical aspect of the MT textual tradition relates to how the Masoretic scribes *invested* in the text. Hebrew is a consonantal language: there are no written vowels. This seems odd to us, but most other Semitic languages, such as Aramaic, Syriac, or Arabic, were or remain *sans* vowels. Because of this, there's a risk that you might misunderstand consonant clusters by supplying the wrong vowels. A playful English example might illustrate the point. Take the following vowelless phrase:

> Jn rn t th str t by brd
>
> Depending on the vowels and punctuation, this could mean any number of things.[8]
>
> John ran to the store to buy bread.
>
> Jon, run to the story to buy bread!
>
> Jon ran to the store to buy a board (or a bird).
>
> Jan ran to the stair, at a bay beard.
>
> Jane, I run to thee, a star to obey, a bride!

You get the point. The Masoretes developed a vocalization system of dots and dashes and applied it to the text to minimize this risk, solidify meaning, and aid in reading.[9] In short, this microlevel *interpretation of the text* and *investment in the tradition* ensures your bread, birds, beards, and brides aren't confused. Thank you, Masoretes.

When it comes to text criticism, the MT tradition is foundational. While this manuscript tradition is from the medieval period, the DSS revealed that, in most instances, its content is a reliable representation of scripture in antiquity. As we'll see, however, this was not the only rendition of scripture on offer in ancient Judaism.

The Septuagint: Antiquity's Most Ambitious Translation Project

It's hard to overstate the significance of the LXX for biblical, theological, and cultural studies. Like the MT, the LXX is a bit of a catchall for a larger extended family of manuscripts. These, however, are not written in Hebrew but Greek.

IMAGE 6.1a, 6.1b, 6.1c: Though the Aleppo Codex is slightly older than the Leningrad Codex, it suffered much damage during riots in Syria after the 1947 United Nations Resolution establishing the modern state of Israel. Thought to be lost, it resurfaced in 1958 when it was smuggled into Israel and gifted to the second president of the state of Israel, Yitzhak Ben-Zvi. Because of the incompleteness of the Aleppo Codex, the Leningrad Codex is the predominant base text for most contemporary presentations of the Hebrew Scriptures.

The Leningrad Codex images here are from a facsimile edition, here of a sample black and white image of Jeremiah 2:11b–2:37a (folio 246, verso) and an adorned, full-color page of Masoretic rules (folio 476, recto). The Aleppo Codex image is also from a facsimile edition, here a full-color image of a sample page from Ezekiel 7:8–8:4. (Image credits: Andrew B. Perrin)

Why Greek?

As Alexander the Great swept across the Mediterranean and Near East in the mid–fourth century BCE, Hellenistic culture spread in his wake. Coinage, dress, architecture, infrastructure, sport, entertainment, and, yes, language were all part of the package. From advanced Greek philosophical thought to Greek graffiti, this ripple effect touched every level of society, including religion. Jews in and beyond their home turf in Judea were now part of this Hellenistic cultural context. This sparked the desire and need to render Hebrew Scriptures into Greek.

The LXX is the single most ambitious translation enterprise of antiquity. Period. The effort began in the third century BCE with the Pentateuch—Genesis through Deuteronomy. By the turn of the Common Era, all the other writings of the Hebrew Scriptures, as well as several other ancient Jewish writings, had donned Greek garb, either through translation or composition.[10] Here we need to keep in mind that, like the DSS, the LXX is not a single collection, object, or artefact.

While we have Greek LXX papyrus fragments at a number of sites and among many collections, our most complete texts of the LXX are the Christian codices of the fourth and fifth centuries CE, such as Vaticanus, Sinaiticus, and Alexandrinus. In addition to the New Testament, these codices also include Greek versions of the Hebrew Scriptures and writings from the Apocrypha, or Deuterocanon.

The DSS discoveries revealed that LXX traditions were very much part of the scriptural world of Qumran and Judea in the Hellenistic period. The DSS include fragmentary copies of several Greek translations of books in the Hebrew Scriptures (for example, Exodus, Leviticus, Numbers, Deuteronomy, and the Minor Prophets), snippets of materials received in the Apocrypha, or Deuterocanon (such as the Epistle of Jeremiah), an even a few fragments of Greek translations of Aramaic literature, typically dubbed "pseudepigrapha" (like 1 Enoch). As we saw in the last chapter, Cave 7 contained *only* Greek texts.

IMAGE 6.2: Given the spread of Greek across the ancient world, it is perhaps not surprising to find fragments of early LXX texts in several locations, such as Qumran, Nahal Hever, and Oxyrhynchus, as early as the first century CE. Fourth-century CE codices, such as Codex Sinaiticus, featured here in a facsimile image of Numbers 17:20–18:12, are among the earliest and most complete exemplars to the ancient Jewish translation of Hebrew Scripture received by the early church. (Image credit: Andrew B. Perrin)

Prior to the discovery of the DSS, the translators of Greek texts were often caricatured. It was assumed that where the Greek texts departed from known Hebrew texts, these divergences were due to the translator being either careless or overly creative. Yet the DSS include Hebrew texts that reflect the structure, shape, and content of the type of texts behind Greek translations. To put it another way, where the LXX *seems* to go in its own direction, the DSS often authenticate those readings in a now known ancient Hebrew text. Such insights indicate the Greek translators weren't reckless; rather they were reliable conduits for the tradition.

The DSS fragments, then, give new insight into the *production* of Greek translations and their *reception* in a known Jewish community. Our Hebrew scriptural scrolls also help us rethink the *process* of Greek translations in ancient Judaism.

The Samaritan Pentateuch: Another Jewish Canon

The SP refers to a particular form of scripture received by a particular expression of Judaism. Today, Samaritan Judaism includes approximately eight hundred followers, living largely in the Qiryat Luza region on Mount Gerizim and the urban area of Hola, near Tel Aviv.[11]

Despite the small size of this community, their scriptural tradition is significant. Scholars debate the date of the SP as a scriptural collection. Our earliest hints of the tradition come from Origen's third-century CE *Hexapla*, which nods to a Greek translation of the Samaritan scriptures known as the *Samareitikon*, although the SP tradition is likely centuries older.[12]

What defines the SP textual tradition? Samaritan scripture is narrower in scope than all other canons. It includes only five books: Genesis through Deuteronomy. But the content and structure of the SP are distinctive.

The SP has a signature theological overlay of textual variants that reflect key aspects of Samaritan belief and practice. For example, Deuteronomy 27:4

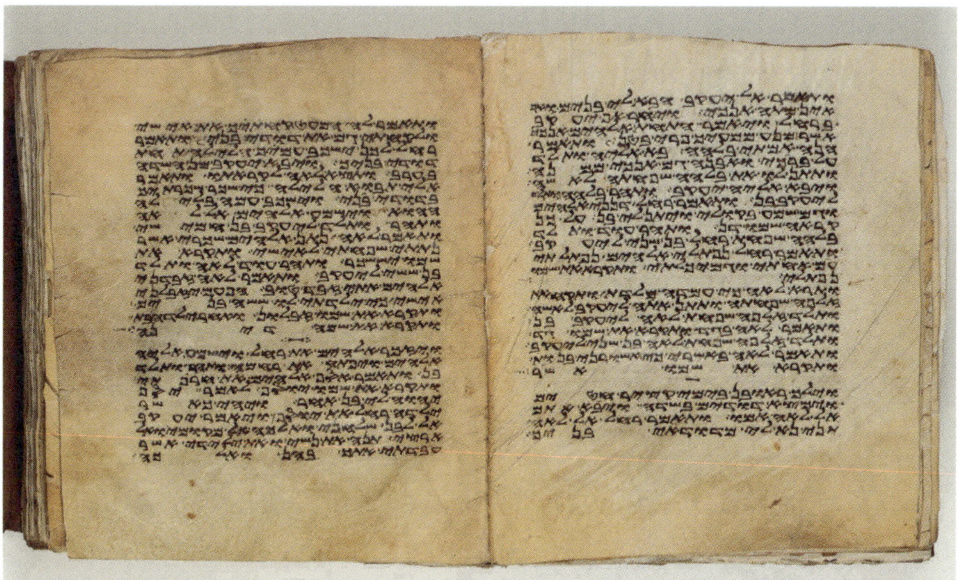

IMAGE 6.3: In addition to their more focused scope, Samaritan Pentateuch manuscripts are distinguished by their scribal features, including their distinctive Samarian script that, while having origins in the ancient world, was retained mostly by Samaritan Judaism. The manuscript featured here dates to approximately 1232 CE. (Image credit: The New York Public Library Digital Collections)

---

in the SP says that on crossing the Jordan the Israelites built an altar at Mount Gerizim, not Mount Ebal. Similarly, Deuteronomy 12:14 subtly swaps verb tenses from "the place that the Lord your God *will choose*" (that is, Jerusalem) to "the place that the Lord your God *has chosen*" (that is, Shechem). In these examples, the SP reframes the scriptural basis to support the origins and ongoing worship of God at significant sites for Samaritan Judaism. This also provides a bit more context for the alleged "new" reading in the modern forgery we explored in the Azusa Pacific University collection a few chapters back.

The structure of the SP is also noteworthy. It results from a creative editorial approach to scripture: scribes of the SP tradition often thematically rearranged related sections of scripture to achieve cogency, harmonized parallel passages to enhance consistency, and augmented law and narrative to ensure coherence.

But we knew all of this about the Samaritan scripture before the DSS. What we didn't know was how far back into the Second Temple period some of these features extended.

On one hand, the DSS don't include any sectarian variants. This means there are no variant readings at Qumran that are theologically motivated to legitimate the thought and practice of the group that penned or preserved the scrolls, whereas the theological overlay of the SP is an innovation of Samaritan culture.[13] Yet beneath this overlay, the SP includes variants that agree with the MT and the LXX, making it an important text-critical conversation partner.[14]

On the other hand, the Qumran materials reveal that the SP's editorial approach has deep roots. Scrolls like 4QpaleoExodus^{m}, 4QNumbers^{b}, and 4QPentateuch—which predate the SP—also feature shuffled, reconfigured, extended, and harmonized passages. Apparently the SP *inherited* this intensive style of interaction with scripture from earlier scribal cultures. Molly Zahn concluded that this suggests the editorial strategies in both the SP and our pre-SP texts at Qumran go beyond "a single editorial moment."[15] They are part of a larger story.

In these ways, Samaritan scripture is integral for retracing both the *formation* and *reception* of the Pentateuch in and beyond the Second Temple era.

Transformations: The Impact of the Scrolls on Modern Scriptures

Now that we've met the main textual traditions from the past that help us write the biography of the Bible, let's explore some details in that story that need to be rewritten because of the DSS.

To illustrate the potential of the DSS for text criticism of the Hebrew Scriptures, we'll work through three case studies of increasing complexity and impact. Admittedly, this is a highly selective sample. There are literally thousands of variant readings when the DSS are compared with other known biblical traditions.[16] Alongside this variety, of course, there is also remarkable continuity.

Our journey will involve the restoration of a single yet profound *word* from Isaiah 53:11 in 1QIsaiah[a], the recovery of a lost *sentence* from Psalm 145:13 in 11QPsalms[a], and the renovation of an entire *paragraph* from 1 Samuel 10:27 in 4QSamuel[a]. Along the way, we'll compare these verses in different ancient manuscripts and track their impact on modern English Bible translations. To keep you motivated, at least one of these will involve a sadistic, eyeball-gouging king. Be on your guard.

A New Outlook from a Single Word?
Isaiah 53:11 in 1QIsaiah[a-b] and 4QIsaiah[d]

Sometimes a small discovery makes a big difference. That's the case with a variant reading in Isaiah 53:11 found in the DSS. For some, this is a theological showstopper. For others, it's oversensationalized. Whether original or not, this variant reading has had a far-reaching impact on modern Bibles.

The verse comes in the last of Isaiah's series of servant songs (Isaiah 52:13–53:12). These oracles speak of a figure emerging to lead the nations who is tragically afflicted, abused, and abased.

Despite this bleak outlook, the passage inspired a number of positive expectations. The atonement projected in Isaiah 53:11 likely inspired the hint at resurrection in the wise who "lead many to righteousness" in Daniel 12:3. For the early church, the figure forecasted in Isaiah's servant songs was none other than Jesus (Acts 8:32–35). Apparently the passage is open to a variety of interpretations.

But does a single word—a tiny textual variant—matter at all in the earliest formation of this historic passage? Let's work through our witnesses to Isaiah 53:11 and find out. The MT reads this way:

> As a result of the anguish of his soul, he will see and be satisfied; by his knowledge the righteous one, my servant, will justify the many, as he will bear their iniquities. (NASB, with slight revision)

Suffering, bearing sin, downward spiral. Almost Stoic. Certainly sad. When we wind back the clock, however, our earliest witnesses to this verse find light on the horizon. Hope. The LXX here reads:

> from the pain of his soul, to show him *light* [φῶς] and fill him with understanding, to justify a righteous one who is well subject to many, and he himself shall bear their sins. (NETS)

In this take on Isaiah 53:11, the Greek scriptures still feature a suffering servant—yet there's a new outlook. Somehow, through suffering, the figure will find illumination: "light." Prior to the DSS, it would have been easy to write off this variant as late, a mere invention attributed to the Greek translator, not the Hebrew text before him. The DSS, however, overturned this idea.

All three of our Hebrew witnesses to Isaiah 53:11 at Qumran read the word *light*. This includes both of our famous Cave 1 manuscripts (1QIsaiah[a-b]) as well as a more fragmentary text from Cave 4 (4QIsaiah[d]). The single word is significant. Here's how the passage reads in the Great Isaiah Scroll of Cave 1:

> Out of the suffering of his soul he will see light (אור) and find satisfaction. And through his knowledge his servant, the righteous one, will make many righteous, and he will bear their iniquities. (1QIsaiah[a] 44:19)

Still suffering. Still bearing sin. Still a spiral. Only now, this individual's satisfaction is in seeing light beyond the present darkness. This discovery proved revolutionary for both ancient and modern scriptures. As VanderKam and Flint remarked, the Qumran Isaiah scrolls show "that the early Hebrew text used by the Septuagint translator actually contained the word *light*, and provides a new reading for exegesis of the passage."[17]

But does this new insight into what Isaiah 53:11 change what the verse means? Perhaps. For example, in view of other ancient Jewish texts associating light imagery with divine presence (such as 1 Enoch 92:3–4), Klaus Baltzer commented that, if Isaiah's servant "can see the 'light,' he has been judged worthy to enter into the immediate presence of God; he has been received into the company of the heavenly beings."[18] In effect, the once-downward spiral has become an elevation.

This ancient variant has had a contemporary payoff in many modern English translations. Several have adopted and integrated the "light" reading as original (CSV, NIV, NRSV), while others nod to it as a possible reading for consideration (ESV, HCSB, LEB, NASB, NKJV)—all thanks to the DSS and LXX. Given this broad acceptance, or at least recognition of the variant reading's importance, there are also ongoing debates among translators and scholars about not over translating the text or overly loading it with theological significance from a Christological perspective.

In the case of Isaiah 53:11, the unexpected discovery of a single word in our Isaiah scrolls at once authenticated the Hebrew text behind the ancient Greek translation and enhanced many modern Bibles by restoring a term that had been lost or overlooked for two thousand years.

A Psalm Completed by a Recovered Sentence? Psalm 145:13 in 11QPsalms[a]

If a single word matters, surely a full sentence would make an even greater impact. This is the case for Psalm 145:13 in 11QPsalms[a], a fragmentary text dated to the mid–first century CE.[19] The newly discovered sentence has been accepted in more modern Bible translations than any other variant reading in the entire DSS collection.

Before we get to the text of this psalm, let's talk about its genre. Remember acrostic poems from grade school? These poems are patterned alphabetically: each new line starts with the next letter of the alphabet. At times, Hebrew poetry also plays at this game. The acrostic structure tells us what to expect. It also makes it obvious when something is missing—like in Psalm 145.

In the MT, this psalm is an incomplete acrostic. Where we would expect a verse starting with the Hebrew letter *nun* (the equivalent of the English *N*), there simply isn't one. It's missing. Our Cave 11 Psalms scroll, however, provides a more complete picture, one that was already hinted at by a fuller verse in the LXX and at least one medieval manuscript (Kennicott manuscript 142). 11QPsalms[a] *includes* the lost verse—exactly where we'd expect it. This ancient text presents Psalm 145:13 as follows, with the recovered *nun* line presented in italics in the translation below:

> Your kingdom is an everlasting kingdom, and your dominion endures throughout all generations. Blessed be the LORD and blessed be his name forever and ever. *God is faithful in his words, and gracious in all his deeds.* (11QPsalms[a] 17:1–3)[20]

What does this detail do for us? Psalm 145 paints a brilliant theological portrait of God. The first half highlights his lofty *reputation*. Verse 13, however, marks a shift. Our *nun* verse is the final statement on the divine character before a section affirming God's promises, provision, and preservation of the faithful. Psalm 145:13, therefore, hinges toward content that underscores God's *reliability*. Or, as Goldingay put it, the more complete divine portrait provided by the DSS and LXX reassures us of "the moral qualities of this being who is trustworthy ... and committed in word and deed."[21]

This recovered sentence—this sound bite from a once-awkward acrostic—has impacted modern Bibles more than any other variant in the DSS. Allen noted that the "accidentally lost" *nun* verse "is generally restored in modern versions, except the NJPS."[22] To give a sense of the scope of this acceptance,

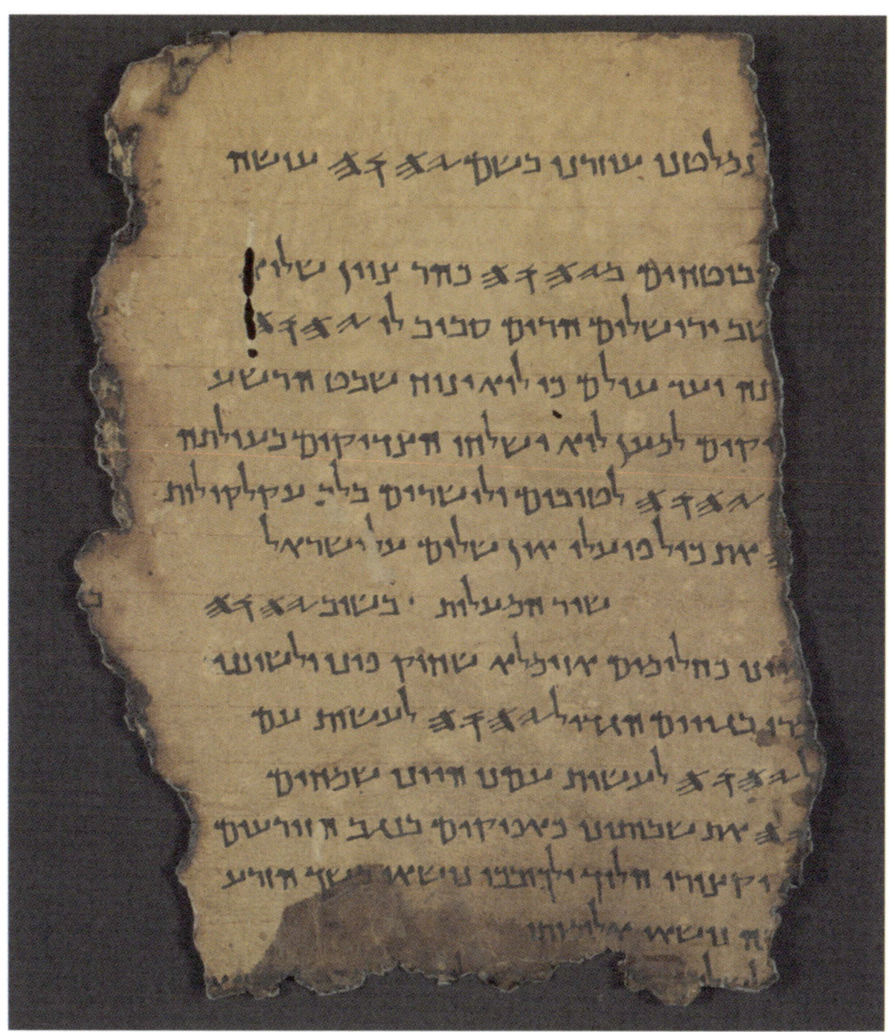

IMAGE 6.4: A sample section of 11QPsalms^{a} (11Q5 4) found in Cave 11 (ca. 50 BCE). As with some other scrolls at Qumran, the scribe or secondary scribe of this manuscript wrote the divine name of God in a more cryptic script, known as paleo-Hebrew, apparently to signify reverence for the holy name. Even to the untrained eye, this distinctive script is evident in the second word from the left in line 1 of the fragment. (Image credit: Courtesy of The Leon Levy Dead Sea Scrolls Digital Library; Israel Antiquities Authority, photo: Shai Halevi)

the variant of 11QPsalms[a] has found a home in the main text of the ESV, CSB, NAB, NIV, NJB, NLT, NRSV, REB, RSV, and TNIV. Several others give the variant reading honorable mention in the footnotes.

This updating-scripture-to-make-it-more-ancient, however, is not only about a restored text. It's about recovering the full theological vision of Psalm 145—a vision that existed before the discovery of the DSS as but a minority report in a few minor medieval manuscripts. We should celebrate this textual discovery. It's a big deal. But not bigger than the theological reality it points toward.

Scripture is always about more than the words on the page. The invitation of this variant is to reestablish the *text* to open new vistas of its *theology*.

A Narrative Gap Filled by a Full Paragraph? 1 Samuel 10:27 in 4QSamuel[a]

Our final sample comes from 1 Samuel 10:27 in 4QSamuel[a]. This first-century BCE manuscript includes a full paragraph of previously unknown material—the largest and longest difference found in the Hebrew Scripture texts at Qumran. Given its scope, the reading is also controversial. Let's get a bit of backstory on the passage before we recover a new insight from an old manuscript.

The first ten chapters of 1 Samuel are critical for the Old Testament story. It's been a rocky road of oppression, crying out, deliverance, and repeat for the twelve tribes. They're sick of it. They want a king: a *human* king. Though God is reluctant—after all, *he* is their king—1 Samuel 8:7-9 relates how he relents and gives them a guy: Saul. However, when it comes time for his installation, tall, handsome Saul is hiding among the baggage (1 Samuel 9:2; 10:22). Awkward.

As Saul emerges, the response is mixed. Some proclaim, "Long live the king!" (1 Samuel 10:24). Yet the chapter ends on a somber and disapproving note:

> But certain useless men said, "How can this one save us?" And they despised him and did not bring him a gift. But he kept silent about it. (1 Samuel 10:27 NASB)

Doubly awkward. Nothing like a bunch of freeloaders without presents to ruin a coronation. Then, without missing a beat, 1 Samuel 11:1–2 reads:

> Now Nahash the Ammonite went up and besieged Jabesh-gilead; and all the men of Jabesh said to Nahash, "Make a covenant with us and we will serve you." But Nahash the Ammonite said to them, "I will make it with you on this condition, that I will gouge out the right eye of every one of you, and thereby I will inflict a disgrace on all Israel.'" (NASB)

Wait, what? How did we go from present-less party crashers to a sadistic, eyeball-collecting Ammonite king? The narrative as it stands in most manuscripts is glitchy and jarring. But 4QSamuel[a] tells a different story—a more complete story. Right between 1 Samuel 10:27 and 11:1, this Cave 4 manuscript includes the following interlude:

> [Na]hash king of the [A]mmonites oppressed the Gadites and the Reubenites viciously. He put out the right [ey]e of a[ll] of them and brought fe[ar and trembling] on [Is]rael. Not one of the Israelites in the region be[yond the Jordan] remained [whose] right eye Naha[sh king of] the Ammonites did n[ot pu]t out, except seven thousand men [who escaped from] the Ammonites and went to [Ja]besh-Gilead. (4Q51 10a:6–9)

This section certainly makes for a more intelligible sequence. And sure, it's ancient. But is it original? 4QSamuel[a] is the only known manuscript to include this paragraph-long passage. It's also our oldest copy of the book.

Think about the implications of this. If the cut scene in our Cave 4 text is original—and there's debate on that point—it means that all the other manuscripts of 1 Samuel in existence, and I mean *all* of them, are corrupt, wrong, incomplete. It also means that most readers, in most places, for most of history, were unaware of this gaping hole in their scriptures. Pretty much everyone. Pretty much everywhere.

Now, it might be easy to marginalize this reading of 4QSamuel[a]. After all, it's just one manuscript. Maybe. Yet sometimes the most illuminating insights on biblical texts come from nonbiblical sources. In this case, it's our old friend from a few chapters back, Josephus. When, in *Antiquities of the Jews*, Josephus retells the tale of Saul's ascendancy to the throne and his eventual overthrowing the Ammonites, he includes an extensive introduction to Nahash and an account of his eyeball-collecting covenant (*Ant.* 6.68–72). Apparently Josephus's scriptural sources in the first century CE also included this lost paragraph. This is a powerful tag team. Our earliest manuscript attests to the paragraph in this passage, and one of our earliest interpreters of the passage is also aware of its existence.[23]

So it was part of scriptural traditions then. But should it impact Bibles now? With a variant of this scope and significance, not everyone agrees. And that's the rub of text criticism: it is both an art and a science. At present, only the NRSV and NLT include this paragraph in translation.[24]

Regardless of the text critical decision in this example, our venture into the world of scribes, scrolls, and scriptures once again involves a delicate balance. The DSS enable us to encounter scripture as it was and rethink how to best restore it today. This leads us to our final topic for this chapter: how the DSS not only revolutionized the text of scripture but challenged text critics to reimagine their tasks and tools.

Text Criticism: Rethinking Aims and Outcomes in Light of the Dead Sea Scrolls

Traditional text criticism is like a mining operation in manuscripts. It is effectively commodity recovery: the task is to source, sift, and secure the earliest readings, then leave the rest as rubble. We saw above that the outcomes of this approach are invaluable. Yet if we ignore the rubble—the majority of variant readings, which are *not* deemed original, early, or best—we've missed an opportunity. In fact, we've set up an unsustainable enterprise.

What if we shift metaphors and rethink the process altogether? What if text criticism is less about the relentless pursuit of rarities and more about the journey into untraveled territory? Sure, our destination might still ultimately be the pursuit of the best readings. But like most expeditions, some of the most rewarding discoveries come from our explorations along the way.[25]

From this perspective, the DSS are about more than new *texts*. They are also about new *contexts* that challenge text critics to develop new approaches and to ask better questions. This approach opens us to the terrain of traditions at Qumran to learn about the practices of *scribes*, the formation of traditions inscribed on *scrolls*, and the development of *scriptures*.

We'll look at four case studies to press in this direction. Only now, we're not concerned with early readings recovered for our Bibles—that is, end *products* for today. Rather, our aim is to restore our relationship with the scribal practices and perspectives that shaped ancient scripture—that is, the ongoing *processes* back in their day. To show that new insights often come from unexpected places, our topics will include variant readings from the rubble. These include fresh takes on asses, assassins, burnt toast, and burning men.

Scribal Errors are Opportunities: Bald and Breezy Asses in Jeremiah 14:6

4QJeremiah[a] is one of six fragmentary copies of Jeremiah in the DSS. This manuscript dates to around 225–175 BCE, making it one of the oldest scrolls at Qumran. It's also one of the most heavily corrected.[26] Now, that's an interesting set of claims to fame: oldest and most erroneous. Think about that for a second.

As I often tell my students, "Messy manuscripts matter." This Jeremiah manuscript has a lot to teach us in our text-critical journey. Let's look at just one variant in Jeremiah 14:6 and see what it reveals about *coherence*, *corrections*, and *conversations* in this early tradition.

Here's a rundown of translations and the isolated textual variant in the relevant manuscripts for Jeremiah 14:6.

> 4QJeremiah[a]: "The wild asses stand on the barren heights and *are bald* (שׁפאו) for air like jackals; their eyes fail [because there is no vegetation.]" (4Q70 22:2)
>
> MT: "The wild asses stand on the bare heights, *they pant* (שׁאפו) for air like jackals; their eyes fail because there is no herbage."
>
> LXX: "Wild asses stood by wooded valleys; *they inhaled* (εἵλκυσαν) wind; their eyes failed, because there was no grass."

Are the asses bald or hyperventilating? (Just to clarify, we're talking about donkeys—now is not the time to confuse imagery!)

While insignificant at first glance, these textual variants relate to big lessons in text criticism. This text is full of creative scribal interventions. Judging by different styles of handwriting, we can also tell that two scribes contributed to the manuscript. Often scribe number two corrected the missteps of scribe number one. In the case of our "bald" reading in 4QJeremiah[a], the first scribe inadvertently wrote the rare form שׁפאו ("bald") rather than the likely intended שׁאפו ("they pant"), as known from MT, and which is likely behind the Greek verb ἕλκω ("to inhale") in the LXX.

This is hardly a theological showstopper of a variant. But what does it reveal about the human hands of holy writ? Simply put: scribal errors are not corruptions—they are opportunities. It might come as news to modern readers that ancient scriptural manuscripts—in this case one of the oldest on earth—include slipups and blunders. However, these connect us to lost

IMAGE 6.5: These fragments of 4QJeremiah[a] (4 i–ii, 10) make up a partial column of Jeremiah 7:28–9:2. In this sample, the scribe clearly optimized the manuscript by writing down the margins. In another fragment from the lower portion of the manuscript, the scribe even wrote content upside down in the lower margin (4QJeremiah[a] 7). It seems these additions were made by the second scribe, who caught the accidental omission of Jeremiah 7:30–8:3 by an earlier scribe. (Image credit: Courtesy of The Leon Levy Dead Sea Scrolls Digital Library; Israel Antiquities Authority, photo: Shai Halevi)

---

scribal worlds. In most cases, scribes are expert copyists. They had a vested interest in the texts they copied. This was serious work that required great skill. Yet they also sometimes made mistakes. After all, like you and I, they were humans. It's fine to have a high theology of Scripture (I do), but not to write out the humans who were part of this process (I don't).

In this instance, and several others in 4QJeremiah[a], we have an ancient typo of sorts by scribe number one. Throughout the manuscript, scribe number two worked in parallel, routinely correcting scribe number one for a more cogent tradition. Yet our variant in Jeremiah 14:6 slipped through quality control.[27]

If we're unsettled by the reality of errors in ancient manuscripts, that's our problem, not theirs. Scribes are not photocopiers. Variant readings originating as errors connect us to the very real, very human, side of sacred scripture. Perhaps it's time our theologies allow for a greater space to embrace both the experience and interactions of ancient scribes with and within the traditions they copied.

Who Wants an Original Text That's Unintelligible? One-Shot Assassins in Psalm 11:2

To interpret something, you typically need to quote it. The *Pesher Habakkuk* text we met back in chapter 1 included selective citations of Habakkuk with a quote-comment-quote-comment style of interpretation. Another style of interpretive literature, called *catena* texts, clusters scriptural sound bites by common themes. In these interpretive writings, scriptural citations come from somewhere—often an older or even unknown scriptural tradition.

At times, these embedded scriptures reveal textual variants. These may be scribal: perhaps the scribe tailored the meaning of the quoted text to fit a desired meaning. Yet more often than not they are textual: that is, the interpreter accessed a manuscript or memory that differed in the details from known manuscripts.[28]

We see this in a sample of 4QCatena A, a manuscript dated to the second half of the first century BCE.[29] When this interpretation presents Psalm 11:2, it includes several variant readings. One of them illustrates how embedded scriptural texts provide unexpected insights.

4QCatena A: "Look, the wicked bend the bow,] and they have fitted *arrows* (חצ֯ים) t[o the string."

MT: "Look, the wicked bend the bow, they have fitted *their arrow* (חצם) to the string, to shoot in the dark at the upright in heart."

LXX: "Look, sinners bent a bow; they prepared *arrows* (βέλη) for the quiver, to shoot in a moonless night at the upright in heart."

A common guideline for text criticism is that "the more difficult text is the earlier one." This maxim is based on modern logic: a scribe is more likely to clarify a text than corrupt it. Every time I hear this "rule," a little part of me dies. Let me show you why. Did you catch the odd imagery required by the MT of Psalm 11:2? We have a cohort of covert, wicked archers taking aim in the night at this poor poet. Yet they lock and load with an "arrow" (singular). The image is inconsistent. The text is incoherent. Yet somehow this is more original, better, preferred?

The embedded text of 4QCatena A and LXX paint a different picture. Our assassins by night set the righteous in their crosshairs with their "arrows" (plural). Makes sense: multiple archers will need multiple arrows. The issue with "the trickier text as earlier" rule is it insists that, for all our efforts in reverse engineering ancient scriptures, what we're chasing, at times, is a biblikal teckst that mehks know cents. See what I mean?

If we insist that the original form of Psalm 11:2 read the more difficult "arrow," as in the MT, we're implying that the reading "arrows" in the DSS and LXX is deficient. Yet it was apparently sufficient for the readers of both collections in antiquity! We can't insist the DSS and LXX support our Bibles on the one hand, while implying they were incoherent on the other.

Ancient scriptures existed with a limited variety. Scribes engaged, even cultivated, that variety. Reading communities embraced it. Scrolls, whether scriptural or interpretive, reflect those encounters, that variety, and that openness. This example underscores that text critics need to diversify their data by considering scriptural quotations in writings that are typically off their radar.[30] It also means perhaps dismantling some basic presuppositions of text-critical rules, which, as we'll see, is also essential in our next sample.

The Samaritan and Septuagint Tag Team: Burnt Toast in Leviticus 2:1

I get it: Leviticus is nobody's favorite book. I want to change your perception that Leviticus is a bore. What if I told you that of the some 930 DSS, a Leviticus manuscript was one of two of the oldest manuscripts? What if I told you that this fragmentary manuscript was a twofer, containing material from both Exodus and Leviticus? What if I told you this text both shared important readings with a number of other known scriptural traditions, and revealed new readings we'd never seen before?

The marvel I'm talking about here is 4QExodus-Leviticus[f]. It's written in an archaic script dated to around the mid–third century BCE. In light of this date, Frank Moore Cross confirmed that "the manuscript of 4QExod-Lev[f] is, along with 4QSam[b], the earliest of the manuscripts found in the caves of Qumran."[31] That's more than a millennium—1250 years, give or take—*older* than our MT codices. Not so boring anymore.

But what about the variants in 4QExodus-Leviticus[f]? Let's talk about burnt toast (also known as grain offerings) in Leviticus 2:1. This passage follows an introductory chapter on animal sacrifice and shifts toward descriptions of other items accompanying the offering. The relevant witnesses present this prescription as follows, with the variant in question presented in italics and original languages when present:

> 4QExodus-Leviticus[f]: When anyone presents his] grain [off]ering [to the Lord, the offering shall be of choice flour; and he shall pour oil on it, and put frank]incense on it—[*it is*] *an offering* (מנחה [היא]).

MT: When anyone presents a grain offering to the LORD, the offering shall be of choice flour; the worshiper shall pour oil on it, and put frankincense on it.

SP: And when any will offer a meat offering unto the LORD, his offering shall be of a fine flour; and he shall pour oil upon it and put frankincense thereon: *it is an offering* (מנחה היא).[32]

LXX: Now if anyone presents a gift, a sacrifice to the Lord, his gift shall be fine flour, and he shall pour oil on it and put frankincense on it—*it is a sacrifice* (θυσία ἐστίν).

Traditionally the shared longer readings of 4QExodus-Leviticus[f], SP, and LXX would be deemed "secondary," effectively an accretion, with the shorter reading of MT declared as the "primary" and likely original reading. This is due to another text-critical guideline devised long before discoveries like the DSS: longer texts are later texts. This is based on similar modern logic to the rule above: the assumption is that scribes were more likely to *add to* rather than *take away from* a text—as if scribes were playing the "telephone game." But this is a really terrible metaphor for thinking about the transmission of scripture. The logic is flawed, and so is the rule.

This is problematic for similar reasons to our assassins example in Psalm 11:2. The bias toward a unified original text effectively writes human scribes and communities who read more diverse texts out of the equation. Here again, this reveals an unsettling idea: some might want the word of God but aren't terribly interested in the people who transmitted it. Theologically, that's dodgy. Ethically, it's dangerous.

Judging from the manuscript evidence above, it seems most readers or hearers in antiquity—across both linguistic and religious traditions—experienced and embraced the "secondary" form of Leviticus 2:1 as scripture. Was Leviticus any less Leviticus for them? Hardly. In fact, one thing we learned from the DSS is that variation among manuscripts of a given book of Hebrew Scripture at Qumran is a *signal* of authority, not a *compromise* of it. Similarly, if scribes continued to invest in (or even extend) texts and traditions, it meant they mattered.

This variety within the unity, then, helps us reorient the aims of text criticism away from restoring a single text—often or assumed to equate with the MT—toward mapping the textual history of scriptural traditions read and received by generations of Jewish and Christian communities. This leads us to our last example, an equally fiery one in the book of Daniel.

Transmission Is Reception: Burning Men in Daniel 3:25

The arc of a scriptural tradition generally involves three phases. *Composition*: writing stuff down. *Transmission*: copying that stuff. *Reception*: interpreting that stuff to make more stuff. Typically, these are understood as separate parts of a longer sequence. In some sense, that's true. But the DSS challenge us to see the interrelatedness of these three in our oldest scriptural traditions.

There is often a long period between when we think a given book was written and our earliest copies of that book. For the book of Daniel, however, the DSS reduced that major gulf to a modest gap.

Daniel was likely written in the mid–second century BCE, and the earliest Daniel manuscript at Qumran, 4QDaniel[c], dates to the late–second century BCE. Frank Moore Cross remarked that this fragmentary scroll is "closer to the original edition of a biblical work than any biblical manuscript in existence."[33] This puts *composition* within a generation of *transmission*. Yet the Daniel DSS reveal that *reception* is also at work from the get-go. Next chapter we'll also see that the transmission and reception of Danielic traditions at Qumran both preceded and extended beyond the book of Daniel itself.

We see this play out at the level of textual variants of Daniel 3:25 in 4QDaniel[d]. The variant revealed by the DSS here has less to do with the sight of these figures in the fiery furnace than the dialogue among the imperial onlookers. The difference is evident even when comparing two key witnesses.

> 4QDaniel[d]: "*Nebuchadnezz*[*ar*] *replied* [*and said*] *to his officials* (ע֯נ֯ה֯ נ֯ב֯כ֯ד֯נ֯צ֯[ר ואמר] ל֯הדברוהי), 'But I see four men loo[se, walking in the midst of the fire, and they are unharmed; and the appearance] of [the fo]urth is lik[e] a son of the god[s.'" (4Q115 2ii:4–5)

> MT: "*He replied and said* (ענה ואמר), 'But I see four men unbound, walking in the middle of the fire, and they are not hurt; and the fourth has the appearance of a son of the gods.'" (NRSV, slightly revised)

How do we account for this variety? If text criticism restores *what the text says* in its earliest form, reception history recaptures *what the text meant* to individuals or communities. Traditionally, text critics and reception historians don't talk to each other. This is a problem, particularly since the scribal world of Qumran was at the intersection of scripture and community. Text critics and reception historians, it's time to buddy up.

The scribe of 4QDaniel[d] made a minor addition to clarify the text. Rather than leave you guessing at the subject and object of the dialogue, he spelled it out: the "he" is Nebuchadnezzar and the implied "they" are his onsite officials. In this, the scribe has carried over the details from Daniel 3:24, which sets up the conversation similarly.

Like our burnt toast example in Leviticus 2:1, the DSS Daniel manuscript includes a *longer* reading. Here too, even though 4QDaniel[d] is our oldest witness to this passage, the reading is likely secondary. For text critics, that's the end of the job.

But reception historians would see this as the start of the job. There are many uses of Daniel in ancient sources—within the DSS, the writings of Josephus, the New Testament, and others—yet these are *not* the first interpretations of Daniel. Our earliest interpretations are the scribal interventions *within* manuscripts like 4QDaniel[d], which add, clarify, or harmonize details of the narrative. The reception history of Daniel is diverse and continues throughout time, communities, and various forms of art and media. As Michael Diamond, Adam Harovitz, and Adam Yauch demonstrated, the inspiration of Daniel's (mis)adventures in biblical traditions reach from ancient Babylon to contemporary Brooklyn.[34]

The big breakthrough here is that interpretation and reception do not only occur *after or apart from* developing scriptural traditions—they are in fact *active within* and *part of* the scribal formation of ancient scripture itself. We might think of scribes as copyists, but scribes are also our first interpreters.

Conclusion

Today we experience the Bible as a book of fixed and finalized scripture. Admittedly this is changing with digital technologies. For many readers on screens, e-readers, phones, and tablets the Bible is no longer a book in the technical sense. We now know that in the days of the DSS books didn't exist either, and neither did canons. The challenge for us is to encounter this world on its own terms, not ours. Scribes were more than copyists. Scrolls varied one to the next. Scriptures were somewhat fluid. As a result, we have both similarities and differences in the details—you can't have one without the other.

To understand scripture not only for what it is, but for what it can be, means that we must train our eyes to see it as has been. The true challenge here is to take ownership of our scriptural heritage, to grow our awareness of its brilliant and complex manuscript history, to encounter the scribes to whom we're indebted for their efforts and interactions, and to assess how our modern perspectives inform what we expect, want, or even need the Bible to be.

The DSS have changed, and will continue to change, the text of the Hebrew Scriptures. Whether it's a restored word, recovered sentence, or renegotiated paragraph, the text-critical advances and updates made possible by the DSS make our modern scriptures more ancient. These changes are akin to artistic restoration. They are positive and undertaken with great care, study, and discernment. If scripture matters, we should rise to the challenge of making the right restorations thoughtfully, carefully, meaningfully. The DSS also sparked a revolution for the text-critical aims and approaches that guide that process. Our job is not only the pursuit of an early or original text—a *product*. Our journey is to profile the scribes who developed scripture, to account for and embrace a *process*.

But when it comes to the potential of the DSS for the Hebrew Scriptures, we can't underscore changes without affirming continuity. Traditionally, text criticism emphasizes differences between manuscripts and traditions. Yet it's easy to lose sight of the remarkable consistency that defines much of the transmission history of biblical manuscripts from antiquity down through the medieval period. As James VanderKam commented, the differences between the DSS and other known manuscript traditions, like the MT, "are indeed numerous though frequently very slight, often ones that do not affect the meaning of the text for most purposes (e.g., spelling changes, omission or addition of a conjunction)."[35]

Variant readings might make us think differently about the formation of texts and even cause us to see differences in the information in texts. But what we aren't seeing is an entirely different text. Most often, our manuscripts agree. If anything, the case studies above underscore the value of the DSS for *supplementing* new details to the larger picture we already knew about from countless other witnesses to the Hebrew Scriptures. Continuity is certainly part of the equation.

So far, our study of scripture at Qumran has put variants under a microscope. The scribal imagination of ancient Judaism, however, means that what we would eventually call "biblical" books were stars within larger constellations of traditions. To account for this larger scope of traditions, in the next chapter we'll exchange our microscope for a telescope to capture the bigger picture before us.

Chapter 7

The Orbits of Traditions: Patriarchs and Matriarchs Before the Bible

The DSS opened new worlds to us—a world of ancient Jewish scribes copying, interpreting, and often extending scriptural traditions and tales inherited from ancient Israel. For all the new texts and contexts these finds revealed, however, our modern minds often struggle to understand how scribes built texts and blended traditions.

How can we overcome this obstacle in understanding? Perhaps the best place and time to start is a long time ago in a galaxy far, far away. While every analogy has its limits, arguably the best contemporary parallel to the ancient formation of texts and traditions is the intergalactic anthology of Star Wars films.

Star Wars purists know that the core and genesis of the authoritative Star Wars canon—yes, it is technically a canon—originally included three films: *A New* Hope (1977), *The Empire Strikes Back* (1980), and *Return of the Jedi* (1983). Over time this authoritative core extended to include now thirteen films, with the latest one in the canon being *The Last Jedi* (2022). The canon also includes a surprising number of books, shows, and even video games.

If you study the development of this modern tradition, you're likely to note two things that are remarkably similar to the scribal cultivation of ancient scriptural traditions. First, rereleases of the earlier films include minor updates—splashes of CGI effects, clever but conspicuous cut scenes, new dialogue to clarify elements of the script, even literal "textual variants" in that iconic yellow script preamble fading into the galaxy at the outset of the films. The films are still Star Wars, they're just made more relevant and relatable to a new generation. You might say that the *texts* that constitute this anthology grew over time. They were updated.

Second, more recent entries in the Star Wars anthology of traditions are almost always inspired by, or even developed around, the authoritative characters of core figures from the oldest and most authoritative cast of the original films. Leia, Luke, Han, Yoda—they're all there, either in lead roles in untold tales or in cameos in critical scenes to anchor a fresh take on this intergalactic tradition. You might say that the authority of the core tradition was extended by reimagining old characters in new narratives.

How does this sci-fi and pop culture analogy help us make sense of scrolls found a long time ago in caves far, far away? Last chapter we saw that scribes were as much participants in the process of passing on scripture as there were preservationists. They were copyists *and* creatives. We also now know that the *texts* that turn up in the Bible are part of larger bodies of *traditions*—at times overlooked or forgotten, and often misunderstood.

This is often news to most modern readers, particularly those of the Bible. We're used to thinking about texts in isolation, as fixed entities between two covers, suspended from the broader set of ideas that gave rise to them. But the DSS reveal that what we've come to know and love as biblical writings often existed in multiple forms—even multiple editions. They've also helped us recover the scribal imagination that crafted and created far more episodes and tales about biblical figures that we ever realized.

This chapter continues the conversation from the last chapter, but takes us into new territory of lost texts and forgotten versions of them. I want to reintroduce you to four personae from the Hebrew Scriptures that you probably already know: Jeremiah, David, Daniel, and Miriam. Yet by arranging this encounter in the DSS, we'll see that these figures are bigger than their scriptural selves. So if you've ever wondered whether all that binge-watching of Star Wars would help you in life, I'm here to tell you it was worth it—and just might help you make sense of the pages that follow.

Burning Braziers and Editions of Jeremiah

The book of Jeremiah is unique among the prophetic literature.[1] It blends narratives *about* the prophet and oracles *attributed to* the prophet. For all this richness, however, what I like most about the book of Jeremiah is his scribal sidekick, Baruch. If Jeremiah was the vocal, controversial, countercultural voice speaking truth from the fringes, Baruch was the edgy, essential, yet underappreciated element of the ensemble.

The misadventures of this dynamic duo told in the book of Jeremiah provide glimpses into the types of scribal processes that eventually resulted in "multiple literary editions." But before we get to those, let's study a scriptural scene of a burning brazier from Jeremiah 36. (Just to clarify, that's a fireplace, not women's underwear.)

Jeremiah 36 includes a scene of the delivery of oracles against Judah's king, who was contending with the Babylonian superpower on their doorstep. When inspiration strikes, Jeremiah enlists Baruch to pen and perform his oracles. Jeremiah 36:1–4 reads:

> In the fourth year of King Jehoiakim son of Josiah of Judah, this word came to Jeremiah from the Lord: Take a scroll and write on it all the words that I have spoken to you against Israel and Judah and all the nations, from the day I spoke to you, from the days of Josiah until today. It may be that when the house of Judah hears of all the disasters that I intend to do to them, all of them may turn from their evil ways, so that I may forgive their iniquity and their sin. Then Jeremiah called Baruch son of Neriah, and Baruch wrote on a scroll at Jeremiah's dictation all the words of the Lord that he had spoken to him.

Turns out, this anthology of doom wasn't received well. Following Baruch's reading of the scroll in the temple courts, the scroll is confiscated and brought to its addressee, King Jehoiakim, who is cozied up fireside in his winter apartment (Jeremiah 36:9–23). In short order, the scroll meets its toasty and untimely end.

> As Jehudi [a courtier] read three or four columns, the king would cut them off with a penknife and throw them into the fire in the brazier, until the entire scroll was consumed in the fire that was in the brazier. (36:23)

This is why you back up your files. The sole copy of the oracle is torched. Gone. Never seen again. But what happens next is an essential lesson in the growth of scribal traditions. Jeremiah and Baruch regroup to both *rewrite* and *extend* the original message.

> Now, after the king had burned the scroll with the words that Baruch wrote at Jeremiah's dictation, the word of the Lord came to Jeremiah: Take another scroll and write on it all the former words that were in the first scroll, which King Jehoiakim of Judah has burned. ... Then Jeremiah took another scroll and gave it to the secretary Baruch son of Neriah, who wrote on it at Jeremiah's dictation all the words of the scroll that King Jehoiakim of Judah had burned in the fire; and many similar words were added to them. (36:27–28, 32)

The big insight from this scene is that there are two versions of the document in the narrative. The two scrolls are united in message, yet varied in their scope and content. Prophets forecast the future, yet they speak into the present. The situation has changed, and so the prophet and scribe rise to the occasion and speak into it. This new rewritten and expanded document reflects development both in changing understandings of revelation in growing traditions as well as the growing authority of scribes to transmit, extend, and interpret texts.[2]

This illustration from within the Hebrew Scriptures parallels one of the biggest lessons about the scribal formation of scriptures that we've learned from the DSS. Scribes participated in the production of texts and traditions as they were brought into ever-changing cultural, historical, social, and political situations. One of the outcomes of this process was many books' emergence and circulation in more than one form.

Eugene Ulrich, editor of the Qumran Biblical Scrolls, pioneered the discovery of "multiple literary editions" of many books of Hebrew Scripture in ancient Judaism. If textual variants are differences on a microlevel (such as spelling, words, and phrases), then these variant editions reflect larger patterns and degrees of differences on a macrolevel. Ulrich described this reality the following way.

> The term *variant editions* refers to two or more literary forms of an entire book or large passage evident in copies of the same work. One form was completed by one author or editor, but another form was intentionally reformulated by another scribe or editor according to a discernible pattern. That extent of the reformulation was large enough that—like a revised, corrected, updated, and expanded textbook—it deserves to be called a *new and revised edition* of the earlier text. Usually one form can be recognized as the earlier one and the other as secondary; in that case they can be termed *successive editions*. If neither form appears to have derived from the other, they can be termed *parallel editions*. The formulation and reformulation of scriptural texts resulting in variant editions is illumined by the collective study of the Dead Sea Scrolls, MT, SP, and LXX.[3]

The two scrolls in Jeremiah 36 are unlikely to relate to the actual origins of the book of Jeremiah, but the scene is heuristically helpful when we encounter the Jeremiahs of the DSS. The processes of revising, updating, and expanding traditions described by Ulrich are evident in our oldest manuscripts of Jeremiah from Cave 4. This is sometimes referred to as "pluriformity."

Caves 2 and 4 included a total of six copies of what we now call the book of Jeremiah (2QJeremiah; 4QJeremiah[a-e]). These date to between 200 BCE and 100 CE. When we set these alongside one another, however, we find two editions of Jeremiah: a longer one and a shorter one. Was this a shocker? Yes and no.

Comparisons of the book of Jeremiah in the LXX and MT reveal that the text of the former was about 13 percent shorter. We already knew this before the DSS. What we didn't know was just how ancient *both* editions were. On one hand, 4QJeremiah[b] and 4QJeremiah[d] reflect the lost Hebrew text form behind the shorter Greek version. Emanuel Tov, chief editor of the Dead Sea Scrolls and editor of the Jeremiah texts, remarked that "no other Qumran fragment is as close to the LXX as these two texts."[4] On the other hand, 4QJeremiah[a] and 4QJeremiah[c] reveal the background of the longer form of the MT. In view of this pluriformity, we can now confirm that both editions of the book are authentic and existed alongside one another in antiquity.[5]

We get a glimpse of this variety in the satire on idols in Jeremiah 10:3–11. Abegg, Flint, and Ulrich observe that, "While the Masoretic Text has all nine verses, the Greek Bible and 4QJer[b] lack verses 6–8 and 10, which extol the greatness of God."[6] To this, we could add that these texts are not only shorter; they also reveal a different order. We can see all these variations in the smaller sample of Jeremiah 10:9–11. Representing the longer version, Jeremiah 10:9 is found only in the MT, and fragmentarily in 4QJeremiah[a] (bolded text below). Representing the shorter version, Jeremiah 10:5b is tucked in between 10:9 and 10:11 in 4QJeremiah[b] and the LXX (italicized text below).

> MT: [10:9] Beaten silver is brought from Tarshish, and gold from Uphaz, the work of a craftsman and of the hands of a goldsmith; their clothing

is of violet and purple; they are all the work of skilled people. [10:10] **But the LORD is the true God; He is the living God and the everlasting King. The earth quakes at His wrath, and the nations cannot endure His indignation.** [10:11] This is what you shall say to them, "The gods that did not make the heavens and the earth will perish from the earth and from under these heavens." (NASB; compare 4QJeremiah[a] [4Q70] 11–12:1–4)

4QJeremiah[b]: [10:9] Beaten silver is brought from Tarshish, and gold from Uphaz, the work of a craftsman and of the hands of a goldsmith;] violet and purple [are their clothing; they are all the work of skilled men. [10:5b] *They must be carried, because they cannot walk! Do not fear them, for they can do no harm, nor can they do any good.*" [10:11] Thus you shall say to them, "The gods that did not make the heavens and the earth] will perish from the earth [and from under the heavens."

LXX: [10:9] Beaten silver will come from Tharsis, gold of Mophas and a hand of goldsmiths—works of craftsmen all; they will clothe in blue and purple. [10:5b] *Raised they will be carried, because they will not walk. Do not be afraid of them, because they shall not do evil, and there is no good in them.* [10:11] Thus shall you say to them: Let gods who did not make the sky and the earth perish from the earth and from under the sky.

This sample represents in a focused way the variation in content and scope that extends to many other areas of the book of Jeremiah. We saw above that the book of Jeremiah includes *memories* of the development of prophetic oracles. Now we've also observed how Qumran includes *manuscripts* of pluriform Jeremiah texts. So what's the upshot of all this for how we understand the constellation of Jeremiah traditions?

First, the existence of concurrent and contemporary versions of Jeremiah at Qumran proves that the long and short Jeremiahs weren't necessarily iterations of each other—they were read and revered in antiquity at the same time.

Our earliest evidence of Jeremiah is pluriform. The Qumranites embraced this variety because the message of the prophet mattered more than the form the tradition took.

Second, the existence of multiple literary editions for any book is a key indicator of the authority of a tradition, not a compromise to it. When gauging the authority of an ancient book, it often isn't the *quantity* of the manuscripts that mattered as much as the generative *quality* of a tradition in a variety of forms.

Third, authority was extended to texts, but it often originated in ancestral figures.[7] In fact, at Qumran a collection of other texts either about or inspired by the figure of Jeremiah outnumber the copies of the biblical book. This includes four copies of the *Apocryphon of Jeremiah C* (4Q385a, 4Q387, 4Q388a, 4Q389), two works of the *Apocryphon of Jeremiah A–B* (4Q383, 4Q384), and a fragmentary Greek text of the Epistle of Jeremiah (7Q2), received later in the Septuagint. The figure of Jeremiah was bigger than the eventual biblical book. And this is to say nothing of the many ways Jeremiah is quoted and interpreted in other writings at Qumran.

Taking these three strands together, the Jeremiah materials among the DSS reveal how ancient scribes and the Qumran community valued the mouthpiece of Jeremiah the prophet and were open to hearing it in multiple forms. In all of this, they got something modern minds often miss: if a tradition mattered, it should continue to speak. The more important the message, the more forms it took. And if this was true in the example of Jeremiah, it was even more true of the Psalms.

Psalms Mixtapes and Memories of David

I grew up in the era of mixtapes. These were the analog predecessors of the playlist. Mixtapes were a way of capturing your favorite songs in the limited amount of space set by the confines of the cassette. Mixtapes are inherently selective and strategically shaped.

The Psalms is not a book. It's a mixtape of prayers and praises from ancient Israel. The Psalms mixtape we're used to listening to has 150 tracks. That's the established scope. These proceed in a certain order which was later numbered. There's an expected sequence. This format was selected, set, sequenced, and shaped by the Masoretic tradition. Yet when we look at other manuscript traditions, we find other mixtapes—other orders, other content.

The DSS revealed a remarkable set of at least thirty-four scrolls that included Psalms materials of varying shapes, sizes, and scope.[8] One of these was that revolutionary scroll from Cave 11 we met in the last chapter, 11QPsalms[a]. This fragmentary scroll included several psalms we already knew about (though set in a different order), a smattering of Hebrew versions of some psalms known previously in the Greek LXX, and still more that were lost until their modern discovery.

Not unlike Jeremiah, the LXX Psalter already hinted at a different scope and structure for the tradition. Items such as Psalm 151 and the "Prayer of Manasseh," as well as a different order in the Greek Psalter, indicated that antiquity's psalms mixtapes were more numerous than today. 11QPsalms[a] also attests to the crossover of ancient psalm, prayer, and poetry collections. For example, it includes fragments of the earliest known form of a poem on the pursuit of wisdom from Ben Sira 51 (again known from the LXX).[9] The Qumran version, however, includes more erotic imagery that was censored at some point in the Greek scriptures. 11QPsalms[a] reads:

> While I was a young man, before I had gone astray, I looked for her.
> She came to me in her beauty, and eventually I sought her out. Even as
> the blossom drops in the ripening of grapes, making the heart happy,
> so my foot trod in uprightness; for since my youth I have known her.
> I inclined my ear but a little, and great was the captivation I found.
> So she became a wet-nurse for me; to my teacher I give my sceptre.
> I decided to make sport: I was eager for pleasure, without stopping.

> I kindled my passion for her, I could not turn away my face. I bestirred my desire for her, and on her heights I could not relax. [I] spread my hand […] and perceive her nakedness. I cleansed my hand […] your reward in its time. (11Q5 21:11–22:1; compare Ben Sira 51:13–30)

In this instance, 11QPsalms[a] shows how a psalm later received among the Apocrypha and Deuterocanon was read in the context of a broader collection of psalmic materials. (In case you were wondering , the Hebrew word יד most often means "hand" but is clearly a euphemism here. It means what you think it means.)

Inching further into the unknown, some lost psalms project voices of blended anguish and hope. Take this other sample from 11QPsalms[a]:

> I was in death's thrall through my sins; my iniquities had sold me to Sheol—but you saved me, O Lord, according to your boundless compassion, your myriad righteous acts. I, too, have loved your name and sought shelter in your shadow. When I recall your might, I take heart and throw myself on your mercy. Forgive, O Lord, my sins, cleanse me from my iniquities! Favor me with a constant and knowing spirit and let me not be shamed by ruin. Let Satan have no dominion over me, nor an unclean spirit; let neither pain nor the will to evil rule in me. Surely you, O Lord, are my praise; in you I place my hope all the day. (11Q5 4–5:9–17)

The themes and theology of this Hebrew poem echo another prayer in Aramaic in a writing called the Aramaic Levi Document. As Levi offered words of wisdom and raised hands to heaven in prayer, he pleaded, "Let not any satan rule over me" (4Q213a 1:17). In this example, 11QPsalms[a] shows how the complex themes and rich theology of ancient psalms flowed across languages and literatures into a writing typically read in other collections.

IMAGE 7.1: The book of Ben Sira was also found in more complete forms in the Cairo Genizah collection. The image here is of Ben Sira 3:6; 3:8–4:10 in a manuscript from that collection (Cambridge University Library T-S 12.863). (Image credit: Syndics of Cambridge University Library)

But what generated this psalmic imagination, and enabled the expansion of its authority? The memory of a persona: David. There's no better place to see this than in a unit of 11QPsalms[a] that retains a scribal comment on the enterprise of psalmic innovation and expansion undertaken in the name of David. Near the end of the scroll, we read the following:

> And David, son of Jesse, was wise, and a light like the light of the sun, and a scribe, and discerning and perfect in all his ways before God and

> men. And the Lord gave him a discerning and enlightened spirit. And he wrote three thousand six hundred psalms; and songs to sing before the altar over the whole-burnt perpetual offering for every day, for all the days of the year: three hundred and sixty-four; and for the sabbath offerings, fifty-two songs; and for the offering of the New Moons and for all the days of the festivals, and for the Day of Atonement: thirty songs. And all the songs that he uttered were four hundred and forty-six, and songs for making music over the possessed: four. And the total was four thousand and fifty. All that he uttered through prophecy which had been given him before the Most High. (11Q5 27:2–11)

Suddenly we're beyond a mixtape, bigger than a greatest hits collection, and bridging into an almost endless anthology of poems and prayers—an imagined endless scroll of inspiration—associated with, and driven by, the memory of David. In this scribal tradition, David was that big a deal. His prolific profile exceeded any single collection. What we learn here is that it was less about Davidic authorship than Davidic authority, and his memory as a revered, ideal scribe.[10]

This perspective helps us see why multiple editions of the psalms circulated. They amplified the authority of David. They accentuated the potential of prayer and poetry for any area of life, from celebration to oppression. They elevated the importance of psalms traditions in community settings. It's perhaps not surprising, then, to find that the Psalms are quoted more than any other writing of the Hebrew Scriptures in both the Dead Sea Scrolls and the New Testament.

These samples from 11QPsalms[a] connect us to an ancient imagination that understood the poetic powerhouse behind the psalms—David—as a prolific scribe and even prophet. This tradition was bigger than any one text. Our next persona, Daniel, also loomed large in ancient Hebrew, Aramaic, and Greek literature.

Transforming Daniel Traditions from an Arabian Spa to Ascetic Qumran

The book of Daniel is a bit of an oddity in the Hebrew Scriptures. It's a linguistic hybrid of Aramaic and Hebrew. It's unabashedly apocalyptic. It's also likely the latest writing in the Hebrew Bible and the Old Testament.

We could compound the book's curious character by browsing the LXX. The book of Daniel in the Greek Scriptures is known in two ancient versions—Old Greek and Theodotian—and it includes three additional episodes not found in the Masoretic tradition but only in the Apocrypha and the Deuterocanon. My personal favorite is when Daniel explodes a dragon by feeding it a giant tar-bound hairball. Then, after Daniel lands in the lion's den yet again, an angel flies the prophet Habakkuk in to deliver a late-night pot of stew.[11]

In the last chapter we saw how the Daniel DSS are closer in *date* to the book's original composition than any other biblical manuscripts in existence. But how do the up to eight copies of Daniel at Qumran match up to the *shape* of the book?

The MT and LXX already evidence multiple literary editions of Daniel in antiquity. While the Daniel DSS include variant readings at a microlevel, their macrostructure aligns with the form of the book known in the later Masoretic tradition.[12]

We've already observed how scribes often harnessed the potential of personae from the past to both extend and generate traditions. The DSS reveal that, like Jeremiah and David, Daniel too was bigger than his eventual biblical self. In the case of Daniel, the Qumran discoveries gave insight into both potential sources *before* the biblical book and reformations of Daniel's character *beyond* it. We can learn some of these lessons by going from arid Qumran to an Arabian spa with the Babylonian king, Nabonidus.

Daniel 4 is a famous passage. King Nebuchadnezzar is unsettled by a nightmare in need of an interpretation. In his dream, he beheld a lush tree

IMAGE 7.2: Manuscript illumination of a late-night stew delivery to Daniel from the prophet Habakkuk while the former is (again) in the lion's den in the Greek tradition of Daniel. This manuscript image is from ms. 0089 f. 029, Marseille. (Image credit: Wikimedia Commons)

that sustained all life. Then, at an otherworldly utterance, the tree was hacked to pieces and shackled to the ground. After the Babylonian magicians fumble at unlocking the meaning of the revelation, Daniel steps in and delivers the hard news.

> This is the interpretation, O king, and it is a decree of the Most High that has come upon my lord the king: You shall be driven away from human society, and your dwelling shall be with the wild animals. You shall be made to eat grass like oxen, you shall be bathed with the dew of heaven, and seven times shall pass over you, until you have learned that the Most High has sovereignty over the kingdom of mortals, and gives it to whom he will. As it was commanded to leave the stump and roots of the tree, your kingdom shall be re-established for you from the time that you learn that Heaven is sovereign. (Daniel 4:24–26)

Daniel 4:33 reports that the portent was realized in short order. Nebuchadnezzar abandoned society and embraced insanity. Long hair, longer fingernails, and an animalized existence in the wilderness. After a season of affliction, Nebuchadnezzar has a moment of lucidity. He confesses the true and enduring sovereignty of God. At this, his composure is restored and his position in Babylon reclaimed (Daniel 4:34–37).

Great story. But, like most epic accounts, it has a prehistory. Scholars had long suspected that the episode of Nebuchadnezzar gone mad in Daniel 4 was based on the bio of another Babylonian king, Nabonidus, who held the helm of the Babylonian empire from 556–539 BCE. According to Paul-Alain Beaulieu's catalog, there are at least twenty-seven known cuneiform tablets and inscriptions of both polemics and personal accounts relating to Nabonidus's ten-year hiatus from Babylon to hole up in the desert oasis of Teima.[13] Apparently, the ancient Near East was abuzz over this odd absence.

What was lacking in this scholarly hunch, however, was an explanation of the *mobility* and *transferability* of the tradition. How did this Babylonian lore land in Judea? And why was Nabonidus recast as Nebuchadnezzar? The Aramaic *Prayer of Nabonidus* found in Qumran Cave 4 both answered these questions, and helped us ask new ones. The work is known mostly by its beginning, which reads as follows:

> The words of the p[ra]yer which Nabonidus, king o[f Bab]ylon prayed, the king [...] with a severe inflammation by the decree of G[o]d in Teima [...]I was afflicted for seven years and from [...] he made ... [...] and as for my sin, he remitted it. A diviner, now he was [...] a Judean fr[om ...] "Pro[cla]im and write to give honour and ... [...] ... to the name of G[od ...] 'I was afflicted with [a severe] inflammation[...] in Teima [...] Seven years [I] was praying [...] gods of [...] silver and gold [...] wood, stone, clay, because [...] ... that gods ... [...][14]

This Aramaic tale may be about a foreign king, but the presence of a copy of the *Prayer of Nabonidus* in Cave 4 confirms it was preserved in the scribal culture in Judea. This is a Jewish text critiquing empire. Script analysis indicates that the *Prayer of Nabonidus* was copied around 75–50 BCE, though the composition itself is perhaps as early as the Persian period.[15] This is an excellent example, then, of how the scribes behind the DSS were simultaneously inheriting traditions from their larger culture and innovating them for their more localized communities. Mobility managed.

What about transferability? This Cave 4 composition features Nabonidus, not Nebuchadnezzar, and casts an unnamed courtier from among the exiles, not Daniel. The Jewish scribes who cultivated the Daniel tradition saw the potential in a tale about Nabonidus losing his wits. They also knew his imperial persona might not mean much in Judean territory. Nabonidus's worst crime was spending a decade at an Arabian spa eight hundred kilometers away from Judea. Nebuchadnezzar, however, was a symbol of the evils of empire. It was Nebuchadnezzar who had demolished the temple, dismantled the dynasty, and dispersed the population. Retelling the "king's gone mad"

IMAGE 7.3: The Aramaic *Prayer of Nabonidus* (4Q242) begins with an ancient title framing its first-person voice and setting. On one hand, this models the direct speech presentation of the imperial propaganda in some cuneiform inscriptions explaining Nabonidus's absence. On the other hand, it reflects a formal trend for titling works in the Aramaic Dead Sea Scrolls. (Image credit: Courtesy of The Leon Levy Dead Sea Scrolls Digital Library; Israel Antiquities Authority, photo: Shai Halevi)

---

tale and reapplying it to Nebuchadnezzar made for a timeless message about God's sovereignty in any time under an empire.

But was a nameless diviner among the exiles a powerful enough protagonist for this new script? Unlikely. The scribes behind this emerging tradition needed a more compelling cast. A lead character with authority. While the diviner of the *Prayer of Nabonidus* is technically unknown, Daniel may have been the right figure given his larger profile as a seer, sage, and scribe in Babylonian court tales.

What does this new network of Danielic literature do for our understanding of the (trans)formation of ancient traditions? Two things. First, it helps us see a potential scenario where scribes navigated the space between sources and scripture. We don't know for sure if the Cave 4 Aramaic *Prayer of Nabonidus* was the actual source that inspired Daniel 4. Scholars have argued for every potential avenue of intertextuality (or none at all) between *Prayer of Nabonidus* and Daniel 4. The issue of influence, however, is less important than the insight this pair of texts offers into how authors, scribes, and editors engaged sources and extended traditions. They did so by making a good story a great one. Most often this was made possible by the growing gravity of an authoritative figure.

Second, it helps us situate writings in the Hebrew Scriptures and the DSS in a shared cultural moment. The Qumran scribes were part of this intellectual and cultural landscape. It should come as no surprise, then, that scribes engaged and added to the literary heritage of antiquity. In fact, if they didn't, we'd have a problem. Regardless of their potential relationship, the Aramaic *Prayer of Nabonidus* and Daniel 4 reveal that scribes spoke into and out of the cultural, historical, religious, and political domains of life under an empire.

In the three case studies so far, it was the memories of major figures that drove traditions forward and generated texts. As we'll see in our final example, however, the DSS reveal how even marginalized figures had the potential to be recast and reimagined in unexpected ways.

Miriam and Ancient Mansplaining

Did you notice that the three case studies above orbit around men? Jeremiah, David, Daniel—they're all gents. It's not that women characters are absent in the traditions, texts, and tales associated with such figures. It's that there's a gendered gravity to these masculinized memories.

The literary heritage of ancient Judaism and Christianity is predominantly authored by men and oriented around them. This includes the Bible. Until relatively recently, the ongoing history of interpretation of these writings also flowed from the pens of men. That includes me (self-awareness is key to interpretation). Our eyes haven't been trained to watch for women in these texts, nor have our voices been trained to invite them into the conversation. Thankfully, this is changing.[16]

While there are minority reports of gendered dynamics across traditions associated with male figures—like those Jeremiah, David, and Daniel[17]—the memory of women also has a generative quality in ancient scribal imagination. One in particular played an essential, though often overlooked, role in Israel's foundational story of deliverance. I'm talking about Miriam.

You're probably familiar with Miriam because you know her brothers, Moses and Aaron. In some ways, these masculine associations defined her memory. This is despite the fact that she is placed on the same level as her siblings *within* the Hebrew Scriptures. Micah 6:4 recalls the Exodus this way: "For I brought you up from the land of Egypt, and redeemed you from the house of slavery; and I sent before you Moses, Aaron, and Miriam." Perhaps this recollection in prophetic literature is a recognition of Miriam's status as a "prophetess" in Exodus 15:20.[18] If we've learned anything about the scribal strategies to extend and reimagine scriptural traditions in the DSS, it's that prophetic voices were often amplified in ancient Judaism. Miriam's was no exception.

We'll see in our next chapter that the Aramaic *Visions of Amram* offered a different take on the life of Miriam, in the celebratory scene of her marriage to Uzziel. In the Qumran Hebrew literature, however, 4QPentateuch[c] extends Miriam's profile with her own words. This text, which John Strugnell once described as a "wild Pentateuch," brilliantly blurs the boundary between scripture and interpretation.[19]

One such item was Miriam's unreleased contribution to the "Song at the Sea" in Exodus 15:1–18. With the Israelites barely evading a massacre and the Egyptians engulfed by the waters of the Red Sea behind them, Moses bursts into song. The scene ends with an afterthought about Miriam's chorus.

> Then the prophet Miriam, Aaron's sister, took a tambourine in her hand; and all the women went out after her with tambourines and with dancing. And Miriam sang to them: "Sing to the Lord, for he has triumphed gloriously; horse and rider he has thrown into the sea." (Exodus 15:20–21)

These lines echo the opening lines of Moses's song in Exodus 15:1. It's as if Miriam and the women are typecast as backup singers—no ideas of their own, just echoes of those offered by the men on scene. Hanna Tervanotko, however, recovered inklings of ancient Jewish traditions in both the LXX renderings and references in Philo that suggest that some understood Moses and Miriam's offerings not as pale echoes of one another but allusions to full performances. 4QPentateuch[c] offers the fullest such perspective.

The scribe of this fragmentary scroll didn't understand Exodus 15:20–21 as a coda, Miriam's repeat of the already-performed piece. Rather, these lines hinted at a lost track. 4QPentateuch[c] presents the Moses and Miriam songs in seamless sequence as follows, with the previously unknown materials in italics:

> [and the water]s [forming a wall for them on]their right and on their left. *vacat* Then[Miriam the prophetess, sister of Aaron,] took [a timbrel in her hand, and al]l the women went after her in[dance with timbrels. And (Miriam) chanted for them: Sing to the Lord, for he has triumphed gloriously; Horse and driver he has hurled into the sea *...]you despised [your enemies ... I will sing to the Lord] for he has triumphed[gloriousl]y. [The Lord is my]s[trength and might ...]You are great, delivering [your people ...]The enemy's hope has perished and[his memory] is for[gotten ...]Your e[nemie]s perished in the mighty waters [... Your people] will exalt you to the heights, [for] you gave[a cove]nant[to our fathers ... the one do]ing glorious things.* (4Q365 6b 5–6; 6a ii + 6 c 1–7)[20]

IMAGE 7.4: The arc of ancestral traditions begins in text traditions from the ancient world but also extends in many directions. The field of "reception history" maps how creatives and communities down through the ages have engaged with and explored meanings of scriptural traditions in any form of media. This example of a manuscript illumination of the Golden Haggadah portrays Miriam and the women by the sea in musical performance (top right) on a page of four images depicting aspects of the preparation for the Passover. The image is from the Golden Haggadah, ca. 1320, Spain, MS. 27210, fol. 15 recto. (Image credit: Wikimedia Commons)

Sidnie White Crawford remarked that these lines reveal that a "song was created for Miriam on the basis of Moses's song."[21] In general, poems and prayers ascribed to women in ancient Jewish and early Christian writings are in short supply.[22] Yet when we stand back and read these synoptically, some intriguing themes emerge, such as the reversal of fortune by divine favor.[23]

But how does Miriam's song of divine favor relate to our topic of developing textual traditions? Simply put: women ancestral figures too generated orbits of tradition. We're just not used to seeing them due to the black hole of masculinized memory and interpretive traditions. The Pentateuch is usually characterized by its predominant association with the Mosaic Torah and its memories of patriarchal tales. And it mostly is—but that's not all it is. 4QPentateuch[c] registers Miriam's material in at least one scribal collection of Genesis and Exodus materials in a manuscript from around 75 BCE.

Last chapter we encountered a full paragraph about our eyeball-gouging king Nahash in 4QSamuel[c] that has begun to impact scriptures today. Now we know that variations of this scope signal authority, and the existence of multiple literary editions. The same is true here. A bonus paragraph. A bigger tradition. A prophetess with a voice amid an anthology defined by mansplaining.

Conclusion

Last chapter we saw that the concept of canon and the media of a Bible didn't yet exist in the world of the DSS. This chapter explored the expanding universe traditions associated with figures deemed prophets and prophetesses. This sample revealed how the scribal imagination enabled these figures to continue to speak in new ways and once-lost texts. The scrolls challenge us to see that it wasn't necessarily some innate quality of a single text that drove ancestral traditions forward. It was the authoritative profiles of famous figures that enabled scribes to bring a message from the past into the present. This is similar to something we're familiar with in modern canons and anthologies like Star Wars.

The Hebrew Scriptures contain essential, authoritative, even foundational examples of traditions set in orbit around such figures from the past. To push the outer space metaphors further, the DSS revealed how ancient scribes encountered and extended those traditions to develop bigger and brighter constellations of texts in the name of ancestors, both men and women. And remember: as with the existence of biblical books in multiple editions, the development of other writings in the name of ancestral figures only further signals the importance of ancestral and scriptural traditions. The memories of these figures in scribal imagination are what drove the development of editions and spinoff stories. The fact is, the majority of writings that are extending and reimaging ancient ancestral tales do so with reference to texts or traditions that later become biblical.[24]

But this scribal imagination was not limited by language. We already saw this with Greek translations in the LXX—but a significant part of the rich and yet unrealized scribal heritage discovered at Qumran was penned in Aramaic. And that's where we're heading next.

Chapter 8

The Aramaic Imagination: Extending Ancestral Traditions in Imperial Language

It's not every day that biblical language debates are front page news. Back in 2014, Pope Francis made a historic visit to Israel. Of the many handshakes and holy sites that were part of his papal itinerary, the one that broke the internet was an age-old debate about the spoken language(s) of Jesus. At a press conference with the pope, Israeli Prime Minister Benjamin Netanyahu remarked, "Jesus was here in this land. He spoke Hebrew,"—to which the pope interjected, "Aramaic." After an exchange with an interpreter, Netanyahu qualified, "He spoke Aramaic, but he knew Hebrew."

Of course, there is a political edge to this dialogue, as language—both in antiquity and today—is associated with identity and land. But we're also hearing echoes of an ongoing debate among biblical scholars about the spoken versus written languages of Second Temple Judea. In many ways, the DSS both added to and complicated this debate.

Readers of the Bible are likely familiar with the Hebrew and Greek heritage of Jewish and Christian scriptures. As the name suggests, the Hebrew Bible was penned predominantly in Hebrew. As we saw a few chapters back, these texts were rendered into Greek in the early translations of the Septuagint. The books the New Testament, of course, were also composed in Greek.[1]

So where does Aramaic enter the equation? Well, there are inklings of Aramaic in both the Hebrew and Greek scriptures as well as hints of it elsewhere in ancient Jewish and Christian writings beyond the Bible. But what we didn't know prior to the discovery of the DSS was the breadth and depth of ancient Judaism's Aramaic scribal heritage. The scrolls revealed both new *texts* and fresh *contexts* for mapping yet-uncharted territory of Aramaic language and literature in the Second Temple period.

In this chapter we'll explore new texts and encounter familiar ancestral figures. We'll also see how scribes crafted and reimagined Hebrew traditions in the Aramaic language to speak to a new generations of readers.

But first, a crash course on Aramaic language and literature at Qumran will set some context and give you some intel unaccounted for in that papal and prime ministerial spat.

Contours and Contexts of the Qumran Aramaic Texts

The Aramaic DSS are some of the latest published and least studied of the entire Qumran collection. But they're great reads, including tales of demonic possession, romantic vignettes, cameos of bloodthirsty giants, visions of imperial upheaval, apocalyptic dreams, wisdom poems, impassioned encounters, and lover's bouts over ancestral paternity tests. (If you're only interested in that last item, fast-forward to the end of the chapter.)

The reality is there's simply too much in the world of the Aramaic DSS to explore in a single chapter. So we'll set the scene with some must-know info and insights into the world of the Aramaic DSS and a few comments on how they fit within the larger Qumran collection.

Between 10 and 13 percent of the Qumran collection was penned in Aramaic.[2] This includes Aramaic originals of texts that were previously known to have been written in Aramaic (like Daniel 2–7 or Tobit), translations of Hebrew works (bits of a Job translation and samples of Leviticus), a few Greek fragments translated from Aramaic originals (snippets of a

Greek rendering of sections of 1 Enoch), suspected Aramaic sources for later works (such as the Aramaic Levi Document behind portions of the Greek *Testament of Levi*), or entirely new works lost until their discovery (for example, the *Genesis Apocryphon*, *Pseudo-Daniel*, and *Visions of Amram*). All told, the Aramaic discoveries at Qumran include approximately twenty-nine identified compositions, some in multiple copies, and (as always) a large number of fragmentary materials of lost, unknown, or yet-to-be-identified writings.

As you can see from this set of stats and few samples, the Aramaic DSS also cut across a variety of later canonical or modern collections: Hebrew Bible/Old Testament, Apocrypha, Deuterocanon, and Pseudepigrapha. This broader collection, then, expanded our view of ancient Judaism's Aramaic scribal heritage, which is known only in patches in biblical literature.[3]

How and *why* did scribes adopt and write in Aramaic? The reach of Aramaic into Israelite and Jewish culture is due to the larger imperial context of the ancient Near East. Starting in the seventh century BCE, Aramaic became both a common and administrative language of imperial superpowers. As the Israelites were shuffled around the map in the Assyrian (722 BCE) and Babylonian (587 BCE) exiles, they became part of this imperial patchwork. We see this, for example, when Sennacherib's Assyrian cronies roll up on Jerusalem, and the Israelite envoys ask them to speak in Aramaic (Isaiah 36:11). The native tongue of Hebrew was apparently somewhat dwindling by the time Jerusalem and was resettled and rebuilt (Nehemiah 13:24). Sometime after this, in the era of the Maccabean revolt (second century BCE), Hebrew evidently saw a resurgence, which parallels the concentration of Hebrew texts among the DSS around this time.

Even with the spread of Greek through the ascendancy of Alexander the Great in the fourth century BCE, Aramaic proved to have lasting power in Judea. This is why the Gospel according to Mel Gibson (also known as *The*

Passion of the Christ) uses a Hollywood-ized version of Aramaic for the majority of its dialogue. It is likely, then, that by penning a work in Aramaic in the mid–Second Temple period, a Jewish scribe could expect the work could be understood by a broad readership, both at home and abroad.

Who wrote the Qumran Aramaic texts, and *where* were they read? There are few firm answers here. Typically, it is assumed the Aramaic texts were not composed at the site of Qumran—although this assumption is increasingly being called into question.[4] In general, the Aramaic texts do not contain any telltale terms that would suggest they are overly sectarian. But many Aramaic writings do include topics and theologies that were likely complementary to the thought of the sectarian movement, such as a disdain for empire, an openness to revelation, an apocalyptic outlook, a penchant for priestly knowledge, and a dualistic view of the world. Aramaic Enoch texts, in particular, had a particular influence on the Qumranites.

In general, the Aramaic texts are older than the majority of Hebrew materials among the DSS. The composition dates of the Aramaic texts span from the third century BCE through first century CE, putting the Aramaic texts among the most ancient writings found among the DSS.[5]

While there is much we don't know about the origins of this literature, and there is certainly some diversity in the Aramaic writings discovered among the Qumran materials, Daniel Machiela outlined a compelling context for these materials. It seems likely that they were penned by some group of priests seeking to develop a new sort of literature, which offered a paradigm for living faithfully in view of God's laws in diverse and often difficult political or cultural settings.[6] This working hypothesis is a good way of anchoring ongoing work on the Qumran Aramaic texts.

With this linguistic capacity, plausible setting, and potential of reach, *what* are the scribes of the Aramaic DSS writing about? A lot of things. The scribes of these materials were well-versed in their ancestral traditions and adept at engaging with the thought of the cultures around them. They creatively crafted or re-presented stories in ways that were both fresh and familiar. The Aramaic DSS tell, retell, and remix stories from two poles of Israelite history and heritage.

On one hand, there are many stories oriented around the distant ancestral past, particularly figures and stories about the flood or early patriarchs and matriarchs. We saw this already in our intro to the *Genesis Apocryphon*, which takes up tales associated with Lamech, Enoch, Noah, and Abraham, and also provides names and voices to some of their wives: Emzera, Batenosh, and Sarah. A cluster of writings, such as the Aramaic Levi Document, *Words of Qahat*, and *Visions of Amram*, also present new takes on the ancestral past with a particular focus on priestly figures.

On the other hand, there are several stories oriented around the more recent exilic past, particularly stories of survival in foreign courts or unfriendly imperial environments that put traditional Jewish ways of life at risk. Writings like *Jews in the Persian Court* casts new characters like the Jewish courtier Bagasraw in a setting reminiscent of the book of Esther. The Aramaic Daniel chapters and Tobit also fit in this literary world.

Almost entirely lacking in the Aramaic DSS, however, are references or stories about the golden age of Israel's monarchies. The Aramaic *Pseudo-Daniel* materials include lists of kings and priests with some famous figures such as David, Solomon, Abiathar, and Hilkiah (4Q243 11:4–13). The only other verifiable reference to this age is the mention of the Kingdom of Uzziah in a highly fragmentary Aramaic puzzle piece from Cave 4 (4Q558 29:4). Otherwise, the focus of our Aramaic scribes fell on the memory of the distant, ancestral past, or reflected on the recent disruptions of diaspora life in the time of the exiles.

With this outline in mind, let's dive into some content of the Aramaic DSS to detail some of the more prominent or defining features of these writings.

IMAGE 8.1: The Aramaic work known as *Jews in the Persian Court* (4Q550) is a narrative set in the exilic days of the diaspora, not unlike the settings of Daniel or the book of Tobit. This work, unknown until its modern discovery in Cave 4, was once thought to be related to the book of Esther (which would have been remarkable since Esther is the only book among the Hebrew Scriptures either not found, lost, or unattested among the DSS). The work, however, is unrelated to Esther and attests to a bourgeoning Aramaic scribal culture of edifying and entertaining narratives of the perils of life in a foreign court and land. (Image credit: Courtesy of The Leon Levy Dead Sea Scrolls Digital Library; Israel Antiquities Authority, photo: Shai Halevi)

Pseudepigraphy: Strategies for Capturing and (Re)Presenting Authoritative Voices

The majority of the writings in the Aramaic DSS are in the first-person voices of ancestral or diaspora figures. The technical term for this is *pseudepigraphy*. Scribes presented their material in this way using various mechanisms for various purposes.

On several occasions, scribes flat-out framed entire writings, or sections within them, as books penned or discourses delivered by these figures, containing the very words uttered by known or notable figures, whether ancestors, angels, or imperial nemeses. Take a look at these snippets and note the close similarity of terms across the writings.[7]

> *Genesis Apocryphon*: "A [c]o[p]y of a 'Writing of the Words of Noah.'" (1Q20 5:29)
>
> *Visions of Amram*: "A copy of 'The Writing of the Words of the Vision(s) of Amram, son of[Qahat, son of Levi.'" (4Q543 1a–c:1; cf. 4Q545 1ai; 4Q546 1:1–2)
>
> Tobit: "The book of the words of Tobit son of Tobiel." (Tobit 1:1)[8]
>
> *Words of Michael*: "The words of the writing that Michael said to the angels." (4Q529 1:1)
>
> *Prayer of Nabonidus*: "The words of the pr[ay]er that Nabonidus, King of [Babyl]on, [the great] kin[g] prayed." (4Q242 1, 2a–b,3: 1–2)

Couching materials in this way was a strategy for collapsing the distance with the past and for claiming authenticity, even authority, for the new writing. Today this approach to pseudepigraphy might sound like trickery at best, and forgery at worst. But in the ancient world it was the exact opposite: this was a way that scribes ensured that the past continued to speak to new audiences and engage new issues. Pseudepigraphy didn't undercut the tradition; it drew upon and extended it.

Some of these writings (and several beyond the Aramaic DSS) purport to have a deep origin in the preflood days, or claim otherworldly revelation. This is particularly the case in Enochic traditions, in which special tablets or books are read, revealed, written, and passed down on a regular basis. Take, for example, the sound bites in 1 Enoch 106:19b and 107:3, which provide knowledge of Noah's birth and the looming destruction in the flood:

> For I know the mysteries of the Lord that the holy ones have revealed and shown to me, and that I have read in the tablets of heaven. ... When Methuselah heard the words of Enoch his father—for (Enoch) revealed them to him secretly—(Methuselah) returned and revealed everything to (Lamech). And his (son's) name was called Noah—he who gladdens the earth from destruction.

These materials in the Enochic booklet of 1 Enoch 106–107 were put in remarkable new perspective by the Cave 4 discoveries of the *Birth of Noah* text (4Q534–536), which include similar material on the miraculous birth of Genesis's champion of the flood.

Enochic books also show up in numerous places in the Aramaic DSS, which provided an even bolder claim to the deep origins of knowledge in the earliest of Israel's ancestors before the flood. The *Genesis Apocryphon* provides a remarkable new example of the scribal creativity and strategy for Enochic pseudepigraphy. In an Aramaic rewrite of Abram's sojourn to Egypt (which we know from Genesis 19), the scribe of the *Genesis Apocryphon* included the following scene:

> Now at the end of those five years ... to me, and three men from the nobles of Egypt ... his [...] ... by Phara[oh] Zoan because of my words and my wisdom, and they were giving m[e many gifts. ... They as]ked scribal knowledge and wisdom and truth for themselves, so I read before them the book of the words of Enoch. (1Q20 19:23-25)

This clever remake recasts Abram as an anchor of ancestral knowledge linked to (and even in possession of) an Enochic book. The scene also makes the not-so-subtle claim that all Egyptian knowledge really originated with Abraham, and ultimately Enoch. This example underscores how pseudepigraphy in its various forms focused on ancestral figures as orbits of authority.

Dreams, Dualisms, Demons, and Destinies: Aramaic Apocalyptic Imaginations

When we say "apocalypse" today, a host of images and ideas come to mind: ecological collapse, nuclear wastelands, pandemic chaos, face-chewing zombies, and R.E.M.'s song "It's the End of the World as We Know It." These contemporary associations, however, are mostly products of the risks and realities of post–Cold War (and now post-COVID-19) life, as well as the imaginative amplifications of modern media. But nukes, zombies, global viruses, and 80s rock earworms didn't mean much in antiquity.

In the ancient world, the term *apocalypse* meant something different: a genre of writing. Apocalypses offered timely answers of hope to timeless questions of loss, chaos, and oppression. Hope that God could still speak through new revelation. Hope that history was all connected, its course directed. Hope that deliverance was nigh. Hope that life wasn't limited by space and time as we know it.

We have a few apocalypses in the Bible. The top tier includes Isaiah 24–27, Daniel 7–12, Mark 13, and the book of Revelation.[9] Eventually, the apocalypse genre grew in popularity. Apocalypses are found across cultures and corpora from antiquity through the medieval period.[10] Jews, Christians, Muslims, and others have all written apocalypses.

The genre is also associated with a way of thinking: apocalypticism. This outlook reflected the core concepts of the genre and provided individuals and communities with a way of ordering the world around them and orienting themselves to it. You don't have to write apocalypses to embrace this outlook.[11] As E. P. Sanders underscored years ago, "An ancient apocalypticist may also have been a legal expert, a priest, or anything else."[12] No single group held a monopoly on apocalypticism.

Yet the library of ancient Judaism's apocalyptic literature was limited prior to the discovery of the DSS. The Aramaic texts in particular expanded the collection of writings radiating with apocalyptic thought and representing the formal genre of the apocalypse.[13] They are even redefining what we thought we knew about the shape and scope of apocalyptic writings and outlooks in the ancient world.

The Aramaic DSS emphasized how an openness to new or ongoing revelation underpinned apocalyptic thinking. Two-thirds of the writings of the Aramaic DSS include dreams or visions and/or their inspired interpretations. To be sure these are *literary* dreams and visions, not experiential accounts. But by creatively and strategically including such episodes and interpretations in writings about figures from the distant past or diaspora experience, the scribes of these texts infused inherited traditions with authority, expectation, and revelatory insight into a diversity of topics.

Some revelations, such as those in the *Visions of Amram*, reveal a view of a divided cosmos ruled by angels of light and darkness. Amram beheld two angels at loggerheads and was struck by their contrasting clothing and countenances: one figure wore dark garb and had a terrifying countenance, the other had light clothing with a smiling and laughing face. Upon engaging the figures, the light angel revealed to Amram that the two oversee opposing domains: "Now, he is given authority over all the darkness. But I[... from] the heights to the depths. I am ruler over all light" (4Q544 2:15–16). These fragments also reveal that the name of the dark angel is "Melchiresha" (מלכי רשע), meaning "king of evil" (4Q544 2:13). Here we find a remarkable blend of apocalyptic elements—dreams, dualisms, and demons—all embedded in a tale told in the first-person voice of a priestly ancestor.

Other revelations in the Aramaic DSS advance an apocalyptic outlook that is more historically oriented, either looking ahead or reflecting on the deep past. Some texts, like *Aramaic Apocalypse*, feature a seer likely relaying or interpreting a dream about the apocalyptic upheaval of nations and divine deliverance for the righteous.

IMAGE 8.2: The *Visions of Amram* is attested by at least five manuscripts from Qumran Cave 4. It is an example of how new discoveries are revolutionizing how we understand the development and formation of apocalyptic thought and literature in ancient Judaism, as well as the centrality of dream-visions and pseudepigraphy for claiming authority and forming identity. The image here is from 4Q543, and includes the opening lines and ancient title of the work. The stitching at the rightmost edge also makes us wonder what came before this opening of the work. Perhaps it was a protective cover sheet, or another priestly apocalyptic writing attributed to another ancestor, such as Levi or Qahat. (Image credit: Courtesy of The Leon Levy Dead Sea Scrolls Digital Library; Israel Antiquities Authority, photo: Shai Halevi)

> O [k]ing, wrath is coming to the world, and your years … your vision, and everything is coming until the world … [g]reat … trouble will come upon the earth … and great carnage in the provinces … kings of Assyria [and of E]gypt. (4Q246 1i:2–6)

The text then speaks of a "son of God" figure (stay tuned for messianism in the next chapter) before refocusing on the meaning of what appears to be dream symbolism:

> Like the meteors that you saw, so their kingdoms will be. For yea[rs] they will reign over the earth. And all will trample: nation against nation, province will trample province. *vacat* Until the people of God arise and all will have rest from the sword. His kingdom will be an everlasting kingdom and all his ways are righteousness. He will jud[ge] the earth with righteousness and he will make everything at peace. The sword will be no more on the land and all the provinces will bow to him. The Great God is his strength. (4Q246 1i:1–7)

Finally, some Aramaic revelations about the past also signal how eschatological destruction or deliverance was set and sealed from the beginning. The Enochic *Book of Giants*, for example, reimagines the experience of the human-angel giants hinted in Genesis 6:4. The ravenous giants receive nightmares with frightful scenes of obliteration—the fiery destruction of trees and the washing of text from a tablet. To seek clarity on the matter, the giants fly—yes, fly—to visit Enoch on the outer reaches of existence for an interpretation. Surprise, surprise: the news isn't good. As an inspired interpreter with authority and heavenly insight, Enoch relates that the dreams signal that the fate of the giants (and the evil they represent) is certain. Their bodies will perish in the flood while their evil spirits will see judgment at the end of time.

IMAGE 8.3: The cryptic and suggestive language of the flood narrative and the reference to the giant Nephilim in Genesis 6:1–4 sparked many diverse reimaginations, from ancient times through the medieval period. The image here is one such artistic depiction of Noah's flood in William de Brailes "Bible Pictures" (ca. 1250). (Image credit: The Walters Art Museum, Creative Commons License)

These examples show us how the scribes of the Aramaic DSS reimagined inherited traditions and crafted new ones that were deeply apocalyptic in outlook and form. New realities, possibilities, and hopes were presented via dream-visions where almost anything was possible.[14]

The Double Helix of Priestly Lineage and Lore

Priestly knowledge and identity are a big deal in the Aramaic DSS. This takes many forms and is deployed for many purposes, from full blown priestly apocalypses to lists of priest's names.

The Aramaic *New Jerusalem*, for example, reads like an inspired-by-Ezekiel visionary journey to eschatological Jerusalem. Oddly enough, the massive city is uninhabited—likely hinting at it being a destination for the nations in the eschaton—but the temple at its epicenter has a vibrant, functioning sacrificial system.

While priestly topics are patterned in various ways in these writings, the cluster of writings associated with the priestly ancestors Levi, Qahat, and Amram offer an intriguing take on how scribes retold or reimagined the priestly past.[15] While Levi is both a famous priest and an infamous ancestor—not least for the slaughter of the Shechemites (Genesis 34; 49:5-7)—his son (Qahat) and grandson (Amram) are known only by name in the Hebrew Scriptures (see Genesis 46:11; Numbers 3:19; 1 Chronicles 6:2–3). A group of Aramaic scribes saw this as an opportunity—a nearly blank canvas—to establish a clear line of priestly lineage and lore passed down through the ages.

The identity of priests was a touchy subject in Second Temple Judaism. As the priesthood became politicized as a pawn for Hellenistic and then Roman rulers, scribes of texts like the Aramaic Levi Document, *Words of Qahat*, and *Visions of Amram* were already firming up their understanding of the priestly family tree (or better, its roots) deep in the past. They did this by underscoring that there were to be no outsiders permitted to the priestly line, and that

IMAGE 8.4: Writings like the Aramaic New Jerusalem text—found in multiple copies in Caves 2, 4, and 1—provided an early example of an apocalyptic and end-times view that included a remarkable, reimagined city of Jerusalem. Other writings that contribute to this type of expectation include Ezekiel, the Temple Scroll, Tobit, and the book of Revelation. The apocalyptic Aramaic texts among the DSS provide examples of the formation of these images and ideas in ancient Judaism. The image here is from a fourteenth-century CE tapestry inspired by the book of Revelation. It demonstrates the ongoing reception of this expectation in art, media, imagination, and culture. (Image credit: Wikimedia Commons)

---

this privileged identity was confirmed by insider knowledge and an unbroken chain of teaching.[16]

The writers of these texts present priestly ancestors and their families as models of "endogamy." This term refers to a commitment to marrying only within one's kinship group, often to preserve an inheritance. We see this, for example, in Levi's statement of marital fidelity and success as a matchmaker in the Aramaic Levi Document:

> I took a wife for myself from the family of Abraham my father, Melcha, a daughter of Bathel, son of Laban, brother of my mother … I to[ok wives] from the daughters of my brothers for my sons at the moment corresponding to their ages, and sons w[ere b]orn to them. (ALD 63, 73)

In *Words of Qahat*, Qahat speaks emphatically against mingling with those beyond the immediate priestly clan:

> And now, my sons, be careful with the inheritance that has been bequeathed to you. Neither give your inheritance to strangers nor heritage to assimilators lest you become debased and disgraced in their eye and they debase you. For they will become resident foreigners to you and become rulers over you. (4Q542 1i: 4–7)

Amram likewise presents himself as a model of endogamous commitment and ensures that his own children, specifically Miriam, are lined up with a next of kin. While sojourning solo in Canaan and unable to return home due to a civil war, he says: "I did [not] take anot[her] wife [for myself" (4Q544 1:8), emphasizing his commitment to Yochebed. The opening scene of *Visions of Amram* puts Miriam's wedding front and center and emphasizes that she married Uzziel, an uncle on Amram's side (4Q543 1 a–c:5–7). In this combo, then, we see both an ancestral model of endogamy and an ancestor advancing this ideal in the next priestly generation, including both sons and daughters.

These sound bites from the rewritten lives and times of Levi, Qahat, and Amram draw a tight connection between priestly generations, and set boundaries between generations of the priestly past and outsiders. These writings treat priestly teachings, knowledge, and even booklore in a similar way to the protection of priestly lineage.

The Aramaic Levi Document presents a scene of Isaac passing on priestly yore to Levi, based on knowledge drawn from the book of Noah (ALD 13)—a pattern Isaac admonishes Levi to continue with his own sons: "All your sons are priests. And so command your sons that they should do according to this law as I have shown you" (ALD 13, 49, 57). Levi obeys this command and gathers his sons to reveal to them knowledge on avoiding evil while seeking truth, and pursuing book knowledge and wisdom. *Words of Qahat* and *Visions of Amram* both pick up on this theme, and feature scenes of passing on the tradition to their own progeny in an unbroken chain (4Q542; ii: 4–5, 12; 4Q543 1a–c:1–2).

Such scenes provide chains of commands to teach the next generation and present a secure line for transmitting priestly knowledge in, and only within, the members of the priestly line. This suggests that for the Aramaic scribes behind these materials, identity was not bound up in DNA alone—it was also formed and maintained through insider knowledge preserved within the priestly line.

International Intellectuals (also known as Giant Bastards, Decoding History, and Where Babies Come From)

We've seen some of the ways scribes of the Aramaic DSS inherited traditions from Israel's past and reimagined them through pseudepigraphic strategies, apocalyptic outlooks, and priestly knowledge. But these scribes were also well-versed in and engaged with the cultures around them. This should not surprise us—ancient Judea was not an island, geographically or metaphorically. The overturning and exchanges of major empires enabled, even assumed, interactions and the exchange of ideas between peoples. The Aramaic DSS evidence this in remarkable ways.

The scribe of the Aramaic *Book of Giants*, for example, cast some characters with names oddly familiar from ancient Near Eastern myths. The most obvious name assigned to one of these illicit, gargantuan monsters born of angels and women (inspired by Genesis 6:4–8) was none other than "Gilgamesh," a name that instantly hearkens to ancient Mesopotamian mythologies such as the *Epic of Gilgamesh*. Not unlike the Aramaic *Prayer of Nabonidus*, discussed last chapter, this levels a clever cultural shot against imperial lore. For the scribe and tradition of the *Book of Giants*, this international hero of ancient empires and epics was nothing more than a mishap monster whose doom and destruction was predetermined in Israel's own origins story. Apparently these Aramaic scribes were a well-read and creatively cheeky bunch.

The scribes of the Aramaic scrolls were also up to speed on various forms of what we might call the protoscience of the day. Several texts, like the *Birth of Noah* (4Q534–536), demonstrate knowledge of physiognomy, the ancient divination practice of deciphering futures by reading signs on the human body, which was a well-established practice in ancient Near Eastern and Mediterranean cultures.[17]

The Aramaic *Four Kingdoms* decodes the past in a dream-vision of talking trees to predict the future. Each tree identifies itself as an ancient empire, resulting in resulting in a four-kingdom chronology of empires rising and falling. This culminates in a utopian or divine age, likely after the Greek or Roman empires fall. This form of ancient historiography has a long history itself in both classical and ancient Near Eastern historiography as early as the fifth century BCE, and is also reflected in the book of Daniel.[18]

I promised at the outset of the chapter that the Aramaic texts include impassioned debates and even controversies over paternity. In one famous scene in the *Genesis Apocryphon* (1Q20 1:1–18) we have a heated exchange between Lamech and his wife Batenosh, in which the former suspects the latter of infidelity.[19] And not just any infidelity, but pregnancy resulting from one of the fallen angels of heaven!

After harboring suspicion "that the conception was from the Watchers," Lamech confronts his wife and demands that she "recount [truthfully] for me, without lies" to determine whether "the son (born) from you is unique."

With tears and in heated reprimand, Batenosh responds, "O my brother and my husband, recall for yourself my pleasure ... in the heat of the moment, and my panting of breath."

There's some ancient science behind this sexy scene. Our scribes are, once again, engaging and integrating wider forms of knowledge into their work. As both Ida Fröhlich and Pieter van der Horst have uncovered, underlying this text is an ancient Greek medical tradition's understanding that connected a women's orgasm with conception.[20] For Batenosh, the paternity proof is in the pleasure. Still, Lamech is unconvinced and seeks knowledge from his father, Methuselah, who in turn consults the all-knowing Enoch. Enoch instructs, "Go, say to Lamech your son,['The chi]l[d is t]r[ul]y from you [and]n[ot] from the sons[of Heaven'" (1Q20 5:10).

These few examples reveal that the scribes of the Aramaic DSS were at once deeply invested in their own ancestral traditions and adept at innovating them in new ways. This included engaging with and threading in knowledge of the cultures around them.[21]

Conclusion

Even the brief and selective tour above highlights that these Aramaic writings are remarkable reads. They have great potential for how we think about (or need to rethink) the life, thought, and literature of that critical period that spans the latter times of the Hebrew Scriptures, and which shaped both Judaism in the Second Temple period and Christian origins.

The Aramaic DSS push us to contend with *what was missing* in our view of this world. In many ways, the Aramaic scrolls provide new views of previously lost or unknown expressions of Judaism in antiquity before and beyond Qumran. They also give new perspective on scribal cultures. Previously, Aramaic literature was thought to be a minority report of sorts in the historical, theological, and literary worlds of ancient Jewish scribes. The Aramaic DSS overturn that idea. The opportunity now is to encounter these materials and rethink what we might have been missing about ancient identity and scribal activity revealed by this Aramaic legacy.

The Aramaic DSS also challenge us to see *what was there all along*, or at least, visible in glimpses or sensed in inklings. As we saw, there are many texts among the Aramaic discoveries that were lost until their modern recovery in the Qumran caves. But there are also several that were known in some form in other canonical or modern collections—whether in the Bible (bits of Daniel and Ezra), the Apocrypha or Deuterocanon (Tobit), or the so-called Pseudepigrapha (1 Enoch). In some cases, texts were circulated in diverse collections such as those of the Manichaeans, or as far as northern China (*Book of Giants*), or they've turned up in other Jewish literary collections, like the Cairo Genizah (the Aramaic Levi Document). While most of the Aramaic originals were lost on us until the DSS discoveries, they apparently had reception histories for communities spanning upper Africa through parts of Asia.

Lastly, the Aramaic texts help us reframe questions of other ancient writings about what we have perhaps *missed or misunderstood* without this Aramaic context. This angle of research is ripe for exploration, not least as it relates to the world of the New Testament—which brings us to the topic of the Qumran discoveries and Christian origins.

Chapter 9

Conspiracy and Opportunity at the Intersection of Qumran and Christian Origins

The DSS are regularly described as either a goldmine of new information and insights for understanding the beginning of Christianity or a landmine of data unsettling, overturning, or exploding core theological and historical tenets of the faith. A pair of items from world media outlets in the 1950s illustrates the full spectrum of rushed conclusions, hopes, and fears regarding exactly what type of mine we're dealing with at Qumran and in the DSS.

On September 3, 1955, *The Illustrated London News* ran an article by British archaeologist G. Lankester Harding. While the insider crew of scrolls scholars sorted and sifted fragments in Jerusalem, Lankester Harding directed a dig at Qumran. His findings? Jesus and his desert-trekking cousin, John the Baptist, likely studied at Qumran. This site is holy ground. The associated scrolls, near relics. Bold assertion.

We find the polar opposite view a few years later in a 1958 issue of the Soviet tabloid paper, *Komsomolskaya Pravda*. This publication too heralded the DSS. Only now, to make an equally sensational counterclaim: these ancient discoveries at last proved that Jesus never existed.[1] Take that, religion!

So, who's right? Neither. The opportunity here is to explore how the DSS help us refine our understanding of Christin origins as part of, not apart from, the context of Judaism in the Second Temple period. News flash: Jesus was a Jew. Same for the disciples. Paul too. Judas, Jairus, Jude? All Jews. It's not until Paul takes the show on the road that the movement becomes increasingly Gentile.[2] So to understand the social history, thought, and practices we find in the pages of the Christian New Testament, we need to see, hear, and think about them in the worlds of ancient Judaism.

The challenge and opportunity are to do this well. Method matters. We must avoid "parallel-o-mania" (seeing continuity and connections everywhere) without succumbing to "parallel-o-phobia" (overlooking crossover from our collections anywhere). Ideally, we land somewhere in the middle.[3] In this chapter, we'll explore three intersections between the DSS and New Testament that reveal how the former enhances our understanding of the latter.

To begin, we'll explore aspects of their shared *conceptual* worlds with an eye for similarities and differences in apocalyptic communal structures and hopes for the messiahs (yes, plural) found in the DSS and the Gospels. Next, we'll encounter the *cultural* expressions of religious practices, specifically Jesus's postures of prayer when exercising demons and perspectives from Paul on religious practice and justification. Last, we'll engage the *compositional* formation of some early New Testament traditions and consider Mary's amazement at Jesus's otherworldly paternity and ancient Jewish projections from scripture to hint at resurrection.

Conceptual Correspondences

We don't need copies of New Testament texts at Qumran to consider the significance of the DSS for providing context for early Christianity. Remember, they simply aren't there.[4] It's also not the case that the Vatican controlled the scrolls for fear that they debunked historic Christian theology. That simply didn't happen, but it is a regular element of conspiracy theories and myths circulating around the DSS. Such sideshows only encourage misunderstanding, and distract from the opportunity ahead.[5] Conspiracies and controversies aside, the DSS are the single most important resource for recovering a historically informed view of the culture that cultivated the ideas of the early Jesus movement. Full stop.

Of the many topics we could explore, two will highlight how the DSS provided new information and perspective on how ancient Jews understood themselves, the world around them, and their relationship to each other. First, we'll talk about how apocalyptic outlooks informed the identity and ethics of both the Qumran and early Christian communities. Second, we'll consider New Testament messianism in light of the patterns of messianic thought among the DSS.

Time and Togetherness: The Idea of Apocalyptic Communities

We saw in the last chapter how the Qumran Aramaic texts cast new light on the development of the apocalyptic worldview and literature in Second Temple Judaism. That background is essential here, since apocalyptic ideas also shaped emerging Christian groups and influenced New Testament writers. However, this is not due to any direct genealogical relationship between Qumran and Christian origins. Rather, it's because both movements drew on and contributed to a common cultural pool of ideas and outlooks. Apocalypticism, therefore, found expression in the lived experience and expectations of both groups: for example, in understandings of *time* and related practices of *togetherness*.

Time is a big deal for formal apocalypses and groups informed by apocalypticism. Past, present, and future form an arc of history. Everything is related. Nothing is accidental. When understood properly, this apocalyptic

EXECUTION PHOTOS STATE BY STATE
Justice for 57 killers—so far
Sun
Sealed in Vatican Vaults...
DEAD SEA SCROLLS
7
Never before revealed prophecies for 1998!
ALSO DISCOVER—
Proof that Jesus has returned
Why Heaven and angels are real
Map of how Earth will change
PLUS MORE

TEEN GODFATHERS TAKE CONTROL OF MAFIA
Sun
Religion in turmoil over discoveries in lost desert city!
NEW MYSTERIES of the DEAD SEA SCROLLS
Startling revelations
Who really wrote Christ's messages to world?
How ancient documents' prophecies affect us all
Incredible challenges to origins of Christianity
The New York Times reports
WOMAN WINS $200,000,000 ON SLOT MACHINES—THEN LOSES IT ALL!
Reveal casinos

U.S. JET SHOOTS AT LOCH NESS MONSTER IN ALASKA LAKE
Sun
FINAL PROPHECY OF...
DEAD SEA SCROLLS
World War III will be started by a woman
December 19, 1999 set as 'new day of infamy'
FIND OUT HOW YOU CAN SURVIVE!
JESUS' RETURN
STORMS
RELIGIOUS LEADERS
EARTHQUAKES

FBI'S real-life X FILES EXPOSED!
Sun
Mutant humans escape from labs
Deadly viruses are unleashed on public
STARTLING REVELATIONS FROM...
DEAD SEA SCROLLS: '1997 WEATHER TO BE WORST EVER'
Forecasts will terrify you!
NEW YORK
BLIZZARDS
FLORIDA
HURRICANES
COLORADO
FIRES
ILLINOIS
TORNADOS
CALIFORNIA
EARTHQUAKES

IMAGE 9.1: Conspiracy theories about the scrolls and their implications for Christian origins have become part of the modern cultural history of the DSS. This includes a spectrum of items, from tabloid takes about apocalyptic weather, geopolitical prophecies, and Jesus's true identity, to unhinged theories from overly creative scholars and tinfoil hat–wearing conspiracy theorists.
(Image credit: Andrew B. Perrin)

historiography reveals patterns of eras or a crescendo of events ramping up toward the end. Typically, the protracted end involves the arrival of the kingdom of God that's always on the horizon.[6]

The Qumran movement and early Christians located themselves on this axis of time in many ways. One was inspired by their shared—yet distinct—interpretation of a passage from Isaiah 40:3–4. The biblical prophecy of Isaiah reads:

> A voice cries out: "In the wilderness prepare the way of the LORD; make straight in the desert a highway for our God. Every valley shall be lifted up, and every mountain and hill be made low; the uneven ground shall become level, and the rough places a plain."

In its original setting, Isaiah's oracle was expectant but not apocalyptic. Isaiah spoke of paving a path back to Judea from the Babylonian exile. That's what it *meant*. But it *came to mean* something different for the Qumran and early Christian movements.

All four of the canonical Gospels quote aspects of Isaiah 40:3–4. Their perspective, however, does not to point to a runway out of Babylon in the past. Rather, the Gospels use it to profile John the Baptist in the present. Take the sample from the early chapters of Luke describing John's ministry:[7]

> He went into all the region around the Jordan, proclaiming a baptism of repentance for the forgiveness of sins, as it is written in the book of the words of the prophet Isaiah, "The voice of one crying out in the wilderness: 'Prepare the way of the Lord, make his paths straight. Every valley shall be filled, and every mountain and hill shall be made low, and the crooked shall be made straight, and the rough ways made smooth; and all flesh shall see the salvation of God.'" (Luke 3:3–6)

Luke is citing a tradition here—one that touches on time. He understood Isaiah 40:3–4 as both *set in* his own time as a Gospel writer and as a *sign of* the times. To outsiders, John's actions in the wilderness were odd. For insiders, like the evangelists and the communities they wrote to, John's actions were ominous. By citing Isaiah, the gospel writers claim a connectedness of past, present, and future. John was the projected way-paver, Jesus the history-maker. That's the axis. This is no mere instance of the "New Testament use of the Old Testament." It's a perspective on the present and a posture toward the past that, when strategically connected, formed larger ideas that informed the identity of ancient Christian writers and gospel communities.

How does this posture toward traditions and time relate to the theme of togetherness? There's a lot to be said about the structure of the early church. One thing's certain: they banded together. The question is, Why? Perhaps to share goods. Definitely to eat together. Maybe to tend to each other's needs. Certainly to worship. Probably a bit of safety in numbers. You see all of this, for example, in the snapshot of an early Christian community in Acts 2, the companion volume to Luke's Gospel.

However, these elements weren't the primary motivation for this incessant togetherness. Expectations were. Early Christian communities found themselves in an awkward in-between. Their founders proclaimed a risen Savior and promised his prompt return. However, the timing of this return was unknown.[8] By plotting themselves at this point on an apocalyptic timeline, they opted to position themselves in shared places—to prepare, together. Therefore, most early Christian churches were apocalyptic communities.

This blending of time and togetherness to form apocalyptic communities, however, was not an innovation of the early Jesus movement. It had been prototyped in ancient Judaism before, not least by the Qumran group. Let's circle back to where we started with a quote from Isaiah and advance from there toward the DSS.

Isaiah 40:3 was also a cornerstone for the Qumran community's self-understanding. Once again, the issue is not simply the interpretation of scripture. Rather, it's about what the tradition has *come to mean* in what is undoubtedly an apocalyptic community. Let's look at the set of citations in the *Community Rule*.

Following a direct quotation of Isaiah 40:3—that text we heard above—1QS 8:15–20 reads:

> This means the expounding of the Law, decreed by God through Moses for obedience, that being defined by what has been revealed for each age, and by what the prophets have revealed by His holy spirit. No man belonging to the Covenant of the Yahad who flagrantly deviates from any commandment is to touch the pure food belonging to the holy men. Further, he is not to participate in any of their deliberations until all his works have been cleansed from evil, so that he is again able to walk blamelessly. They shall admit him into deliberations by the decision of the general membership; afterwards, he shall be enrolled at an appropriate rank. This is also the procedure for every initiate added to the Yahad. These are the rules by which the men of blameless holiness shall conduct themselves, one with another.

At first glance, this might not sound like an apocalyptic take on Isaiah 40:3. Part of what we have here is another essential strand in Qumranite DNA: living out the legal prescriptions of scripture in accordance with their insider understanding. But even this core idea is imbibed with apocalyptic themes. Revealed knowledge, boundaries of time and space, and authoritative perspectives on imminent expectations—all part of the package.

The *Community Rule* extends these concepts with a second tier of interpretation on Isaiah 40:3. Following a rundown of membership hierarchies and a rehearsal of messianic job descriptions (more on that in a minute), the scroll reads:

> He (the Instructor) shall ground them in knowledge, thereby instructing them in truly wondrous mysteries; if then the secret Way is

> perfected among the men of the Yahad, each will walk blamelessly with his fellow, guided by what has been revealed to them. That will be the time of "preparing the way in the desert" (Isaiah 40:3). He shall instruct them in every legal finding that is to regulate their works in that time, and teach them to separate from every man who fails to keep himself from perversity. These are the precepts of the Way for the Instructor in these times. (1QS 9:18–21)

Once again, an old passage from an age past finds new meaning in a different time. The Qumran community understood themselves to be on the edge of the eschaton. We saw this already, for example, in the *War Scroll*. The community's ideas, structures, and expectations reflect this conviction. Qumran was hardly an all-inclusive resort. Long-term desert living can't be easy. But if you're planning a short-term residency on the brink of something big, your time together takes on a different meaning.

This understanding of time and tradition puts the Essene emphasis on togetherness in fresh perspective. Our archaeology chapter demonstrated that this movement preferred clustered living, shared meals, and common property. Do such perceived parallels with the early church provide the background to Christian practices and structure? In a way. But more importantly, they demonstrate how such similarities are due to a common or shared heritage in this period.

However, too often that approach results in caricatures of Qumran, sketched in view of images torn from later Christian tradition. It doesn't really matter, for example, that the communal meals of the ancient Jewish community at Qumran remind us of the Eucharist of the emerging Christian church. Surface level comparisons like this miss the point. These were and are Jewish texts.[9]

The better, more balanced, approach is to recognize the culturally crafted ideas that underlie such perceived parallels. In this case, it's that joint meals—whether for sustenance or symbolism—had an eschatological orientation within these distinct apocalyptic communities. Their understanding of time dictated their practices of togetherness. The parallel isn't *what* they did, it's *why* they did it, in their understanding of the *when*. Apocalypticism was (and is) an open-source way of coordinating lived experiences with a boundless reality imagined by writers and movements.

The Messianic Matrices of Ancient Judaism

"Christ" isn't Jesus's last name. (I'm sorry if nobody told you that.) Starting with the LXX, the Greek term Χριστός ("Christ") begins to be used to approximate the Hebrew משיח ("messiah"). By the mid– to late–Second Temple period, both are commonly understood as "messiah." We have become so accustomed to this term, however, that we've lost touch with its origins and implications.

In the Hebrew Scriptures, the term משיח refers to individuals anointed for a role of leadership or deliverance. Though varied, such "anointed ones" or "messiahs" were predominantly priests, kings, and prophets of the *past*.[10] However, as later groups looked back on this heritage, they developed these categories with *future* hopes for reestablished institutions and restored leadership. In a sense, then, the traditions gained a messianic momentum.

Take Balaam's oracle of a "scepter" and "star" in Numbers 24:15–19. Though the passage doesn't include the term משיח, and was hardly read as messianic its earliest formation, its messianic malleability is evident in a variety of later texts at and beyond Qumran.[11] Such reflections capitalize on the potential of "messianic moments," when scribes and interpreters identified either passages or persons for their messianic potential.[12] In this example and others, it's mostly in hindsight that passages are assigned a messianic character. How is it that a particular messianic identification became the hallmark of Christianity? You can't have Christians without a—well, *the*—Christ. Here again, we need to find context in a void in most modern Bibles.

The DSS revealed two key things about messianic perspectives in the Second Temple period. First, messianism wasn't really a defining feature of group identity. Perspectives on purity, calculations of calendar, and pragmatics of religious practice were what formed and divided groups. There isn't a single ancient text that suggests the Pharisees, Sadducees, Essenes, and Zealots drew a line in the sand over their messianic hopes.[13] As Michael Bird remarked, this means "messianism remained only one way of telling the story of Israel's hope for the future."[14]

Second, while messianism was relatively minor, sections of the DSS revealed that there were many patterns and profiles for messianic figures in ancient Judaism. We are simply the most familiar with one that worked for Jesus and his followers. This also becomes a matter of perspective. As George Nickelsburg once remarked, "Different ancient Jews expected different types of Jewish messiahs."[15]

If messianism was less about *claims* and more about a *conversation* in ancient Judaism, then the opportunity of the Qumran texts is to hear other voices. When we listen to sound bites of these discussions in the DSS, we hear a remarkable variety of messianic expectations for royal, priestly, and prophetic figures.

In one place, the *Community Rule* anticipated a messianic tag team. As the community went about their business anticipating an imminent eschaton, they would know the beginning of the end was upon them when a pair of priestly and royal messiahs (yes, plural) emerged. The relevant text in the Cave 1 copy reads:

> They shall govern themselves using the original precepts by which the men of the Yahad began to be instructed, doing so until there come the prophet and the messiahs of Aaron and Israel. (1QS 9:10–11)

Before the discovery of the DSS, this sort of dual eschatological agents model was rare.[16] The *Community Rule*, therefore, connects us with the inception of this idea in an age *before* the New Testament.

But you can't go into a messianic age hungry. The *Rule of the Congregation*—that work included on the same scroll as the Cave 1 *Community Rule*—described the procession up to an eschatological meal, again featuring multiple messiahs. Only now, the royal messiah of Israel is subordinated to the priestly leader.

> The procedure for the [mee]ting of the men of reputation [when they are called] to the banquet held by the party of the Yahad, when the messiah (המשיח) has been revealed among them: [the priest,] as head of the entire congregation of Israel, shall enter first, trailed by all [his] brot[hers, the Sons of] Aaron, those priests [appointed] to the banquet of the men of reputation. They are to sit be[fore him] by rank. Then the [mess]iah of Israel (מש]יׄח ישראל) may en[ter]. (1QSa 2:11–14)

These samples give glimpses into the messianic ideas of the insider community at Qumran. As we know from our tour through the Aramaic DSS, this community also received and read writings from beyond their own enclave. When these texts outline their future expectations, the roles reserved for eschatological agents extend the gallery of ancient Jewish messianic portraits.

At least one Aramaic text, the *Apocryphon of Levi*, references an eschatological high priest. Though he is not labelled a "messiah," the figure clearly plays a role of revelation and deliverance in a turbulent future age.

> And he shall make atonement for all those of his generation, and he shall be sent to all the children of his [peo]ple. His command is like the command of heaven, and his teaching is like the will of God. The sun everlasting will shine and its fire will give warmth to all the ends of

> the earth. It will shine on darkness; then will darkness vanish [fr]om the earth, and mist from the land. They will speak many words against him, and many [falsehood]s; they will concoct lies and speak all kinds of slander against him. His generation is evil and perverse […] will be; his term of office will be marked by lies and violence [and] the people will go astray in his days and be confounded. (4Q541 9i:2–7)

Apparently both *insider* and likely *outsider* texts at Qumran were thinking in terms of future figures of priestly significance. This trend suggests that when some New Testament writers explore and describe aspects of Jesus's priestly identity (such as Hebrews 2:17; 4:14; 7:13–17; 9:11–12), they're speaking into and out of a context where conversations over priestly figures of the future are already taking place. In this case, the payoff is not direct *connections* but discerning *context* for *concepts*.[17]

The significance of this new context at times also adds to our understanding of ancient Jewish terms used to talk about expected eschatological figures before the New Testament. Take, for example, the Cave 4 work *Aramaic Apocalypse* (or, as it is more sensationally known, the "Son of God" text). This fragmentary writing features a dream-vision interpretation, where a Jewish courtier unlocked the meaning of a king's revelation that featured shooting stars. The most significant section refers to an anticipated authoritative figure using loaded language.

> [Also his son] will be called *The Great* (ר]ב̊א), and be designated by his name. He will be called the *Son of God* (ברה די אל), they will call him the *Son of the Most High* (ובר עליון). (4Q246 1:8–2:1, italics for emphasis)

The New Testament is shot through with references to Jesus as the Son of God. The challenge is knowing how to understand those claims in their time. One interpretive angle hears hints of rhetorical counters to the Roman imperial cult. Some Roman emperors, such as Julius Caesar and his son Augustus, asserted their divine sonship. Claims of Jesus's Son of God status, therefore, presented an affront to both emperor and empire.

But is that *all* that inspired the Son of God language in the New Testament? An example from Luke's gospel now read in light of our *Aramaic Apocalypse* fragment suggests otherwise. Luke launches his gospel biography of Jesus with some bold claims and big language. For example, note the italicized terms below:

> He will be *great* (μέγας), and will be called the *Son of the Most High* (υἱὸς ὑψίστου), and the Lord God will give to him the throne of his ancestor David. ... The angel said to her, "The Holy Spirit will come upon you, and the power of the Most High will overshadow you; therefore the child to be born will be holy; he will be called *Son of God* (υἱὸς θεοῦ). (Luke 1:32, 35)

The Greek terms underlying the italicized English texts above are remarkably similar to the terms in *Aramaic Apocalypse*. Because of this tight correspondence, John Collins argued that Luke knew the Cave 4 text and redeployed its language for his own purposes.[18] That doesn't mean our Cave 4 text is about Jesus. It does mean, however, that we've recovered the earliest known usage of specific divine sonship language in Jewish sources prior to the emergence of Christianity. These terms weren't only against the emperor over in Rome—they were inspired by language domestic to intellectual culture in Judea.

So where does this leave us for rethinking New Testament messianic claims in the Jewish conceptual context provided by the DSS? The oft-repeated idea that Jesus didn't fit the mold of a dominant Jewish hope for a militaristic messiah is misguided. There was no mold. The DSS reveal an unforeseen variety and malleability of messianic ideas, both at Qumran and beyond. This should change the way we engage in research on Christian origins. The object isn't to plunder Second Temple period writings for proofs of New Testament

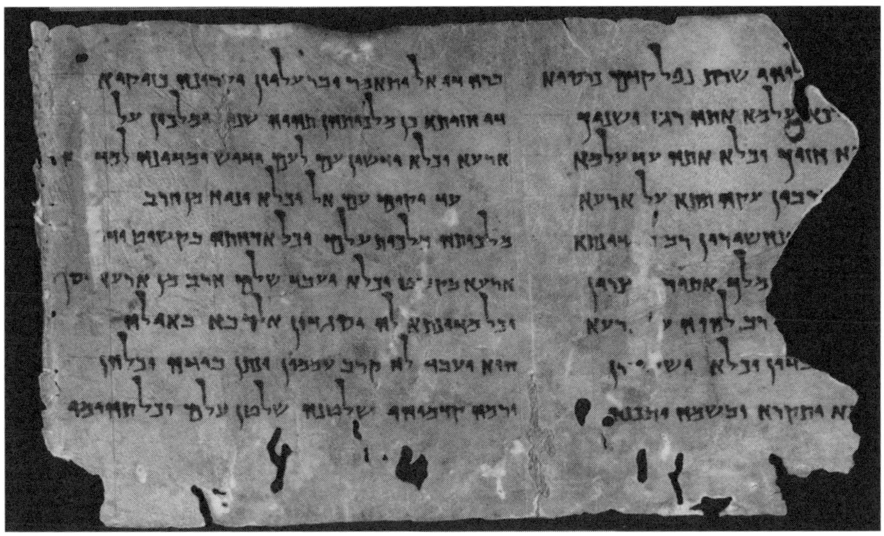

IMAGE 9.2: Sample fragment of the so-called "Son of God" text from Qumran Cave 4 (4Q246). This Aramaic apocalyptic text features a dream-vision and/or its inspired interpretation in a foreign court, some of which included language of divine sonship of some envisaged or expected figure. (Image credit: Courtesy of The Leon Levy Dead Sea Scrolls Digital Library; Israel Antiquities Authority, photo: Shai Halevi)

---

messianic concepts. Rather, the opportunity is to rethink our relationship with the ancient Jewish conceptual world that both informed and formed the ideas New Testament writers advanced. Recovered ideas are not enough. What we really need is a connection to that culture.

Cultural Intersections

Readers of the New Testament today should feel a bit of culture shock when reading these ancient writings—but most of us think we're immune. The world of Jesus, Paul, and others may feel familiar, but it's actually foreign. This is particularly the case when it comes to religious expressions and experiences found in the New Testament. Culture informs thought and practice. Since we're not part of the first-century CE context of emerging Christianity, we're uninformed readers, ill-prepared travelers into a foreign space. That is, until we do some homework in the cultural heritage of Second Temple Judaism.

We'll look at two New Testament passages in tandem with a set of Dead Sea texts that illustrate the potential of this cultural context for both religious practice and perspectives. One example is from the Gospels and pertains to prayer and exorcism. The other example comes from Paul's letters and reveals a major course correction after centuries of misinterpretation.

Exorcising Unsexy Demons and Laying On Hands in Prayer

Prayer is a common practice across ancient cultures, yet *how* people pray is less consistent. Practices of prayer develop over time and look different depending on the where, when, and why of your utterances. Take, for example, saying grace before meals. Seems standard enough. But people didn't always clench their hands and close their eyes. My hunch is that these practices began when some genius parent realized they meant kids couldn't see or swat each other during a premeal prayer. This playful modern example highlights that there's a connection between bodily *posture* and *perspectives* for specific types of prayer in a culture or confessional tradition.

Prayer is all over the Bible. But the books in the anthology of Scripture have their own cultural contexts and places in time. The patterns of prayer in biblical scenes, then, reflect cultural scripts—scripts that we don't have because we're not first-century Jews. We gain glimpses of these, however, by studying portrayals of prayer in the New Testament.

Take Jesus, for example. He prayed a lot, particularly for healing. The Gospels often portray him as a hands-on healer (Mark 1:41; 5:41; 6:5). His words of power are often paired with laying on hands to restore health and dispel sickness. This reputation, apparently, preceded him. Just ask the crowds in Mark:

> Then one of the leaders of the synagogue named Jairus came and, when he saw him, fell at his feet and begged him repeatedly, "My little daughter is at the point of death. Come and lay your hands on her, so that she may be made well, and live." (Mark 5:22–23)

> On the sabbath he began to teach in the synagogue, and many who heard him were astounded. They said, "Where did this man get all this? What is this wisdom that has been given to him? What deeds of power are being done by his hands! (Mark 6:2)

> They brought to him a deaf man who had an impediment in his speech; and they begged him to lay his hand on him. (Mark 7:32)

This posture of prayer—laying on hands—might seem commonplace. But we don't find anyone anywhere else in the Bible doing this. Just Jesus. Was this his proprietary prayer innovation, his signature move? Some used to think so. But then that "dried-up cigar" of a scroll—the *Genesis Apocryphon*—provided a new perspective.

In this Aramaic retelling of Genesis 12, Sarai is trafficked into Pharaoh's house due to the lusty reports of one of Pharaoh's chief courtiers.[19] With Sarai's safety and purity at risk, Abram reportedly lived under a torrent of tears, begging God for her safe return. God listened and responded, but not in the way you might expect. He dispatched an "unclean spirit" to afflict Pharaoh and, for added precaution, every other man in the house. The *Genesis Apocryphon* drives the point home:

> Consequently, he was unable to have sexual relations with her; indeed, he did not have intercourse with her even though she was with him two full years. (1Q20 20:17–18)[20]

When the Egyptian house couldn't take it anymore, they sent a runner to Abram, who reflected on the situation as follows:

IMAGE 9.3: Images of Jesus's prayerful laying on of hands in healing abound in later icons and art. The sample here is from an Ethiopic tradition, seemingly depicting Mark 8:22–26, where the act of healing a blind man is at first unsuccessful but a second attempt of laying hands on the man's eyes affects healing (without an explicit mention of prayer). (Image credit: unknown)

> Then Hyrcanos came to me, asking me to come pray for the king, and to lay hands upon him and cure him—for [he had seen me] in a dream. But Lot replied, "My uncle, Abram, is unable to pray for the king while Sarai, his wife, remains with him. Now, go tell the king to send his wife to her husband. Then he will pray for him and he will be cured." When Hyrcanos heard Lot's words, he went and told the king, "All these smitings and plagues by which my lord the king has been smitten and afflicted are because of Sarai, the wife of Abram! Let him return Sarai to Abram, her husband, and this plague will depart from you, that is, the spirit causing the discharges of pus." (1Q20 20:21–26)

Abram obliged and made a house call:

> So I prayed for him, that blasphemer, and laid my hands upon his [he] ad. Thereupon the plague was removed from him, the evil [spirit] exorcised [from him,] and he was healed. (1Q20 20:28–29)

In the *Genesis Apocryphon*, it's this action that earns Abram his riches, not his trickery, as in the familiar version of the story in Genesis. Clever. But there's also an irony here: Pharaoh is unable to lay a hand on Sarai, yet Abram is able to exorcise the evil spirit by laying on hands in prayer.

So what does Pharaoh's unsexy itch have to do with Jesus the healer? Context. There's that word again. The *Genesis Apocryphon*'s portrayal of laying on hands in prayer for the purposes of dispelling a demon—called "apotropaic" prayer—predates the gospels by about two centuries. Because of this, Joseph Fitzmyer and Daniel Machiela have underscored that the *Genesis Apocryphon*'s portrayal of this posture of prayer undoubtedly reflects the cultural practices now also found in Jesus's hands-on healings in the Gospels.[21]

This means that when Jesus showed up blasting demons and curing diseases by a subtle touch *and* a spoken word, it wasn't novel. Not everything has to be new in the New Testament to have meaning. This posture of prayer for that particular purpose was already part of the culture. Jesus's actions weren't what shocked people. It was that they knew what this practice promised. Why else would random strangers keep requesting he come quickly to lay hands on the sick?

Fresh Perspectives on Classic Paul: "Works of the Law" in 4QMMT

The apostle Paul wrote a lot of long sentences. He also dropped some small words that turned out to have major theological significance—like "righteousness" (δικαιοσύνη). There's been a tidal wave of ink spilled over this word from the Protestant Reformation onward. But it's not only this word that matters. It's how Paul understood the process, outcomes, and activities of being made right—justified—in relation to another concept scattered across his writings: "works of the law" (ἔργων νόμου).

Paul uses variations of this expression eight times in his letters.[22] To streamline things, let's watch Paul in action in a sample passage, Galatians 2:15–21, with key terms in italics and in Greek:

> We ourselves are Jews by birth and not Gentile sinners; yet we know that a person is justified not by the *works of the law* (ἔργων νόμου) but through faith in Jesus Christ. And we have come to believe in Christ Jesus, so that we might be justified by faith in Christ, and not by doing the *works of the law* (ἔργων νόμου), because no one will be justified by the works of the law. But if, in our effort to be justified in Christ, we ourselves have been found to be sinners, is Christ then a servant of sin? Certainly not! But if I build up again the very things that I once tore down, then I demonstrate that I am a transgressor. For through the law I died to the law, so that I might live to God. I have been crucified with Christ; and it is no longer I who live, but it is Christ who lives in me. And the life I now live in the flesh I live by

> faith in the Son of God, who loved me and gave himself for me. I do not nullify the grace of God; for if justification comes through the law, then Christ died for nothing.

Paul put a lot of pieces together here. Yet he didn't pause to define what he meant by "works of the law." Why? Because he's writing to an early gospel community which, like him, was part of a cultural mosaic of shared ideas and understandings.

Here's the problem: until recently, many studies of Paul's understanding of "works of the law" have proceeded *apart* from that context. Classic interpreters emphasize the theological, yet were unaware of the cultural. Luther. Calvin. Zwingli. These were all heavy on the theology but were less aware of or interested in ancient Jewish culture. What we needed was a fresh perspective—one afforded by a new discovery, like 4QMMT.[23]

We know from chapter 5 that 4QMMT was a type of letter that outlined key issues of Qumranite purity practices, beliefs, scriptural interpretation, and hallmarks of identity. Perhaps it was once dispatched, but its presence in six copies penned over a longer time period (between 75 BCE to 50 CE) suggests it was also studied.[24] As the scribe of 4QMMT wrapped things up, he brought it home with an epilogue. Watch those key terms in italics and the original Hebrew.

> Now, we have written to you *some of the works of the law* (מקצת מעשי התורה), those which we determined would be beneficial for you and your people, because we have seen that you possess insight and knowledge of the law. Understand all these things and beseech him to set your counsel straight and so keep you away from evil thoughts and the counsel of Belial. Then you shall rejoice at the end time when you find the essence of our words to be true. *And it will be reckoned to you as righteousness* (ונחשבה לך לצדקה), in that you have done what is

right and good before him, to your own benefit and to that of Israel. (4Q398 14–17 ii:2–8)

You probably picked up on the oddly similar use of terms and topical interests between Galatians 2:15–21 and the epilogue of 4QMMT. Let's unpack the implications of this overlap with three questions.

First, why do the similar terms matter? Before the discovery of the scrolls, no other ancient writer apart from Paul was talking in these terms. Yet 4QMMT revealed the corresponding Hebrew (מעשי התורה) to Paul's Greek lingo (ἔργων νόμου). Suddenly, Paul's terminology doesn't sound so proprietary. And that's okay. He neither lived nor wrote in a cultural vacuum.

It would be easy to say Paul is "borrowing" from 4QMMT. He's probably not. We could also quickly conclude that this Cave 4 text is "background" for the New Testament. That too misses the mark. Rather, overlapping terms and thought in 4QMMT and Paul reveal an ongoing cultural conversation about the legal framework and specific religious practices that fell under the category of the "works of the law." This discovery was revolutionary.

Second, what about the list of practices? In a fuller (though still fragmentary) scope, 4QMMT touches on at least twenty-four items of religious practice and thought. We could cluster these in some larger categories: (1) calendar calculations for Sabbath and festivals, (2) purity of the priests, sacrifices, and participants in the temple, and (3) legal interpretations of transmitting and removing ritual impurity. And don't forget, 4QMMT refers to these as but "*some* of the works of the law." Paul's list was apparently shorter. The identity markers that caught his attention were mostly circumcision, food laws, and festivals (see, for example, Galatians 2:1–14; 4:10; Colossians 2:16).

These lists aren't the same. But they don't need to be. Martin Abegg demonstrated that "the concept of 'works of the law' is quite agile and allows for any number of structures, the only condition being that they find their source in Torah and are concerned with practice which defines relationship to God in a particular sort of Judaism."[25] He also noted that both texts anchor their argumentation in some common blessing/cursing formulae inspired by Deuteronomy 27–28. James Dunn added that both works feature the phrase "reckoned as righteousness," which is likely drawn from the blessing of Abraham in Genesis 15 (Gal 3:6; 4QMMT 31).[26] Standing back from the texts, then, while it was the similar *terms* that first caught our attention, it's the interpretive *tools* in Torah that have held our focus and revealed a shared infrastructure that runs deeper than a surface level parallel idiom "works of the law."

Third, what do the compositional dates of these texts tell us? While dating Paul's letters is not always a simple task, Galatians was likely written around 50 CE. Regardless of the date of this particular dispatch, one thing is certain: when Paul writes, he writes as a first-century Jew. The Qumran copies of 4QMMT are mostly from this period, though the work itself is older. Scrolls scholars generally think 4QMMT is either a foundational text to the Qumran group or even pre-Qumranic in origin, sometime in the mid–second century BCE.[27] This means the idea had time to take hold in ancient Jewish culture well before Paul inked the idea for the early Jesus movement.

The upshot of all this is simple yet profound: Paul is not speaking into silence. He's joining a discussion in process. Sure, the gospel is something new. But the challenge and opportunity ahead of Paul was communicating a timeless message in timely terms. Some of those terms were familiar to them, yet are foreign to us. Until now.

Compositional Patterns

Very few New Testament writers reveal their workflow. Luke tells us his "orderly account" is based on research and interviews (Luke 1:1–4). Paul hints that on occasion he used a scribal amanuensis—a hybrid dictation assistant and collaborator—to help get the message across (Romans 16:22). The writer of Revelation wrapped up his apocalyptic end times expectations with a colophon of sorts—a scribal statement ensuring the next guy didn't mess with your masterpiece (Revelation 22:19).[28]

Apart from these few stray *internal* details, most of our knowledge of the composition of New Testament books comes from *external* sources. The reality is that there was no single, set workflow for ancient scribes, authors, editors, etc. Yet there's one universal we can count on: when composing their works, biblical writers both inherited ideas from culture and encountered traditions from sources. This underscores, yet again, the importance of recovering the Second Temple Jewish context of the New Testament.

For our purposes, we'll look at two samples from Luke. The first shows how Luke actively engaged *sources* when composing his biography of Jesus. The second reveals how Luke deployed a compositional *strategy* for deciphering the signs of the messianic age based on scriptural interpretation and the expectations of the day. These examples come at critical moments, starting with the birth of Jesus (Luke 2:19–51) and ending on death row for John the Baptist (Luke 7:18–23).

Mary's Heart-Hiddenness and Aramaic Revelatory Responses

Let's begin, as most biographies do, at the beginning. Luke is the only canonical gospel to include scenes of Jesus's infancy *and* childhood. Matthew fast-forwards from manger-side to midlife. Mark launches into a ministry in full momentum. John starts somewhere in outer space. Luke, however, begins with two stories of family road trips: the first to Bethlehem, the second to Jerusalem. Mary has breakthrough realizations at two points in this itinerary. In both, Luke captures the moment with a peculiar phrase—a phrase that isn't easily interpreted without a little outside help.[29]

First up, a detail in the Christmas story about baby Jesus that you've probably missed. Let's set the scene. Mary's by the manger, presumably exhausted.

Joseph is settling in as a new dad.[30] Then shepherds show up unannounced. No gifts, just news. During their evening watch, an angelic host had heralded the birth of the Messiah. That one, right there, cozied up in linen strips. Then Luke includes this little aside: "But Mary treasured all these words and pondered them in her heart" (Luke 2:19). No explanation, just introspection. At this, everyone returns home.

Next up, a detail from a Passover journey with twelve-year-old Jesus. Let's jog our memory. The trip's going fine until the return journey to Nazareth, when Mary and Joseph lose Jesus. Panicked, they search among the caravan, then retrace their steps to Jerusalem. Three days later, they find Jesus. He's in the temple, teaching a captive audience. After a little motherly scolding, Jesus retorts that his folks probably should have looked there first—after all, it is his Father's house! With the misunderstanding between preteen and parents hanging in the air, Luke offers a familiar insight into Mary's amazement: "His mother treasured all these things in her heart" (Luke 2:51). A verse later, we're launched into the adult days of John and Jesus. Childhood is short, especially in the Gospels.

Generally, writers repeat things for emphasis. Generally, writers repeat things for emphasis. In the above statement, Luke is intentionally giving readers a sense of déjà vu. He's crafting a story. He's making a point. The echoed phrases in Luke 2:19 and 2:51 are in response to revelations about Jesus's destiny as messiah, and his paternity as the son of God. By deploying this phrase for that purpose, however, Luke hints at his homework in ancient Jewish Aramaic sources, some of which turn up among the DSS.

Last chapter, we saw that dream-visions play a big part in the Aramaic Dead Sea texts. At least two Aramaic writings feature revelations about the otherworldly identities or associations of children. Both depict gobsmacked parents who respond to such divinely dispatched news by tucking away the knowledge in their hearts.

IMAGE 9.4: Images of the Immaculate Heart of Mary in Catholic tradition have developed over centuries for many reasons. Part of this tradition is rooted in the recognition that by pondering special moments and sacred memories in her heart from the life of Jesus, Mary's heart became something that could be a focus or model for our own daily practice. The painting here is by Leopold Kupelwieser (1796–1862) from a side chapel of St. Antony in St. Peter's Church in Vienna, Austria. (Image credit: Wikimedia Commons)

Let's start with Noah traditions in the *Genesis Apocryphon*. Suspicious that his wife Batenosh has been sleeping around with fallen angels, and that Noah is the result of the angelic paternity fiasco of Genesis 6:4, Lamech laments his inner turmoil.

> Then suddenly I thought in my heart that the conception was from (the) Watchers, and the seed from (the) Holy Ones and of (the) Nephil[in ...]and my heart wavered concerning this infant. (1Q20 2:1–2; see also 1Q20 2:11)

That's a tough conversation to have. Later on in the *Genesis Apocryphon*, Noah himself learns of the intermixing of Watchers and women, again a la Genesis 6:4. In a dream-vision, however, God assures him his kids are entirely ordinary, this worldly, and not sons of the wayward Watchers. At this, Noah remarked: "And I hid this mystery within my heart, and did not make it known to anyone" (1Q20 6:12).

But Noah's not the only one hiding heavenly knowledge. The Aramaic Levi Document also featured a response of heart-hiddenness. Only now, the formula follows Levi's revelation that associates his priestly role and lineage with the heavenly host. After ascending to heaven for his priestly ordination, Levi remarked: "Then I said, 'This is the vision, and at this I was amazed that I had any vision!' And I hid this too in my heart, and did not reveal it to anyone" (ALD 7; 4Q213b 1:3).

How do these Aramaic phrases help us rethink the compositional layers of Luke? The curious phrases of Luke 2:19 and 2:51 do achieve emphasis by repetition. But more importantly, they establish Jesus's identity by using a response formula common to revelations about the destiny of infant prodigies and their otherworldly paternity. Whether by cultural awareness or source interaction, Luke is encountering ideas borne out of Aramaic scribal settings of ancient Judaism.

John's Leading Question and Ancient Jewish Exegesis

John the Baptist was always on the fringes in fashion (camel hair belts) and diet (high-protein locusts). But it was his controversial critique of Herod's marriage to his brother's wife, Herodias, that landed him on death row (Matthew 14:1–12; Mark 6:14–29; Josephus, *Ant.* 18.116–19). As he awaited the inevitable, John also sought certainty on matters of ultimate significance. Was Jesus *the* guy?

Luke 7:18–23 tells the story this way. John's in prison. He knows his days are numbered. His last request is to verify that the things he's seen are signs of the messianic age. He sends a few disciples as runners to Jesus. They carry a simple, yet loaded, question: "Are you the one who is to come, or are we to wait for another?" (Luke 7:19). Seems like a simple "yes" or "no" question. Perhaps. Unless you're Jesus. Rather than give a direct nod, Jesus did what first-century rabbis do: answer a question with a conversation. He tells them to report back what they have seen. Luke relates Jesus's reply as follows:

> And he answered them, "Go and tell John what you have seen and heard: the blind receive their sight, the lame walk, the lepers are cleansed, the deaf hear, the dead are raised, the poor have good news brought to them. And blessed is anyone who takes no offense at me." (Luke 7:22–23)

This list of the signs of the times that Jesus sends back to his cousin in the clink is mostly from two passages in Isaiah. See if you can spot the similarities and differences:

> Then the eyes of the blind shall be opened, and the ears of the deaf unstopped; then the lame shall leap like a deer, and the tongue of the speechless sing for joy. (Isaiah 35:5–6)

> The spirit of the Lord God is upon me, because the Lord has anointed me; he has sent me to bring good news to the oppressed, to bind up

> the brokenhearted, to proclaim liberty to the captives, and release to the prisoners; to proclaim the year of the Lord's favor, and the day of vengeance of our God; to comfort all who mourn. (Isaiah 61:1–2)

You probably noticed that one crucial item is *not* inspired by Isaiah: the promise of the resurrection of the dead. Remember, John is on death row. Yet Jesus's answer assumes this critical element won't confuse John. You don't get a second phone call for clarification on death row. So, where did this resurrection motif come from?

I want to introduce you to the Hebrew text of 4Q521, generically called the *Messianic Apocalypse*. This fragmentary text expresses hope for an age when "the hea]vens and the earth shall listen to his messiah" (4Q521 2 ii + 4:1). The hope, however, is not abstract. Rather, it comes from a smattering of (mostly) quotations of Isaiah and the Psalms. These are patterned together as follows:

> and the Lord shall do glorious things which have not been done, just as He said. For He shall heal the critically wounded, He shall revive the dead, He shall send good news to the afflicted, He shall sati[sfy the poo]r, He shall guide the uprooted, He shall make the hungry rich, and [...] disc[erning ones ...] and all of them as the ho[ly ones] (4Q521 2 ii + 4:11–14)

Sound familiar? This fragmentary Cave 4 text represents an ancient Jewish interpretive tradition that was in place *before* the time of the New Testament. It reveals that certain passages in the Hebrew Scriptures were understood for their messianic flare in the mid–Second Temple period. Beyond this, it shows that the hope for resurrection—a rarity in the Hebrew Scriptures—was a part of this package.

This is a game changer. Without 4Q521, we wouldn't understand the true impact of Jesus's response to John. Jesus's message back to John is culturally encoded and conceptually loaded. There are many questions we could ask

IMAGE 9.5: The Hebrew text of 4Q521 engages in a similar style of recombining scriptural samples from Psalms and Isaiah as found in Jesus's response to John on death row in the Gospel, as well as the shared secondary expansion calling out the expectation of the resurrection of the dead in the messianic age. (Image credit: Courtesy of The Leon Levy Dead Sea Scrolls Digital Library; Israel Antiquities Authority, photo: Shai Halevi)

---

about this similarity. Was John the Baptist an Essene who knew this theology? Nope. Is 4Q521 a prophecy about Jesus? Wrong again. Did Luke swing by Qumran and plagiarize 4Q521? Unlikely. Here's a better question. Is Luke's composition informed by an ancient Jewish pattern of interpretation that is lost on us but assumed in his answer to John? Absolutely.

Conclusion

Maybe we've missed or misunderstood aspects of the New Testament. If so, perspective matters. I broke down the sample sets of texts from the DSS and New Testament above into conceptual, cultural, and compositional categories for convenience. The reality is, they're all related. The items discussed above represent different dynamics of the same world, a world that is lost on most modern readers. A world we can now recover, at least in part, from the fragments found in caves in the Judean wilderness.

Sure, we want to know the meaning of scripture *today*. But this must be built on a foundational knowledge of its meaning in *its own day*. That requires historical homework. It also means we need to adapt our reading strategy toward a novel approach to the New Testament that accounts for and encounters the Jewish world within which Christian ideas, communities, and eventually scripture originated. This approach doesn't pull the rug out from under the writers of the New Testament. Quite the opposite: it puts their feet on the ground.

This shift in perspective also demands a different posture toward sources like the DSS. The life and literature of the Second Temple period weren't the "background" of early Christianity. The New Testament is *part of* the heritage of antiquity, not developed *apart from* it. All these sources share the stage. If this is the case, then, ironically, one of the best ways to make sense of what's inside Christian scripture is to read around it.

At the same time, it's easy to run the risk of oversimplification, connecting dots that are too distant, or claiming literary "borrowing" at every whiff of a perceived parallel. If each of the sources outlined above—including the DSS and the New Testament—are actors on the same stage, we certainly need to hear them in dialogue. But we also need to retain the integrity of their monologues. Luke is Luke. The *Community Rule* is the *Community Rule*. We should hear them in conversation, but also let them speak for themselves.

Before Christianity became a religion of the book, it was a movement that followed a guy. But Jesus wasn't a Christian. He was the Christ. A Jew. And both of those things mean something. That "something" only makes sense when we stand back and account for the richness and embrace the complexity of the concepts, cultures, and compositions of the Second Temple period. Otherwise, "Christ" is just a confusing last name.

Finis (for Now): Closing Thoughts from the Unfolding History of the Dead Sea Scrolls

"No matter at what point one brings the record of the Dead Sea discoveries to a provisional conclusion, it will be very many years before the word 'Finis' can be written after the record. Perhaps indeed all that is contained in the foregoing pages is only the beginning."
F. F. Bruce, *Second Thoughts on the Dead Sea Scrolls* (1955)

I opened this book with an invitation to a lost and forgotten world—an ancient world that was something of a time capsule of puzzle pieces, dawning in our day by an unexpected discovery some seventy-five years ago. The DSS texts and associated site of Qumran are at once among our most ancient discoveries illuminating the life, thought, and culture of ancient Judaism, and the most late-breaking sources for studying this world. The story is an ongoing history. Research continues. Old questions are answered and new ones emerging.

But even ongoing history and unfolding stories have lessons to provide. Or, to revisit the alliterated words that started our invitation, the DSS have *challenged*, *changed*, and *confirmed* what we knew about the *words* and *worlds* before, in, around, and beyond the Bible.

Insights into these three areas have been sprinkled throughout the book on focused topics, particularly in the conclusions of the foregoing chapters. But since every book needs to come to an end, I'll stand back here to distinguish the forest from the trees. The refocus is on those categories—the challenge, the change, and the confirmation. I will provide two insights, observations, or recommendations in each area that extend from the more focused and detailed conclusions throughout the book.

What has been challenged?

First, it might be better to shift the relative pronoun there to ask *who* has been challenged. The short answer: us. If your interest in the scrolls is faith-based (that is, you want to explore them to see if and how they might inform your understanding of the Bible, theology, or God) then the DSS present both opportunities and challenges. If your interest in the scrolls is cultural (that is, you want to appreciate how these discoveries might enhance or update our understanding of Judaism and Christianity in antiquity as a bedrock of Western civilization) then they offer a similar blend of challenges and opportunity. Either way, the scrolls touch something that is of great significance to individuals, traditions, communities, and culture. Wherever you locate yourself in that scope of "us", the *words* of the DSS and the *world* of Qumran do challenge us to be open, interested, and even excited about thinking differently. This is very much about us and our time, as well as our perspective on ancient finds.

Second, arguably the biggest challenge of the scrolls is how they press us to rethink the common conceptions or closely held positions about the formation of biblical texts. We saw that for most of the books of the Hebrew Scriptures attested at Qumran, there was more diversity than we might have expected. There were differences in words and phrases among the DSS as well as multiple editions of many books when compared with other known traditions, like the Septuagint, the Samaritan Pentateuch, or the later Masoretic Text.

We also saw that the community of Qumran was likely a scribal one. At a minimum, they preserved texts, but were likely also involved in transmitting them. We observed this scribal community was intellectually engaged and theologically competent and creative. We don't need to agree with or even like all the details of their thought or practice, but it is clear they had their heads in the game and saw a tight connection between what they thought and how they lived.

The scribes of the scrolls were not photocopiers. They participated in crafting a tradition: preserving yet enlivening it. This was not interference. On the contrary, it was an investment. If we want a stable, consistent, word-for-word cloning of ancient words from antiquity through to today, that is neither what we find nor what we should expect to find. Statistically, there is great continuity, but that should not overshadow the differences in texts. This reflection, then, is very much about a challenge about renovating the *words* of scripture as well as our understanding of ancient *worlds* that shaped it.

What has changed?

First, we saw several examples where the DSS have both made modern scripture more ancient by restoring lost or confirmed readings (remember those "textual variants"), and enhanced our understanding and context for the ideas, expressions, and practices of Christianity and Judaism that emerge from the Second Temple period. The content of modern scripture has changed in light of these discoveries, as has the context we now have for understanding scriptural texts.

The "us" element introduced above also comes into play here. With these changes to words, we can reencounter a text and hear it anew, perhaps see it differently, or glean something ancient for the first time. We can and should appreciate the remarkable continuity along with this diversity. Similarly, with this changed context for writings like the New Testament or Mishnah, we can perhaps find a fresh perspective or even recover a bit of backstory about the worlds that shaped the big debates and seemingly minor details of those traditions and the conversations, controversies, and communities behind them.

Second, the way we understand our relationship to ancient finds has changed, is changing, and needs to change. We saw this, for example, in the chapters on discovery stories and the emergence of modern forgeries. It is apparent that the way we describe, remember, and even recreate stories around famous discoveries like the DSS matters. It also reveals a lot about what some might want them to be about. The DSS and Qumran do have historical value, but we are only recently seeing that this can't be abstracted from the modern historiography about what the texts are, why they matter, and who they matter to.

It is also apparent that some of that modern historiography has fueled a market for forgeries. With such a lofty value assigned to the DSS, it's perhaps not surprising (though hugely problematic) that both a supply and demand for "new" DSS and Qumran artifacts (or better, expensive souvenirs) has emerged. The hard lessons learned here should also extend beyond DSS studies, as other fields have or will encounter similar issues. This is a modern reality of studies on antiquity. It should also make us more aware of the ethics, politics, economics, and legal implications of something that was lost and is now found or potentially forged. When ancient or allegedly ancient artifacts suddenly turn up in our world, there needs to be a much longer pause to measure both the opportunity and risks the materials pose for academic research, faith communities, and culture.

What has been confirmed?

First, the DSS have confirmed that the world of Second Temple Judaism was even bigger than we previously knew. Sure, we had decently detailed profiles of ancient groups (Sadducees, Pharisees, Essenes, and others) from classical, Christian, and Jewish sources. In a way, however, the DSS personified some of these profiles by providing insight into the life and thought of at least one group. This group was also in conversation with others in this period. This Essene or Essene-ish group spoke to, about, and against several other groups in the period. Even as insiders, they were engaged and vocal. It wasn't that long ago that it was common to dub the Second Temple period the "years of silence," as if nothing of note happened during this time for two-testament oriented readers. The DSS obliterated this understanding. These years were loud. There were far more conversation partners than previously known.

These conversations also resulted in a much bigger library of texts, of which we only had glimpses before the DSS. Sure, we knew Enoch was a big deal from later pseudepigrapha and hints in biblical writings like Genesis or Jude. But we didn't know Enochic literature was part of a much larger Aramaic anthology of traditions set in orbit around ancestors (men and women) that revealed an uncharted landscape of scribal activity, creativity, intellectual history, and imagination. Examples like these indicate that the DSS aren't providing background for biblical *words* as much as they are foreground impressions, insights, and information into the *worlds* that shaped the texts and traditions that are foundational to Judaism, Christianity, and Western culture.

Second, for all the insights and answers of the last seventy-five years of DSS and Qumran research, the invitation of this book confirmed that there is still work to be done. Publishing the texts was job one. That was long, arduous, complex work. Thanks to those who committed their careers to this task, we can now confirm that we know what the DSS say. As text analysis gave way to synthesis in recent scholarship, however, we're now accounting for what the DSS mean. The meaning of these textual and archaeological discoveries is complex and dynamic, and can only be mapped by ongoing research into both the *words* and *worlds* of the DSS and Qumran. This is just the start of such work.

Perhaps the best image from the DSS to create this impression of ongoing work is what is likely the least celebrated or studied part of the Great Isaiah

Scroll (1QIsaiah[a]) from Cave 1: the final column of the scroll, column 54, some twenty-four feet after the opening of the book. Here the scroll wraps up with the words of Isaiah 66:24, the final verse of the book.

But I'm not concerned here with text or textual variants. Rather, I'll draw your attention to how this scroll was well-worn and well-used, its text faded even in antiquity. Presumably this was the result of being unfurled, read, heard, studied, rerolled, stored ... and repeat. So much so, it seems, that the text itself grew dim, faded. At some point, an ancient scribe reinscribed the words. They invested. They ensured that the end of the scroll did not meet an untimely end, that it was neither lost nor forgotten.

This scribe understood the importance of preserving, of passing along. They understood that for the next generation to find and make meaning would mean ongoing work on their part. That is endless work.

This chapter started with a quote from F. F. Bruce, from the very same 1955 book quoted at the beginning of my introductory chapter. Bruce's words are as true seventy-five years on as they were then: "The story of the Scrolls continues to unfold itself." There will be more that is challenged, changed, and confirmed. The invitation to the world of the DSS and Qumran must remain open.

Finis, for now.

IMAGE 10.1: The fifty-fourth column of 1QIsaiah[a] includes content of Isaiah 66:14–24, and evidences the use and reuse of the scroll as well as several scribal corrections, instances of reinscribed text, and marginal markings. (Image Credit: John C. Trever)

Notes

Preface

1. For a helpful resource demystifying the texts, titles, and scroll references, see Fitzmyer, *A Guide to the Dead Sea Scrolls.*

Introduction

1. The talk was delivered by Martin Abegg and Peter Flint, then co-directors of the Dead Sea Scrolls Institute at Trinity Western University. Eventually Marty and Peter would become my graduate supervisors, mentors, colleagues, and friends.

2. In this book, I use the term *Hebrew Scriptures* to refer to the shared heritage in the Hebrew Bible and Old Testament. Though the books are the same in both collections, their order and shape have important differences. As chapters six and seven show, the DSS come from a time *before* the Bible (Jewish or Christian) existed as a canonical collection and even before books were invented. Throughout this exploration of the DSS, we need to keep that important distinction in mind. When referring to the Bible, I most often mean the two-testament Christian Scriptures, but I will regularly point to the "Hebrew Bible," "Old Testament," or "New Testament" when specificity is needed.

Many of the texts of the DSS beyond the Hebrew Scriptures (which became the Old Testament for Christians) also have importance, authority, and significance for different Christian traditions. While Protestants might not revere, or in many cases be aware of the writings in the Apocrypha, this collection of the Deuterocanon is revered as Scripture by Catholic and Orthodox Christians alike. The DSS of books like Tobit and Ben Sira in their original languages are incredibly important for readers of these traditions. Similarly, writings among the DSS such as Jubilees or 1 Enoch were of great value and even authoritative for some in antiquity—yet it is primarily the Eastern Orthodox tradition, specifically Ethiopic Orthodox Christianity, that received and reveres these writings as Scripture. In these respects, the diversity of canonical contexts is important to recognize, as well as the ways these canons shape and inform theological reflection for the many constituent groups within Judaism and Christianity. Part of the opportunity here is that all these groups, traditions, and communities can look back to the formative period and writings of the DSS for fresh insights from a shared heritage of ancient texts.

3. Before the discovery of the DSS, our earliest and most complete copies of the Hebrew Scriptures were medieval, from about 1000 CE. The most important manuscripts in this regard are the Aleppo Codex and the Leningrad Codex. The DSS provided insights into both the stability and development of scriptural texts from about a millennium earlier.

4. The Second Temple period is the period after the Babylonian exile (587 BCE), when the Jewish communities resettled and rebuilt Jerusalem in the then-Persian province of Judea. Their return during the reign of Cyrus the Great included the endorsement and resources to rebuild the dilapidated Jerusalem temple (538 BCE). This "Second Temple" was a centerpiece of communal, social, religious, and political life in Judea well into the Greco-Roman period. It saw significant expansion under Herod the Great and was the setting of many scenes in the Gospels. The Second Temple was destroyed in 70 CE during the siege of Jerusalem by Titus to quell a Jewish revolt against the Romans. Today, the Western Wall is the primary remains of this structure. The oldest texts of the DSS date to as early as the third century BCE, hence the focus on the mid– to late–Second Temple period in this book.

5. Burrows, *The Dead Sea Scrolls*, foreword, n.p.

Chapter 1

1. The DSS were penned and/or preserved by an ancient Jewish group that lived at the site of Qumran from around the mid-first century BCE to 68 CE. This means their library of texts included many books that would *become* biblical for later traditions as well as many that were not accepted into the canons of Judaism and Christianity. While some of the writings of Paul date to the mid- to late-first century CE, the DSS collection does not include any New Testament writings. The discoveries do, however, add new Jewish texts and contexts for research on Christian origins.

2. This expedition was under the joint direction of Oren Gutfeld and Randall Price. This has been but one of the more recent operations to (re)comb the desert for overlooked scroll caves. For details, see Amanda Borschel-Dan, "In the Qumran Cliffs, an Expedition Digs Up New Dead Sea Scrolls Caves," *The Times of Israel*, January 24, 2019, https://www.timesofisrael.com/in-the-qumran-cliffs-an-expedition-digs-up-new-dead-sea-scroll-caves.

3. The study of paleography is one of the methods for securing approximate date ranges of the DSS. Not unlike pottery styles, Hebrew scripts develop and change over time. The palaeographic typologies for dating manuscripts are typically assigned to different stages (early, late, and mid) of different national periods: archaic scripts (ca. 250–150 BCE), Hasmonean scripts (ca. 150–30 BCE), and Herodian scripts (ca. 30 BCE–70 CE). Scientific methods, such as Carbon-14 testing, have also been applied to some scrolls to confirm or conflict with palaeographical methods. It is important to keep in mind, however, that dating a given *copy* of a text is not the same as dating the actual *composition*. As a rule, most writings at Qumran are older than the copies preserved there.

4. Formally, this style of interpretation is related to ancient forms of dream-vision interpretation or omen divination. In both the Hebrew Joseph narratives and the Aramaic Daniel tales, for example, symbolic elements are often separated from their interpretation by similar phrases: *pishron* in Hebrew or *pitaron* in Aramaic (see Genesis 40:12, 18 and Daniel 5:26; 7:16). The *pesher* interpretive genre at Qumran signals that, in this era, scribes were increasingly understanding the actual text of scripture as containing omens or revelations from the past that now needed to be uncovered and interpreted. This understanding of texts as revelation may seem commonplace for some later traditions, yet in this period it was revolutionary.

5. We don't know as much as we might like about gender identities at Qumran or, more broadly, scribal roles in antiquity. In this volume I will refer to scribes with masculine pronouns. As Charles Halton and Saana Svärd have noted, there is a strong connection between several goddess figures, such as the Sumerian deity Nisaba and the craft of writing, ancient epigraphic evidence for female scribes as early as the Akkad and Ur III eras (ca. 2350–2000 BCE), and diverse sources for the scribal role of women in the "continuum of authorship" of texts (e.g., writing, commissioning, or dictating content). Yet, as they conclude, one of the main reasons scribal craft is predominantly associated with male figures is the "social uses of writing" as "most activities which required reading and writing were male-dominated fields." For these insights as well as current bibliography on the scribal culture of the ancient Near East and women's roles in it, see Halton and Svärd, *Women's Writing of Ancient Mesopotamia*, 25–36.

6. We'll circle back to this term and the mechanisms for establishing a pseudepigraphic perspective a few times. In simplest forms, the term *pseudepigraphy* refers to "the ascription of a literary work to another author by way of title, content, or tradition" (Lange, "In the Second Degree," 40). While it has become common to think

of the Pseudepigrapha as a collection of writings, Reed ("The Modern Invention of 'Old Testament Pseudepigrapha'") demonstrated that it is at best an eighteenth-century CE innovation and something of a catchall category for texts eventually outside the Bible, which is disconnected from how these texts were developed, used, and received in antiquity.

7. This is particularly the case given the variations in content between this Cave 1 exemplar of the *Community Rule* and associated *serekh* traditions found in the Cave 4 fragments. Among the more obvious yet confounding differences is the fact that two manuscripts, 4QS[b] and 4QS[d], are shorter than the form in 1QS, yet seem to have been copied later than the Cave 1 manuscript. As Metso noted, "The evidence of the Cave 4 copies both illuminates and complicates the textual history" of this tradition (*The Serekh Texts*, 17).

8. A second copy of the *Hodayot* (1QH[b]) was subsequently found in Cave 1.

9. Schuller, "Hodayot (1QH and Related Texts)," 748.

10. While the term does not occur in the *Hodayot*, several other places in the DSS reference knowledge of the "secret of the way things are" or, in Hebrew, רז נהיה. For example, the Hebrew text *Instruction* speaks in several places of the centrality of this special understanding, in one instance admonishing the hearer to "Seek the secret of the way things are, and give careful thought to all the ways of truth, look long at the roots of wickedness" (4Q416 2 iii:14). Edward Cook noted that this term expresses the "knowledge of the inflexible purposes of God acquired by study of Scripture and the laws of the sect" (Wise, Abegg, and Cook, *The Dead Sea Scrolls: A New Translation*, 481). The term רז ("mystery") seems to have entered into ancient Jewish thought and language via Aramaic, which carried the concept over from Persian religion. We see it, for example, in the dream-vision narratives of Daniel 2, where both the content and inspired interpretation of Daniel's revelations are described as "mysteries."

11. Like the *Community Rule* and the *Hodayot*, fragments of *War Scroll* traditions were later found in Qumran Cave 4. The variety of content, structure, and detail among these writings found in multiple copies reminds us to think less in terms of fixed forms of *texts* and more about trajectories of *traditions*. This preliminary insight will also help us explore the development and shape of traditions in the biblical scrolls in chapter six.

Chapter 2

1. It is only recently that scholars of biblical studies have started to interrogate the discovery narratives of several key collections of ancient Jewish and Christian texts. In this chapter I will think alongside several of these, but I highly recommend the articles by Goodacre ("How Reliable is the Story of the Nag Hammadi Discovery?") and Mroczek ("True Stories and the Poetics of Textual Discovery").

2. For sample news coverage, see Alexis C. Madrigal, "Do Not Try to Recreate This 16th-Century German Cat Bomb at Home," *Atlantic*, January 23, 2013, and "Young Yoda Turns Up in Medieval Manuscript," *Telegraph*, April 18, 2015.

3. The best and most accessible takes on the discovery tales are those found in Collins, *The Dead Sea Scrolls: A Biography*, 1–32; Schuller, *The Dead Sea Scrolls: What Have We Learned?*, 1–33; and VanderKam, *The Dead Sea Scrolls Today*, 1–20. The most comprehensive and detailed volume of the modern history of the DSS is found in Fields, *The Dead Sea Scrolls: A Full History*.

4. Frank Moore Cross Jr., *Ancient Library of Qumran*, 5. John Trever's early introduction to the DSS launches from a similar point of uncertainty: "Through many retellings, the fragmentary early published accounts concerning what transpired in the scroll story prior to February, 1948, have become legendary" (Trever, *The Untold Story of Qumran*, 101). Not far behind these, F. F. Bruce collected some of the questions over the details of discovery and commented that "no doubt by the time it attained this form, Muhammad's [the initial discoverer] narrative had undergone something of the stream-lining process which form-critics assess as oral tradition tends to undergo as time goes on; even so, it suggests that the precise details of the discovery may be impossible of recovery" (Bruce, *Second Thoughts on the Dead Sea Scrolls*, 14). While details on many fronts have become clearer, it is remarkable that across our earliest DSS introductions there is a recognition of both the varieties of accounts and the challenge of discerning the *actual* circumstances of the early discoveries.

5. Harrison, *The Dead Sea Scrolls: An Introduction*, 2.

6. To complicate matters further, the very first public announcement of the DSS did not involve caves at all. On April 11, 1948, Millar Burrows of Yale University issued a press release from the American School of Oriental Research in *The Times* of London announcing the discovery of four ancient texts "in the Syrian monastery of St. Mark in Jerusalem." This might seem like an odd locale for discovery, yet since the early modern

period, historic libraries of monasteries had become the go-to spot to recover "lost" Jewish, Christian, and classical texts. To correct the confusion over the site of the first DSS finds, on April 26, 1948, Eleazar Sukenik of Hebrew University of Jerusalem issued another release announcing he too had scrolls, but that they seemed to have come from caves in the Judean wilderness. Burrows later noted that the published release did not reflect his original content, which had specified the texts were *acquired* by St. Mark's, not *discovered* there. Was there perhaps some drama behind this edit? Collins noted that, "In view of the intrigue surrounding the discovery, it is also quite conceivable that someone changed the wording deliberately" (Collins, *The Dead Sea Scrolls*, 3–4).

7. Davies, *The Meaning of the Dead Sea Scrolls*, 9.

8. Davies, *The Meaning of the Dead Sea Scrolls*, 9.

9. Allegro, *The Dead Sea Scrolls*, 17–18.

10. Allegro, *The Dead Sea Scrolls*, 19.

11. The Nag Hammadi texts are highly recommended reading— they're confounding and creative. For an introduction and translations, see Myer, *Gnostic Discoveries: The Impact of the Nag Hammadi Library*, and Myer, ed., *The Nag Hammadi Scriptures*. A third modern manuscript find, the Cairo Genizah, could also be considered here, both for the sensational quality of aspects of its find story and for its echoes with the Qumran and Nag Hammadi tales. For more, see Hoffman and Cole, *Sacred Trash: The Lost and Found World of the Cairo Genizah*.

12. The excerpts here are from Pagels, *The Gnostic Gospels*, xiii. See also, Goodacre, "How Reliable is the Story of the Nag Hammadi Discovery?" 304.

13. Mroczek, "True Stories and the Poetics of Textual Discovery," 22

14. The concept of orientalism was first developed in Edward Said's landmark 1978 book, *Orientalism*. Said unpacked the concept as a way of accounting for Western culture's common conceptions or caricatures of the people and places of North Africa, the Middle East, and Asia. The images projected or imagined via orientalism smack of colonialism and political power dynamics from British, French, or American interests. In the case of *The Thousand and One Nights*, an Arabic form of the tales was collected as early as the ninth century CE, from Indian, Persian, Baghdadi, and Cairene traditions. In their most familiar (and often unfortunate) forms in Western culture, we're talking genies, Aladdin, Ali Baba and the Forty Thieves, and Sinbad the Sailor. In a more technical sense, the collection is remarkably diverse, including seductive romances, poems, legendary tales of heroes and heroines, fables with didactic aims, and anecdotes with

comedic flare. By the time white Europeans "discovered" this epic anthology, they were about a millennium late.

15. Both the colonial histories and modern political realities of these regions are complex—there are and will be countless books written on this essential topic. My aim here is not to rush through or diminish this complexity, but to provide a basic context of how colonialism and politics are part of the way find stories develop and are told.

16. My treatment here relies heavily on the account of the DSS discovery by Fields (*The Dead Sea Scrolls*) with some details on the *Genesis Apocryphon* drawn from the following: Avigad and Yadin, *A Genesis Apocryphon: A Scroll from the Wilderness of Judea*; Fitzmyer, *The Genesis Apocryphon of Qumran Cave 1*, 13–25; and Machiela, *The Dead Sea Genesis Apocryphon*, 21–30.

17. Avigad and Yadin, *A Genesis Apocryphon*, 12.

18. In the next chapter we'll see that the Kando family continues to play a role in the ongoing story and controversy of the DSS, as its future generations are still involved in brokering sales, one of which likely involved tiny bits of our Aramaic *Genesis Apocryphon*. For nuance, I should also note that at this point the *Hodayot* scroll was also in two separate "bundles" of sorts prior to its unrolling and deciphering, so it likely appeared as two separate scrolls.

19. Fitzmyer emphasized that the *Genesis Apocryphon* "was found in the early spring of 1947" (*The Genesis Apocryphon*, 13).

20. Trever, *The Dead Sea Scrolls: A Personal Account*, 26.

21. Machiela, *The Dead Sea Genesis Apocryphon*, 21.

22. Trever indicated that he made this observation on a second viewing of the scroll at St. Mark's the same week as his initial impressions and photographs (*The Dead Sea Scrolls: A Personal Account*, 52). However, Yadin has said that the Aramaic identification did not take place until Trever's work on the text in the United States (Yadin, *The Message of the Scrolls*, 144).

23. Trever, "Preliminary Observations on the Jerusalem Scrolls."

24. The rumor of texts hidden in caves in the Judean wilderness dates back many centuries. Joseph Patrich ("Archaeology") tallied at least four such notices. According to a colophon on Origen's *Hexapla*, the Greek version of the Psalms in his translation was said to be found in a jar in a cave of other manuscripts near Jericho (see also Eusebius, *Ecclesiastical History* 6.16.1). Mention of another cave holding biblical manuscripts and other texts in this region is known from a 785 CE letter by Nestorian patriarch Timotheus

I to Sergius, the metropolitan of Elam. The lost "Jericho Pentateuch" of Masoretic tradition was reportedly discovered in a cave. Finally, an inscription from the monarchic period was also found within a cave south of Naḥal Yishai. To these we can add the mysterious case of the Shapira Deuteronomy scroll from 1883. Well before the discovery of Qumran, Moses Wilhelm Shapira approached the British Museum with a scroll he claimed Bedouin retrieved from a cave overlooking Wadi Mujib, a desert stream that runs from the Jordan River into the Dead Sea. The story of Shapira and this scroll are ultimately tragic, as the item eventually disappeared and, following questions over its authenticity, Shapira was driven to suicide in 1884.

25. White Crawford, *Scribes and Scrolls at Qumran*, 138. This figure indicates that, once again, the Ta'amireh Bedouin found the cave first and removed many scrolls found on a surface level. Some also found their way into the hands of Kando, presumably by the same channel. Unfortunately, Kando tucked some scrolls away for a rainy day in a tube buried beneath the stoop of his house. When the capsule was recovered in 1953, humidity had so damaged the finds that they had been reduced to jelly (Fields, *The Dead Sea Scrolls*, 505). So early on we are already contending not only with natural deterioration but also with modern damage due to mishandling.

26. For this figure and historic exchange rate calculation, see Fields, *The Dead Sea Scrolls*, 33.

27. As detailed below, the series title would later change to *Discoveries in the Judean Desert* (DJD for short) to reflect the political realities and shifts in borders in Israel's War of Independence. The DJD series was published by Oxford University Press over several decades. For a full bibliography, see the Hebrew University of Jerusalem's online index at orion.huji.ac.il/resources/djd.shtml. I will periodically cite and reference entries in this series. For simplicity's sake, I will do so by referring to the DJD volume number, not the specific title and editor of the individual texts within the volumes. For the Hebrew University scrolls, see Sukenik, *The Dead Sea Scrolls of the Hebrew University* (1955), with the Hebrew edition of this work published in 1954.

28. Avigad and Yadin, *A Genesis Apocryphon*, 13.

29. Barthélemy and Milik published the text as "Apocalypse de Lamech" (DJD 1, 86). For a complete publication history of the *Genesis Apocryphon*, see Machiela, *The Dead Sea Genesis Apocryphon*, 21–26.

30. For a perspective on the DSS from this angle, see the excellent essay "The Real Question: The Nation, The Object, and Owning the Past," by Kalman and du Toit in *Canada's Big Biblical Bargain*, 123–34.

Chapter 3

1. The story around this forgery is almost too bizarre to be true. See now the excellent treatment by Ariel Sabar, *Veritas: A Harvard Professor, A Con Man and the Gospel of Jesus's Wife*. For discussion of the features debunking this modern forgery, see Bernhard, "The *Gospel of Jesus' Wife*;" and Bernhard, "Postscript: A Final Note About the Origin of *The Gospel of Jesus' Wife*."

2. With rapid changes in technology, I suspect that artificial intelligence will have a much larger role to play in the analysis and authentication of "new" finds. In the future, technologies based in blockchain will also contribute to enhancing claims or documentation related to authentication or even chain of custody.

3. The year 1978 is another important date, as it marks the introduction of Israeli Antiquities Law 5738. Similar to the UNESCO convention, this places strict limits on the discovery and movement of artifacts found in the modern state of Israel.

4. Publications of these materials to this point is limited to the following, many of which have since had to be revised or reframed in the published or public record due to verification of forgeries after publication. See: Elgvin, Davis, and Langlois, eds., *Gleanings from the Caves: Dead Sea Scrolls and Artefacts from The Schøyen Collection*; Tov, Davis, and Duke, eds., *Dead Sea Scrolls Fragments in the Museum Collection*; and Tov, "New Fragments of Amos." While the general content of the Azusa and Southwestern fragments are known from exhibition catalogs and media coverage, they are yet to be published. For good measure, we could also note that the Oriental Institute of the University of Chicago has an authentic Qumran fragment of *Sapiential Admonitions* (4Q184) in their holdings. Thanks to Årstein Justnes for also pointing out to me that Craig and Joel Lampe purchased fragments in 2002, later selling them to a collector in New Zealand in 2014. Bruce Ferrini also brokered a sale of a fragment to Ashland Theological Seminary in 2004.

5. For example, the rumored "Aramaic Enoch Scroll," which has an almost mythic quality in DSS lore. See the comments by John Strugnell in Shanks, "An Interview with John Strugnell." This unicorn of an artefact is so fabled that, at the time of my writing, it even has its own Wikipedia page: "Aramaic Enoch Scroll." Another fabled text is the so-called "Angel Scroll," which reportedly almost surfaced in 1999.

6. The legal status and behavior of modern corporations has been critically and creatively engaged by Joel Bakan in the book turned documentary, *The Corporation*.

7. For appropriately critical yet nuanced views regarding processes of acquisition and the curation of the collection by the Greens, focusing on some of their more (in)famous items, see the Associated Press coverage of "Ancient Tablet Acquired by Hobby Lobby Going Back to Iraq" (https://apnews.com/article/ancient-assyrian-tablet-hobby-lobby-repatriated-iraq-ee765961c1cd91226c8c734dadda0596) and "Bible Museum Admits Some of Its Dead Sea Scrolls are Fake" (https://apnews.com/article/b5cfe168fb004f229634ebe6f3fe57ac).

8. Talking about these fragments can become rather cumbersome. Rather than redundantly using the vocabulary of "alleged," "so-called," "potential," or "claimed" DSS fragments through this chapter—which, trust me, will get annoying—I'll use the term "new/old" fragments. By this I mean all the fragments that have surfaced since the mid-1990s, in particular those now held in private collections. The list below includes those items confirmed as forgeries for the collections now published, as well as insights from ongoing study and general consensus over the likelihood of particular items as fakes in yet-to-be published materials. For the record, I'm of the position that even those marked in the table as "to be determined" are likely to be forgeries.

9. VanderKam, *The Dead Sea Scrolls and the Bible*, 210.

10. Tov, "Introduction," in *Dead Sea Scrolls Fragments in the Museum Collection*, 11.

11. Duke Helfand, "Southern California Universities Acquire Rare Religious Texts," *Los Angeles Times*, September 14, 2009.

12. In this section, I cite several sections from Schøyen's published essay on "Acquisition and Ownership History: A Personal Reflection," in Elgvin, Davis, and Langlois, eds., *Gleanings from the Caves*, 27–32.

13. For an exceptional interrogation of the acquisition narratives of the private collections, see the essay by Årstein Justnes, "Fragments for Sale: Dead Sea Scrolls" in *Marginalia*, available online at https://tinyurl.com/w8y9f92a.

14. Fields delivered the lecture, "Dead Sea Scrolls: Significance of the Latest Developments," on April 16, 2011. The full video can be viewed online at https://www.youtube.com/watch?v=cOcNhHsGKu4.

15. As Årstein Justnes reminded me, Frank Moore Cross apparently had a different recollection that did not include a meeting under a bridge. See Moore Cross, "Reminiscences of the Early Days in the Discovery and Study of the Dead Sea Scrolls."

16. One overlooked fact of the Daniel discoveries is that 4QDaniel[a] (4Q112) was among the lot of fragments that McGill University in Montreal offered funds to secure in the early years of acquisition (Kalman and du Toit, *Canada's Big Biblical Bargain*, 60, 166, 174). Details of other potential Daniel acquisitions, however, are less secure and more sordid. In the appendix of Fields's history of discovery, he claims knowledge of a Daniel scroll photographed by then–CIA representative to Damascus, Miles Copeland, on the rooftop of the American Legation. When the scroll was unrolled, the wind reportedly picked up and ripped off a large portion, which was permanently lost. The photographs were said to be shown later to an American Embassy official in Beirut, who identified the item as coming from Daniel. Fields concludes, "The merchant [showing the item and images] never returns to claim his scroll, and both photographs and scroll disappear" (Fields, *The Dead Sea Scrolls*, 498). These events are said to have taken place in August 1947. Fields also notes that when Sukenik purchased 1QIsaiah[b] fragments and a set of scroll jars via an intermediary who went by the codename "Mister X," the purchase "possibly [included] some Daniel fragments as well" (Fields, *The Dead Sea Scrolls*, 499). Though these hints of Daniel fragments are unverifiable—and have many sensational qualities—they underscore how the authenticity, origins, and chain of custody of many early finds is far from secure.

17. Tov, "Introduction," 3.

18. Duke, Holt, and Russell, "Daniel 10:18–20," in *Dead Sea Scroll Fragments in the Museum Collection*, 200–209.

19. Yardeni's analysis and report on the script are included in Duke, Holt, and Russell, "Daniel 10:18–20," 202–203.

20. Davis, "Palaeographical and Physical Features," 26.

21. Duke, Holt, and Russell, "Daniel 10:18–20," 204.

22. Davis, "Caves of Dispute," 248.

23. The note in the critical apparatus of BHS reads: "prp c pc Mss 𝔊 וֶאֱמָץ vel וְהִתְחַזֵּק." The editors of this edition are suggesting, "Perhaps we should read with a few other known Masoretic manuscripts and the Septuagint, which include 'and be strong,' or 'and strengthen yourself.'" The latter option clearly coheres with the exact reading and reconstruction of the Museum of the Bible fragment. For the earlier reading and proposal, see the German language commentary by Marti, *Das Buch Daniel*, 76).

24. The apparent deployment of readings from earlier Hebrew Bible editions in the new/old fragments was noted already by Elgvin, "Texts and Artefacts," in Elgvin, Davis,

and Langlois, eds., *Gleanings from the Caves*, 51–60, esp. 53. For a description of many of the features noted here in the larger context of the private collections, see also Davis, "Caves of Dispute," and Elgvin and Langlois, "Looking Back."

25. The most relevant academic articles for our topic include Trever, "Completion of the Publication of Some Fragments from Qumran Cave 1" and "1QDan[a]: The Latest of the Qumran Manuscripts." For his expertly researched and written popular introductions, see Trever, *The Untold Story of Qumran* and *The Dead Sea Scrolls: A Personal Account.*

26. In his foreword to Trever's volume, Trever's colleague Frank Moore Cross commented on the scholarly acumen and photographic skill of Trever, specifically Trever's ability to bring many details of the manuscripts into view that are "not apparent in black and white reproduction." Moore Cross underscores the lasting importance of the images for capturing "the appearance of the scrolls at the time of their optimal condition" (Foreword, *Scrolls from Qumrān Cave I from Photographs by John C. Trever*).

27. These fragments were published by Torleif Elgvin and Årstein Justnes, "1QDan[a] (1Q71) with MS 1926/4a (Dan 2.4–5)," in Elgvin, Davis, and Langlois, eds., *Gleanings from the Caves*, 247–56; and Kipp Davis and Torleif Elgvin, "1QDan[b] (1Q72) with MS 1926/4b (Dan 3.26–27)," in *Gleanings from the Caves*, 257–70.

28. See Lönnqvist and Lönnqvist, "Parallels to Be Seen: Manuscripts in Jars from Qumran and Egypt," and Magness, *The Archaeology of Qumran*, 84–119.

29. Trever, "Completion of the Publication," 327.

30. For paleographic descriptions, see Trever, "Completion of the Publication," 333–34; Trever, "1QDan[a]," 279–82; Elgvin and Justnes, "1QDan[a]," 249–50; and Davis and Elgvin, "1QDan[b]," 259.

31. Davis and Elgvin, "1QDan[b]," 261–62. For the text of this section of 1QDaniel[b], see Ulrich, *The Biblical Qumran Scrolls*, 760.

32. Elgvin and Justnes, "1QDan[a]," 247.

33. Elgvin and Justnes, "1QDan[a]," 247–48.

34. It is now apparent that there were many such fragments floating around in the early days of discovery and acquisition, often gifted but rarely studied. Fields notes, for example, another instance of this, when the young German scholar Claus-Hunno Hunzinger received "a few small uninscribed fragments as a souvenir," apparently to mark the occasion of his twenty-eighth birthday while in Jerusalem on September 5, 1957 (Fields, *The Dead Sea Scrolls*, 513). These are now on display at the Qumran & Bible Exhibition. The private collection of Alexander Shick too has some uninscribed DSS

fragments as part of a travelling collection. Canadian scholar R. B. Y. Scott of McGill University also made early purchases in Jerusalem, including a few small fragments with only a few letter traces, which were later donated to McGill University.

35. For this date, see Trever, *Scrolls from Qumrān Cave I*, 7.

36. Davis and Elgvin, "1QDan[b]," 257.

37. Legal scholar Lisa Borodkin found that the economics of antiquities trading in Peru in the mid-1990s generated almost as much revenue as the regional cocaine trade, yet with far fewer occupational hazards ("The Economics of Antiquities Looting and a Proposed Legal Alternative," 378). Make no mistake: antiquities trafficking is as illegal as the drug trade. When it comes to the movement of illicitly acquired artifacts of cultural heritage, Mackenzie, Brodie, Yates, and Tsirogiannis overviewed how an item "undergoes a complex series of negotiations and transformations." It changes hands and experiences degrees of "cleansing" in a transnational crime process.

> Starting as an archaeological artefact, it then becomes loot, then contraband, then a commodity, then finally a collectible object of artistic or historical interest. ... That a looted and illegal antiquity can, through this process, become a legal commodity based on the transnational nature of the crime is a nearly unique feature of the illicit antiquities trade. Most other illicit commodities remain illegal through the course of their smuggling and are always illegal at their point of sale. ... To labour the point, perhaps more than is necessary: the Metropolitan Museum of Art is not in the position to spend $1 million on 50 kilos of trafficked cocaine, to put it on public display, to then defend the purchase in the newspaper as a 'public good', and only turn the cocaine over to the authorities 30 years later without anyone facing punishment." (*Trafficking Culture,* n.p.)

Chapter 4

1. Navigating classical sources can be a task in and of itself. A collection of all the relevant materials can be found in Vermes and Goodman, *The Essenes According to the Classical Sources*. The most relevant passages to the overviews presented in this chapter are Josephus, *Jewish War* 1.78–80; 2.113; 2.119–61; 2.567; 3.11; 5.145; *Antiquities of the Jews* 13.171–72; 15.371–79; 18.18–22; *Life* 10–11; Philo, *Every Good Man is Free* 75–91; *Apologia pro Ioudaeis* (i.e., *Hypothetica*); Pliny, *Natural History* 5.15.70. Pliny acknowledges that his work is based on sources and not on firsthand experience. Other later writers, such as Dio Chrysostom, Synesius, and Julius Solinus provide similar perspectives to Pliny's writings.

2. While the writings, culture, and thought of Second Temple Judaism were once thought of as background for the New Testament, Richard Bauckham captured well the more nuanced approach of contemporary research: "Most New Testament scholars would now agree that the New Testament writings belong wholly within the Jewish world of their time. However much some may be in serious conflict with other Jewish groups, these disagreements take place within the Jewish world. Even New Testament words authored by and/or addressed to non-Torah-observant Gentile Christians still move within the Jewish world of ideas" (*The Jewish World around the New Testament*, 1). A great resource for seeing the New Testament in its Jewish context is Levine and Brettler, eds., *The Jewish Annotated New Testament*—an NRSV Study Bible with introductions and footnotes on items of Jewish thought, culture, and practice in the contextual world of the early Jesus movement. In chapter 9, we'll bring the New Testament and the DSS into a direct encounter with each other.

3. For readers less familiar with the rabbinic writings, the best guide to the Mishnah is Strack and Stemberger, *Introduction to the Talmud and Midrash*. Also, the online project *Sefaria* (www.sefaria.org) now includes open-access introductions and translations of countless key Jewish texts covering more than three thousand years of scripture, literature, liturgy, philosophy, and beyond.

4. Many texts in the DSS interpret the scriptures by rewriting them. Most often the points of departure are narratives of the Pentateuch, but the *Pseudo-Ezekiel* materials (4Q385, 4Q386, 4Q388, and 4Q391) are an example of both the reuse and adoption of the first-person voice of a scriptural source. For comment on this instance of prophetic writing and details of the phenomena in other texts, see Zahn, *Genres of Rewriting in Second Temple Judaism*, 45, 172. We'll come back to this approach of rewriting and extending the scriptures in chapters 7 and 8.

5. Earlier writings in the Hebrew Scriptures have a more limited view of expectations for existence beyond death. The most notable views of the afterlife reference Sheol, a seemingly murky underworld of varied understanding across texts (Genesis 42:38; Numbers 16:30; Psalms 6:5; 9:17; 89:48; Proverbs 15:11; Isaiah 14:9; Hosea 13:14). The Hebrew Scriptures don't have a term or concept equivalent to "hell." It is not until the translation of the King James Version in 1611 that most occurrences of the Hebrew term *Sheol* are rendered with the English term *hell*. This is highly problematic, as Israelite religion and thought had no such category. It is only later texts in the Hebrew Scriptures, such as Isaiah 26:19 or Daniel 12:2, that have hints of resurrection hopes. On afterlife outlooks in the Hebrew Scriptures, see the excellent treatment by Johnston, *Shades of*

Sheol. It is generally not until the writings of the Second Temple period that we have more advanced ideas of postmortem fates or abodes. Some of the earliest such views from this period speak of raising bodies, but not general resurrection (1 Enoch 22 or Jubilees 23:31). It is also important to note the diversity of thought in this era: the wisdom tradition of Ben Sira, for instance, retains the finality of the grave and the end destination of Sheol (Ben Sira 15:16–17; 41:4). For a treatment of ancient Jewish texts and outlooks, see Elledge, *Resurrection of the Dead in Early Judaism: 200 BCE–CE 200*. In chapter 9, we'll see that the Hebrew text of *Messianic Apocalypse* (4Q251) includes an explicit reference to resurrection in terms very similar to what we find in the Gospels.

6. Incidentally, this text provides a different interpretation of Miriam's marriage, as Josephus states her union with "Hur" (*Ant*. 3.2.4).

7. VanderKam, *An Introduction to Early Judaism*, 30.

8. This abbreviated title is based on key content of the opening lines of the text, which indicates that the writer is communicating to an external group or groups regarding "some works of the law." The transliterated Hebrew of this line is *Miqsat Ma'ase ha-Torah*—hence the shorthand "MMT."

9. Fields, *The Dead Sea Scrolls*, 58.

10. For additional details on early Essene identifications—and tensions over who had the idea first—see Collins, *The Dead Sea Scrolls: A Biography*, 32–35.

11. Cross, *Ancient Library of Qumran*, 54.

12. VanderKam and Flint, *The Meaning of the Dead Sea Scrolls*, 241.

13. This point is worth a pause: both Josephus and Philo's perspectives on marriage and family are colored by their views of women, which are at best less than positive and more often openly misogynistic. Like all our sources, we need to interpret them critically and evaluate what they are reflecting from the worlds around them versus what the authors themselves are projecting into their materials.

14. This model likely evolved or was described differently by different scribes. We sense this by references to another group within the group in some *Community Rule* manuscripts (such as 4QS[b]), referred to as "the many."

15. The *Damascus Document* (CD for short) is a text found at Qumran in multiple fragmentary copies, but also known in more complete form in two manuscripts from the Cairo Genizah discoveries. The Qumran and Cairo materials are complementary in many ways, but they also reveal development and diversity. The CD "describes how a group was formed as the elect remnant in the wake of the destruction of the First Temple, its

establishment as a separatist community, and the events of its early history," and outlines the group's end-time beliefs, legal ordinances, and admonitions (Goldman, "Damascus Document (D)," 306).

16. That pithy description of liturgy is mine, and it's meant to capture the gist of what liturgy is and does. A more detailed definition is "any set of rituals (voluntary, repeated bodily actions that are assigned spiritual or cosmic significance) meant for public or communal performance. Liturgies can be part of a calendrical cycle of rights, or mark key turning points in the life of a community or an individual in relation to the community. Liturgies provide time with a structure, give the community an identity, coordinate different types of experience in order to present reality as a unified and comprehensible whole, and serve as paradigmatic patterns of actions that may be drawn on even outside the sacral or religious sphere" (Davila, "Liturgical Works from Qumran," 890).

17. Schiffman, *Reclaiming the Dead Sea Scrolls*, 304.

18. It seems that the Teacher was attacked by the Wicked Priest on the Day of Atonement, which is only possible if the two were functioning on different calendars: while one was pursuing in attack, the other was recognizing the holy day according to the sectarian calendar (1QpHab 11:4–8).

19. Collins, *Beyond the Qumran Community*, 209.

Chapter 5

1. This also means that our tour de Qumran will rely on the expertise of others. I've had the great pleasure of experiencing the site in person. I've also had the opportunity to learn from others in my research and teaching. Throughout this chapter, you'll hear echoes of archaeological experts and footnotes of observations, insights, and questions from what I have found to be the strongest reports and summaries of Qumran archaeology. Primary conversation partners, and recent yet accessible resources you might want to explore further, include: Hanan Eshel, *Qumran: Scrolls, Caves, History*; Flint, *The Dead Sea Scrolls*, 11–27; Magness, *The Archaeology of Qumran*; Mizzi, "Archaeology of Qumran;" Schiffman, *Reclaiming the Dead Sea Scrolls*, 37–61; VanderKam, *The Dead Sea Scrolls Today*, 2–46; and White Crawford, *Scribes and Scrolls at Qumran*, 115–216.

2. The primary materials used for the scrolls at Qumran included prepared sheets of leather stitched together (using hides from sheep, calves, goats, gazelles, or ibex) or papyrus (an Egyptian invention using stripped and squashed reeds from the *Cyperus papyrus* plant, which exudes a glue of sorts to solidify the sheets). The *Copper Scroll*, as

its name suggests, is an exception, with its content pounded into what appears to be a one-of-a-kind scroll of copper. Leather scrolls often have rule or margin lines lightly cut or drawn on to guide the scribe's work. Writing on the correct side of papyrus would allow for natural horizontal lines of sorts to inscribe content. Inks were typically carbon based, developed from charcoal or soot, diluted with water and possibly other elements, such as botanical gall. A very few texts at Qumran have words, phrases, or headings in red ink (for example, 4QNumbers[b] and 4QDamascusDocument[e]). Unfortunately, some elements of scroll preparation (cut rule lines) or execution (inks) are the causes of deterioration over the centuries. For a more detailed overview, see Ingo Kottsieper, "Physicality of Manuscripts and Material Culture."

3. The summaries and figures for Caves 1 through 11 are drawn, with some revision, from Flint, *The Dead Sea Scrolls*, 11–12, and White Crawford, *Scribes and Scrolls of Qumran*, 115–65. For basic details of the latest cave discovery, see Ilan Ben Zion, "New Dead Sea Scroll Cave Found Near Qumran, But Scrolls Are Gone," *The Times of Israel*, February 8, 2017, www.timesofisrael.com/new-dead-sea-scroll-cave-found-near-qumran-but-scrolls-are-gone.

4. White Crawford (*Scribes and Scrolls of Qumran*, 121) noted that the private collection of Martin Schøyen also includes a linen scroll wrapper, cord, and fiber palm tool from Cave 11.

5. Note that the numbering of the caves reflects a now-larger constellation of some six hundred caves in the Judean wilderness and Dead Sea region that have been identified or revisited in ongoing archaeological surveys following the initial wave of discoveries in the 1940s and 50s. My focus is on the caves from the initial wave of discoveries and on the "twelfth" cave (technically Cave 53), which has evidence suggesting the presence of scrolls in the past, and contained artifacts similar to those found in the first eleven caves.

6. Citing the research of Hebrew University of Jerusalem archaeologist and archaeometries Jan Gunneweg in Flint, *The Dead Sea Scrolls*, 21.

7. While the connection between the Qumran archaeological site itself and the scrolls found in the caves has been contested, the scholarly consensus today is that there is undoubtedly a connection between the two. Collins remarked, "It obviously makes a huge difference whether the Scrolls are thought to have come from the site. Most scholars remain persuaded that the proximity of the Caves to the ruins was not mere coincidence" (*The Dead Sea Scrolls,* 84). Flint (*The Dead Sea Scrolls*, 19–21) summarized additional key factors pointing to a connection, including the physical evidence of shared pottery styles and ancient pathways, as well as shared concerns for purity in the DSS and the evidence for purity pools throughout the Qumran site. Some have critiqued the

connection, noting that scrolls were found in caves but not at the site. But this is a moot point. Any scrolls that may have been within the settlement would have been damaged, destroyed, or deteriorated, starting with the onslaught of the site by the Romans in the first century CE and continuing with the exposure to the elements since. As we will see later in the chapter, there is important evidence for scribal activity at the site of Qumran.

8. Much of my summary here is informed by Magness, *The Archaeology of Qumran*. For a summary of de Vaux's proposals and subsequent or alternative theories of the archaeology of Qumran, see VanderKam, *The Dead Sea Scrolls Today*, 20–33.

9. While the function of the site at this early time is unknown, Schiffman suggested that "the site may have served as an outpost of the Judean military" (*Reclaiming the Dead Sea Scrolls*, 38).

10. That the figure of 390 is not strictly a chronological marker is also suggested by its reuse here from earlier texts such as Ezekiel 4:4–6. In this way the materials in the *Damascus Document* interweave a group self-understanding with scriptural interpretation and a memory of their foundations.

11. The most stark evidence of this destruction are finds of Roman tri-barbed arrowheads at Qumran. After this destruction, the Qumran site was used by the Romans as an outpost, which is evident from "the large number of bronze and other metal items, especially twelve buckles associated with Roman armor, and some weaponry" (White Crawford, *Scribes and Scrolls at Qumran*, 82). Following this Roman occupation, the Qumran site was briefly used by members of the Bar Kokbha revolt (132–135 CE).

12. Magness, *The Archaeology of Qumran*, 201.

13. Magness, *The Archaeology of Qumran*, 211. Similarly, White Crawford noted that "one remarkable feature of the material finds is the almost complete absence of gendered objects associated with women" (*Scribes and Scrolls at Qumran*, 202).

14. White Crawford, *Scribes and Scrolls at Qumran*, 182. The possibility that the caves or more temporary structures such as tents served as dwellings has also been debated. But the size of the caves is not conducive to occupation, and there are no material remains of tent structures (Schiffman, *Reclaiming the Dead Sea Scrolls*, 42–43). We'll see below that the large communal spaces and dishware discoveries also suggest the community was home to (or hosted) larger gatherings.

15. Hanan Eshel, *Qumran: Scrolls, Caves, History*, 61.

16. White Crawford called attention to the stepped pool installations "throughout Judea, and especially those in the priests' quarter in the Upper City of Jerusalem prior to

the fall of the temple in 70 [CE], which have been identified as ritual immersion facilities" (*Scribes and Scrolls at Qumran*, 206).

17. Our classical sources are also relevant for this timestamp on the archaeological record. Josephus referenced a quake in the region in the seventh year of Herod's rule (*Ant.* 15.121).

18. Schiffman, *Reclaiming the Dead Sea Scrolls*, 42.

19. These figures are from Magness, *The Archaeology of Qumran*, 144, which summarizes the first (and only) analysis of the animal bone deposits from de Vaux's early dig. That analysis was undertaken by Frederick Zeuner in 1960.

20. Items such as the inkwells are relevant for providing some potential implements for scribal activity. The scribal character of the DSS manuscripts themselves is also an intriguing area of study for exploring what may be distinctive features of so-called "Qumran scribal practice." This can range from items such as spelling to spacing of words to the execution of the writing itself (for example, in the use of four dots or paleo-Hebrew script to write the divine name of God). For a deep dive into the scribal world of the DSS, see Tov, *Scribal Practices and Approaches Reflected in the Texts Found in the Judean Desert*.

21. See the excerpt from de Vaux's proposal in VanderKam and Flint, *The Meaning of the Dead Sea Scrolls*, 40, who remark that de Vaux's proposal aroused much controversy.

22. Schiffman, *Reclaiming the Dead Sea Scrolls*, 48.

23. Magness, *The Archaeology of Qumran*, 121.

24. For a news article summary of this recent discovery see Alan Boyle, "Toilet Tied to Tale of Dead Sea Scrolls," *NBC News*, November 13, 2006, nbcnews.com/id/wbna15689591.

25. Incidentally, Josephus commented on Essene practices for relieving themselves in the wilderness that did *not* include a toilet. According to him, new Essenes were provided with a small hatchet on admittance to the sect (*War* 2.137), one of the uses of which was to dig a hole for relieving themselves outside the camp. Josephus' descriptions also note the importance of Essenes covering themselves with a garment to avoid exposing nakedness in this process (*War* 2.148).

Chapter 6

1. *Revised Standard Version Holy Bible* (New York: Thomas Nelson and Sons, 1952), iv.

2. Remember that there were no New Testament books found at Qumran, so the conversations around biblical scrolls refer to those writings that contain texts and traditions relevant to the Hebrew Bible and Old Testament. Remember also that I refer to the common heritage of these canons as "the Hebrew Scriptures."

3. Metzger and Ehrman, *The Text of the New Testament*, 12.

4. The process and outcomes of canonization vary between religious traditions in Judaism and Christianity. There are also debates on when clusters of authoritative texts emerge for writers and communities in antiquity. Compare, for example, the references to emerging categories of scriptures in Prologue to Ben Sira; 2 Maccabees 2:13–15; 4QMMT C 10–11; Luke 24:44; Mishnah Yadayim 3.5; *Against Apion* 1.38–42; *Contempl. Life* 25. For a detailed discussion on the formation of Jewish scriptures, see Lim, *The Formation of the Hebrew Canon*, 1–53. For discussion of both Hebrew Scripture and the Christian canon, see McDonald, *The Biblical Canon: Its Origin, Transmission, and Authority*.

5. Mroczek, *The Literary Imagination in Jewish Antiquity*, 4.

6. This statistic is based on the collations of Emanuel Tov, who tallies 930 scrolls among the DSS collection, 210 to 212 of which he classifies as "biblical scrolls" (*Textual Criticism of the Hebrew Bible*, 94–95).

7. For the origins and features of the MT tradition, see Tov, *Textual Criticism of the Hebrew Bible*, 24–74. While it is common to underscore the importance of the MT tradition for our earliest and most compete manuscripts of the Hebrew Bible, scholars routinely overlook the essential resources for the Hebrew Scriptures attested in the Cairo Genizah. This collection includes biblical manuscripts which provide insight into what is often a gap in time and data between the DSS and the Masoretic codices. Take, for example, the important Ashkar-Gilson scroll with text of Exodus 9:13–13:2. The manuscript dates to the seventh or eighth centuries CE. For a profile of this scroll and its significance, see Sanders, "The Ashkar-Gilson Manuscript."

8. This clever English example comes from Brown, *A Handbook to Old Testament Exegesis*, 47. Some Greek manuscripts of both the LXX and the New Testament present a similar challenge. "Uncial" manuscripts present the running scriptural text with reduced space between words, written in all caps. This leaves it to the reader to discern divisions in the text. Metzger and Ehrman illustrated this challenge with a famous English example: GODISNOWHERE (*The Text of the New Testament*, 22). What could this mean? Split one way, the text could mean, "God is now here." Divided differently, it could say the opposite, "God is nowhere." To this, I would add the distinctly Canadian reading, "God,

I snow here!" In most cases, of course, the common sense divisions of a passage are evident. When they're not, we can determine the best reading from other Greek manuscripts.

9. Take, for example, the Hebrew consonants ספר. Depending on the vowels supplied, this could be many words: סַפָּר ("he wrote" or "he counted"), סֵפֶר ("book"), סֹפֵר ("scribe"), סְפָר ("calculation" or "coast"), or סִפּוּר ("story"). In fact, one medieval Jewish mystical text, *Sefer Yetzirah*, plays with three of these meanings—"book," "count," and "story"—to explain the foundations of God's creative acts.

Note also that vocalization was only one of the investments the Masoretes made in their scriptural texts. They also included markings for accents and syllables, cantillation guides for liturgical readings, marginal markings or comments, and a series of notes of symbols that are effectively proto–linguistic analytics.

10. The alleged origins of the LXX are related in the Letter of Aristeas, which though legendary in many respects, includes important insight into aspects of the early initiative. As the story goes, at the request of Alexander's librarian, the High Priest in Jerusalem dispatched seventy-two men to Alexandria to render the Pentateuch into Greek. They each stole away to their solitary study spaces for seventy-two days on the island of Pharos. Upon regrouping, the translators found their work was truly miraculous: they had all individually translated the exact same thing! The rhetoric of the account, of course, is meant to instill divine providence in the human task, and to present the Greek scriptures as a reliable and authentic representation of the Hebrew ancestral traditions in an age of increasing Hellenization. For more on the historical setting of the earliest Greek translations, see Jobes and Silva, *Invitation to the Septuagint*, 29–44. For another excellent introduction to the content and significance of the LXX, see Law, *When God Spoke Greek*. For English translations of the Septuagint, see Pietersma and Wright, eds., *A New English Translation of the Septuagint*, and Penner et al., eds., *The Lexham English Septuagint*.

11. For the social, archaeological, and historical background of Samaritan Judaism, see Knoppers, *Jews and Samaritans*; and Pummer, *The Samaritans: A Profile*.

12. On the dating of SP texts and traditions, see Anderson and Gils, *The Samaritan Pentateuch: An Introduction*, 137–46; and Lim, "The Emergence of the Samaritan Pentateuch."

13. Ulrich, *The Dead Sea Scrolls and the Developmental Composition of the Bible*, 169–86.

14. VanderKam and Flint noted that of the some six thousand variants between the SP and the MT, nineteen hundred agree with the LXX (*The Meaning of the Dead Sea Scrolls*, 92). As Knoppers noted, for example, the "Mount Gerizim" reading of Deuteronomy 27:4 discussed above finds some support in the Greek Papyrus Giessen 19, the Greek *Samareitikon*, and *Vetus Latina* ("Toward a Critical Edition of the Samaritan Pentateuch: Reflections on Issues and Methods," 169).

15. Zahn, "The Samaritan Pentateuch and the Scribal Culture of Second Temple Judaism," 308. For additional examples of the editorial features of the SP and their heritage in select Qumran manuscripts, see Tov, *Textual Criticism of the Hebrew Bible*, 81–93.

16. For the complete data in the original languages, see Ulrich, *The Biblical Qumran Scrolls*. To encounter the forms of scripture at Qumran with variant readings in English translation, see Abegg, Flint, and Ulrich, *The Dead Sea Scrolls Bible*.

17. VanderKam and Flint, *The Meaning of the Dead Sea Scrolls*, 133.

18. Baltzer, *Deutero-Isaiah*, 423–24. Other commentaries confirming the text-critical impact of the "light" reading in the DSS and LXX include: Oswalt, *The Book of Isaiah*, 399 and Paul, *Isaiah 40–66*, 411–12.

19. Sanders, *The Dead Sea Psalms Scroll*, 10.

20. The phrase "Blessed be the Lord and blessed be his name forever and ever" is also a noticeable difference from other witnesses. Variations on this phrase feature throughout Psalm 145 in 11QPsalms[a] as a sort of recurring motif or rhythmic marker. Features like this suggest that 11QPsalms[a] may have functioned in liturgy. For discussion on this point, see Flint, *The Dead Sea Psalms*, 209.

21. Goldingay, *Psalms*, vol. 3, 702. As with the Isaiah 53:11 variant, not everyone agrees on the originality of the *nun* verse in Psalm 145. For views and debates, see Hossfeld and Zenger, *Psalms 3*, 144–45.

22. Allen, *Psalms 101–150*, 367.

23. This isn't the only place where Josephus and the scriptural DSS join forces to provide us with new insight into the scope and shape of scripture in ancient Judaism. The Greek LXX and Hebrew MT often reflect what is now known as a shorter version of the book of Joshua. While 4QJoshua[a] (dated to about 100 BCE) shares many details with the LXX and MT, it also reveals important differences in structure and scope. Most notably, this manuscript includes the sequence of building an altar right after the entry into the promised land in Joshua 5:2–7; 8:34–35. This sequence also appears in Josephus's

retelling of the Joshua narrative (*Ant.* 5.16–20), which suggests the text he worked with also had the order of events as now known from the Qumran Cave 4 text of Joshua.

24. Commentators who argue for the originality of the paragraph from 4QSamuel[a] include McCarter, *1 Samuel*, 200; and Klein, *1 Samuel*, 102–3.

25. This approach also challenges us to rethink the theologies that drive traditional text critical aims at securing an original. Eugene Ulrich reflected, "Because the text of each book [of the Hebrew Scriptures] was produced organically, in multiple layers, determining 'the original text' is a difficult, complex task; and theologically it may not even be the correct goal. How do we decide which of the many layers that could claim to be the 'original reading' to select? Often the richer religious meanings in a text are those that entered the text at a relatively late or developed stage. Do we choose the earlier, less rich reading or the later, more profound one?" (Ulrich, "The Bible in the Making," 65). We should locate ancient forms of scripture along a larger arc of meaning and interpretation, as each generation of readers and communities encounters and extends their inherited traditions. Brennan Breed pointed in this direction by advocating a fresh approach to text criticism that does not pick or pursue a singular form of the text and elevate it above others. Rather, our task is to understand the processes of textual formation and reception without prioritizing readings as early versus late, better versus worse, or original versus erroneous (Breed, *Nomadic Text*, 52–74).

26. For a palaeographic date and description of the scribal corrections in 4QJeremiah[a], see DJD 15, 150–51.

27. As it turns out, scribe number two was so preoccupied with correcting a similar error in the previous word that he missed this "bald" ass. Scribe one wrote שפאים, but scribe two recognized that the א was unnecessary. To correct this, he placed a dot above and below the figure (known as a "cancellation dot") to communicate the form should be read as שְׁפִים ("heights"), as we find in MT. Scribe number two's focus on correcting the first form caused him to miss the error in the following word. In both cases, the words of 4QJeremiah[a] start with the same characters: שפאים שפאו. When a scribe's mind or eye skips over a word, phrase, or section due to the presence of similar characters at the front of nearby word, text critics refer to this as "parablepsis due to homoioarchton." Next time you need to call in sick, just tell your boss you came down with a case of parablepsis due to homoioarchton—I bet they won't bat an eye.

28. In light of some variations within cited texts in *Pesher Habakkuk*, Lim observed that "even if the comment depends upon a variant it is not necessarily exegetical" (Lim, "Biblical Quotations in the Pesharim and the Text of the Bible," 76). For a list of significant

variant readings found in the interpretive texts of the DSS, see the index by Novakovic, "Text-Critical Variants in the Pesharim." Perhaps the most famous instance of a variant in a quoted text is from beyond the DSS. When Matthew 1:22–23 cites Isaiah 7:14 to confirm the prophetic fulfillment of Jesus's birth, the gospel writer cites the LXX version, which reads, "Look, the virgin (παρθένος) shall conceive and bear a son, and they shall name him Emmanuel." The Hebrew form of the passage, as in the MT, references merely a "young woman" (עַלְמָה). The question is whether Matthew's use of that form of the Greek scriptures was to advance a particular theology of the virgin birth, which is a point of debate (see Law, *When God Spoke Greek*, 96–97)

29. Strugnell, "Notes en marge," 236.

30. Many of the next generation of critical editions of the Hebrew Bible take this stance, or at the very least engage a diversity of texts in biblical manuscripts and citations embedded in interpretive texts. See, for example, the overview of the method and scope of five ongoing projects including *Biblia Hebraica Quinta*, *Biblia Qumranica*, the Hebrew University Bible Project, the Oxford Hebrew Bible (now Hebrew Bible Critical Edition), and the critical edition of the Samaritan Pentateuch published in the collection of essays in the journal, *Hebrew Bible and Ancient Israel* 2 (2013).

31. Cross, DJD 12, 134.

32. Translation adapted from the Samaritan Pentateuch in English (SPE), with a slight modification to reflect the shared language with the DSS and LXX.

33. Cross, *The Ancient Library of Qumran*, 43. For all the Daniel manuscript dates, see Ulrich, "The Text of Daniel in the Dead Sea Scrolls," 574. The book of Daniel is a linguistic hybrid. Daniel 2–7 is penned in Aramaic and framed by Daniel 1, 9–12 in Hebrew. There's a long scholarly debate with many different explanations about how, when, and why the book came together in this bilingual structure. It's clear that the Aramaic sections are older, and were encased by the Hebrew content during the cultural, political, and religious crises experienced in Judea under Antiochus Epiphanes IV in the mid-160s BCE.

34. I'm referring here to the lyrics of the Beastie Boys song "Shadrach," off their album *Paul's Boutique* (1989). The inspiration behind the song is complemented and contextualized in the Beastie Boys's brilliant rewritten take on Daniel 3 in Diamond and Harowitz, *Beastie Boys Book*, 276. This is but one of countless examples from modern media and pop culture that reimagine or reference the personae, tales, or themes of Daniel traditions.

35. VanderKam, *The Dead Sea Scrolls and the Bible*, 7.

Chapter 7

1. Jeremiah's prophetic career began in the southern kingdom of Judah about a century after the exile of the northern kingdom of Israel in 722 BCE. Jeremiah's oracles reflect the prospect of a similar fate for the southern kingdom if Judah doesn't straighten up. In 597/87 BCE the Babylonians took over the shrinking southern kingdom (now effectively a city-state in Jerusalem), dissolved the Israelite monarchy, and exiled the upper echelon of its society. Jeremiah and his scribe Baruch were reported to have been caught up in a wave of refugees who fled to Egypt against Jeremiah and Baruch's advice and will (Jeremiah 43:5–7).

2. Leuchter, "The Pen of Scribes," 22–23.

3. Ulrich, "Variant Editions of Biblical Books," 14. In the next chapter we will encounter so-called "rewritten" texts that seem to add to and adapt scriptural traditions in various ways. Examples of this phenomenon in the Hebrew Scriptures, LXX, and at Qumran led text critic Emanuel Tov to a similar conclusion on the pluriformity of authoritative scripture in antiquity (Tov, "Reflections on the Many Forms of Hebrew Scripture").

4. Tov, "The Jeremiah Scrolls from Qumran," 198.

5. Dimant, "From the Book of Jeremiah to the Qumranic *Apocryphon of Jeremiah*," 453.

6. Abegg, Flint, and Ulrich, *The Dead Sea Scrolls Bible*, 382.

7. Or, to put it another way, Davis commented, "Jeremiah's prophetic persona was attested and echoed in a number of important texts" (Davis, *The Cave 4 Apocryphon of Jeremiah*, 303). Not unlike Jeremiah, Jeremiah's scribal sidekick Baruch also had an extensive literary afterlife, not least in the apocryphal book of Baruch (dated sometime between 300–50 BCE) and the later apocalyptic writing of 2 Baruch (the composition date of which is difficult to determine, but was sometime after the fall of the Jerusalem temple in 70 CE but before the Bar Kokbha revolt of 132–135 CE).

8. VanderKam notes up to thirty-six, as the content of some scrolls is uncertain (*The Dead Sea Scrolls Today*, 48).

9. The wisdom book of Ben Sira (also known as Sirach) was received among the Apocrypha and Deuterocanon via the LXX, but was also discovered in Hebrew among the Qumran fragments (2QBenSira) and atop Masada (Mas1h). Important Hebrew fragments of Ben Sira are also present in the Cairo Genizah materials. The composition itself was certainly popular in ancient Judaism and likely originated in the early second

century BCE. For an overview of Ben Sira's composition, translation, and reception, see Wright, "Ben Sira."

10. See Mroczek, "Moses, David and Scribal Revelation: Preservation and Renewal in Second Temple Jewish Textual Traditions," and *The Literary Imagination in Jewish Antiquity*.

11. The three so-called "additions" to Septuagint Daniel include The Prayer of Azariah and the Song of the Three Youths, Susanna, and Bel and the Dragon.

12. This number of Daniel texts is from Flint, 'The Daniel Tradition at Qumran." While this observation on the content and shape of Daniel stands, it's important to show nuance in accounting for, or better, counting, the "biblical" manuscripts among the DSS. There are up to eight scrolls with Daniel content at Qumran: 1QDaniel^{a-b} (1Q71–1Q72), 4QDaniel^{a-e} (4Q112–4Q116), and 6QpapDan (6Q7). As hinted above in the section on Jeremiah and Psalms, one of the challenges of simply "counting" copies of scriptural books among the DSS is that we aren't always sure of the scope of their content. For example, 4QDaniel^{e} has content only from the prayer of Daniel 9. We can't infer that these slender bits indicate another full copy of the book. It is equally possible they are excerpts of the passage, perhaps in an interpreted text. Similarly, 4QDaniel^{a-b} both have extensive content from most chapters. However, it is possible that the uses of blank space in these manuscripts indicates the scribe understood the material as a collection of Danielic tales rather than a unified book. On these trends and open questions related to Daniel, see Perrin, "Redrafting the Architecture of Daniel Traditions."

13. Beaulieu, *The Reign of Nabonidus*, 1–42.

14. Translation mine, adapted from Perrin, "Symptoms and Symbols, Prayers and Portents," 46.

15. Loren Stuckenbruck confirmed that this Cave 4 Nabonidus text is earlier than the convergence of the Hebrew and Aramaic Daniel materials in the biblical book, which took place in the mid-160s BCE (Stuckenbruck, "The Formation and Reformation of Daniel in the Dead Sea Scrolls"). On the dating of the biblical book of Daniel, see Collins, *Daniel*, 24–38). Carol Newsom also noted that the propaganda of the Aramaic *Prayer of Nabonidus* must have been developed while the memory of that figure was somewhat fresh, suggesting its origins in some exilic or early postexilic group (Newsom, "Why Nabonidus?").

16. For developments and insights as it relates to Jewish writings from the Second Temple period, see Schuller and Wacker, eds., *Early Jewish Writings: The Bible and Women.*

17. Despite being the only prophetic book to include a memoir, Jeremiah's mother is unnamed (Jeremiah 1:5; 15:10). Jeremiah's oracles also innovate new images that blur gender roles (Jeremiah 30:6; 31:22). For all the outcry and controversy around David's rape of Bathsheba, she utters but a single phrase in response: "I am pregnant" (2 Samuel 11:5). When the story is rewritten after the exile, Bathsheba's assault is erased altogether, her voice silenced (1 Chronicles 20:1–3). If we read closely, Daniel traditions also intersect with gendered identities or issues. In the biblical book, Daniel is trained under the chief eunuch of the Babylonian court (Daniel 1:3). In the LXX addition, as Susanna's assailants extort her to cover up their sexual advances, Daniel advocates for her in a contrived trial to cover up the plot (Susanna 48–62). Clearly in these cases the minority reports are precisely minor, suggesting the shaping of traditions by a predominantly male scribal culture.

18. Other prophetesses of the Hebrew Scriptures include Deborah (Judges 4:4), Huldah (2 Kings 22:14; 2 Chronicles 34:22), Noadiah (Nehemiah 6:14), and an unnamed yet acclaimed figure (Isaiah 8:3).

19. Quoted in Wacholder, *The Dawn of Qumran*, 206, 278). This scroll is part of a loose collection of Pentateuchal scrolls that remix and expand materials in a way not unlike the later SP.

20. Translation adapted from Feldman, "The Song of Miriam," 906–7.

21. White Crawford, "4Q364 & 365: A Preliminary Report," 222.

22. See Judges 5:1–31; 1 Samuel 2:1–10; 18:6–7; *Tg. Neof.* and *Targ. Ps-J.* to Exodus 15:21; and Luke 1:46–55.

23. Brooke, "Power to the Powerless."

24. Andrew Teeter is correct that "Certainly the external boundaries and the precise transmission-historical shape of the scriptural corpus are somewhat undefined, even fluid, during this period. Yet nothing could be clearer than that the literature that constitutes the Hebrew scriptures was an absolutely determinative force in the life of these authors" (Teeter, "The Hebrew Bible and/as Second Temple Literature," 354).

Chapter 8

1. There is a much larger debate about the fine or foggy linguistic lines between Hebrew and Aramaic in the Second Temple period. 2 Maccabees 7:8 and 15:36 link Hebrew to nationalism by referring to it as "the ancestral language (ἡ πάτρος φωνή)," while Aramaic is noted as "Syrian (Συριακή)" (see Schwartz, "Language, Power and Identity in Ancient Palestine"). The book of Jubilees takes it a step further by presenting Hebrew as both

a divine tongue and a language revealed to Abraham (Jubilees 3:28; 12:25–27). Several scholars have observed that the group behind the DSS seems to have had a penchant for Hebrew as a compositional language, seemingly as part of a conscious linguistic revival in the mid–second century BCE (see Weitzman, "Why Did the Qumran Community Write in Hebrew?" and Schniedewind, "Qumran Hebrew as an Antilanguage"). Later, the apostolic father, Papias of Hierapolis (ca. 60–130 CE), nodded to a possible Semitic language version or source of Matthew (Eusebius, Eccl. 3.39.14.17). New Testament scholarly debate is ongoing as to whether Papias's reference (1) is to be accepted and (2) refers to Hebrew or Aramaic (see Black, *An Aramaic Approach to the Gospels and Acts*, 35; Casey, *An Aramaic Approach to Q*, 54–60; Kloppenborg, *Excavating Q*, 80).

2. My range here is based on three proposed calculations: Dimant, "The Qumran Aramaic Texts and the Qumran Community"; Berthelot and Stökl Ben Ezra, "Aramaica Qumranica: Introduction"; and Tigchelaar, "The Dead Sea Scrolls."

3. The Hebrew Scriptures contain a word of Aramaic in Genesis 31:47, a line in Jeremiah 10:11, and portions or patches of books in Aramaic like Daniel (Daniel 2:4b–7:28) and Ezra (Ezra 4:8–6:18; 7:12–26). The New Testament includes several Aramaic words carried over into Greek, which are at times clarified for readers, as in the Gospels (for example, Matthew 10:4; Mark 5:41; John 12:13). Note also the form Ἀββᾶ (Mark 14:36; Romans 8:15; Galatians 4:6), which, contrary to the cozy sermon imagery, doesn't mean "daddy"—it's an Aramaic form of the word "father." It's also debated whether references to Ἑβραϊστί in the New Testament point to Hebrew, Aramaic, or some intermingling of both (see John 5:2; 19:13, 17, 20; 20:16; Rev 9:11; 16:16). For a recent take on these texts and issues, see Buth and Pierce, "*Hebraisti* in Ancient Texts."

4. Several scholars have called for nuance about the assumption that the Aramaic DSS came exclusively from beyond the Qumran community (see Lim, "The Qumran Scrolls, Multilingualism, and Biblical Interpretation"; VanderKam, *An Introduction to Ancient Judaism*, 114–15; and García Martínez, "Aramaica Qumranica Apocalyptica?," 439). We can't assume that the Qumranites only wrote in Hebrew, or that Aramaic composition disqualifies a text from association with the Qumran community. But since the compositional dates of the Aramaic DSS in general predate the sectarian group at Qumran (as per the date of the "revised chronology" outlined in chapter 5), these Aramaic texts may provide important insight into the thought, practice, and scribal culture of the larger or earlier movements associated with the group that eventually called Qumran home. Given the dates of the Aramaic DSS into the first centuries BCE and CE, it is entirely possible, even likely, that some were copied there.

5. The oldest ones being *Astronomical Enoch* (third century BCE) and the Aramaic Levi Document and Tobit (mid–third to mid–second century BCE). Most of the other Aramaic DSS were likely composed in the second to first centuries CE.

6. Machiela, "The Compositional Setting and Implied Audience," 180.

7. These samples are unpacked in greater detail in my article, "Capturing the Voices of Pseudepigraphic Personae."

8. The opening lines of Tobit are lost in the Qumran finds, but the longer Greek version of the text behind my translation above tracks closely to Tobit texts found among the DSS. The Qumran Tobit fragments are themselves an incredible discovery: not only did the finds include at least four Aramaic Tobit manuscripts (4QTobit[a-d] and possibly some Cave 3 fragments in 3Q14), they also included one fragmentary Hebrew manuscript and version (4QTobit[e]). This suggests that at least one scribe understood Tobit as having special significance and rendered the work from Aramaic (the imperial language of the day) into Hebrew (the ancestral idiom of Israelite tradition and Jewish culture). On this, see Perrin, "From *lingua franca* to *lingua sacra*."

9. The Book of Revelation is the first ancient writing to self-identify as an apocalypse. Revelation 1:1 dives straight into the genre, introducing itself as "The revelation (ἀποκάλυψις) of Jesus Christ." Paul claimed that his authority and knowledge of the gospel derived from an ἀποκάλυψις, that is, a revelatory encounter (see Galatians 1:12; Ephesians 3:3). It's also clear that some New Testament writers drew on or conversed with other known apocalyptic writings of the day. Jude 6 cites the Enochic Book of Watchers. Jude 9 alludes to the Apocalypse of Moses.

10. My paraphrase above is based on the most accepted definition, from the *Semeia* 14 genres project. As captured by Collins, an apocalypse is "a genre of revelatory literature with narrative framework, in which a revelation is mediated by an otherworldly being to a human recipient, disclosing a transcendent reality which is both temporal, insofar as it envisages eschatological salvation, and spatial insofar as it involves another, supernatural world" (Collins, *The Apocalyptic Imagination*, 5). David Hellholm's addendum to the definition is also helpful, as he notes apocalypses are also "intended for a group in crisis with the purpose of exhortation and/or consolation by means of divine authority" (Hellholm, "The Problem of Apocalyptic Genre," 27). Of course, as new texts are discovered and old texts reconsidered, even this genre must remain organic. As Collins put it recently, this reality means that "no matter how we define them, [genres] always have fuzzy edges, borderline cases, and related types" (Collins, "Epilogue," 420). The Aramaic DSS are the primary discovery that is now driving this redefinition of the ancient apocalypse.

11. Carol Newsom is correct that "there is a fairly widely accepted description of the Qumran sect as an apocalyptic community that did not write apocalypses" (Newsom, "Apocalyptic and the Discourse of the Qumran Community," 135). This impression is because, while core Hebrew sectarian writings such as the *War Scroll* or the *Community Rule* embrace an apocalyptic outlook, they are not formal apocalypses. Most scholars also now recognize that our oldest apocalyptic writings from ancient Judaism are written in Aramaic, not Hebrew.

12. Sanders, *Judaism: Practice and Belief*, 8.

13. My own contributions in this direction include comprehensive lists of texts and their apocalyptic contours (Perrin, *The Dynamics of Dream-Vision Revelation*, 238–47; and Perrin, "The Aramaic Imagination"), which are now also taken up by Collins (*Apocalyptic Imagination*, 181).

14. Frances Flannery-Dailey referred to this as "dream logic" (*Dreamers, Scribes, and Priests*, 249).

15. You can learn more about this trifecta of priestly texts in my recent commentary, *The Horizons of Ancestral Inheritance*, and my open-access essay "Charting Constellations of Aramaic Jewish Pseudepigrapha at Qumran."

16. One *Pseudo-Daniel* text (4Q243) includes a list of prominent priestly leaders alongside that of kings, reaching into the Second Temple period. This presentation underscores that priestly duties and royal offices were not to be intermingled, which was a contentious issue with some Maccabean kings around the turn of the Common Era.

17. As demonstrated by Popović in *Reading the Human Body*. Although Noah is not named per se in the fragmentary *Birth of Noah* texts, the similarity of the Cave 4 Aramaic finds to the birth of Noah in 1 Enoch 106–107 suggests he, or someone like him, is the personality in view. The "chosen one" of the Qumran *Birth of Noah* materials is recognized by his remarkable white skin, bright red hair, and the moles and marks on his body which portended his destiny and future deliverance. He is also lauded as having special knowledge in his heart, insight into secrets of men, ability to read special books, visionary potential, and wisdom. Not bad for a newborn!

18. For a comprehensive set of studies on the origins, development, interpretation, and reception of four kingdoms themes, see the open-access volume Perrin and Stuckenbruck, eds., *Four Kingdom Motifs before and beyond the Book of Daniel*. For an excellent short overview of the patterns of kingdom counts in antiquity, see Collins, *Daniel*, 166–70.

19. One of the remarkable features of several Aramaic writings—like the *Genesis Apocryphon*, the Aramaic Levi Document, Tobit, and others—is they elevate the characters of women into roles with actual names and lively dialogue. In several instances, unnamed women are given names as well as voices and roles in these rewritten Aramaic narratives, as is the case here in the *Genesis Apocryphon*. The identification of unnamed women ancestors in the reception history of biblical traditions continues in some other texts beyond this period. Perhaps most notably, Job's wife is nameless in that epic biblical tale of suffering, yet several sources identify Dinah, from Genesis 34, as Job's wife (*Testament of Job* 1:5–6; *Biblical Antiquities* 8:7–8; Talmud Bava Batra 15b). For the development of this phenomenon in the Aramaic DSS, see the study by Shelby Bennett, "Silenced Voices: Hearing Biblical Women through the Genesis Apocryphon Scroll."

20. See Frölich, "Medicine and Magic in the Genesis Apocryphon" and van der Horst, "Bitenosh's Orgasm."

21. The Aramaic *Book of Giants* features the figure of Enoch and demonstrates the broader diversity of Enochic tales and traditions in ancient Judaism. Some manuscripts, such as fragments of 4QEnochGiants[a] (4Q203), also contain content from the *Book of Watchers* known later in 1 Enoch. This revealed how the Enoch pseudepigrapha, or Enochic lore, were either collected or created in groups in some scribal settings.

Chapter 9

1. This claim in the Soviet tabloid was reported in the British press. For this reference, I am indebted to Bruce, *Second Thoughts on the Dead Sea Scrolls*, 138.

2. In its earliest forms, what we now call Christianity was part of the developing diversity of ancient Judaism. It's not until at least the end of the second century CE that Christianity is a distinct movement apart from its Jewish origins. As Robert Kraft remarked, "Prior to the emergence of self-conscious 'Christianity,' and even after that, there was significant diversity within the seedbed from which classical Judaism emerged" (Kraft, "The Weighing of the Parts," 92). Our task, then, is to see how the New Testament speaks into and out of the commonalties and complexities of ancient Jewish life, thought, and practice of this era. For forays into this world, see the essays in McCready and Reinhartz, eds., *Common Judaism: Explorations in Second-Temple Judaism*.

3. My examples from the 1950s above are meant to illustrate extreme examples of over- or under-reading the Qumran texts for or against Christian origins. There have, however, been several important and insightful contributions along the way. See Brooke,

The Dead Sea Scrolls and the New Testament, esp. 3–18; Stuckenbruck, "The Dead Sea Scrolls and the New Testament"; VanderKam and Flint, *The Meaning of the Dead Sea Scrolls*, 311–78; and many well-integrated contributions in the *T&T Clark Encyclopedia of Second Temple Judaism*, edited by Stuckenbruck and Gurtner.

4. Jose O'Callaghan claimed that Cave 7 held Greek fragments of 1 Timothy, Mark, and James, as well as possible snippets of Acts, 2 Peter, and Romans (O'Callaghan, "New Testament Papyri in Qumran Cave 7?"). On closer read, however, the fragments in question are likely from Greek translations of a book of the Hebrew Scriptures or 1 Enoch (Flint, "The Greek Fragments of Enoch").

5. The Vatican conspiracy theory never fails to entertain, and also never seems to go away. The clearest articulation of it is found in Dan Brown's *The Da Vinci Code*. There are countless other conspiracy theories on the impact of the scrolls on the history and theology of Christianity, or even broader fringe topics. In some ways, this continues to be part of the allure and appeal of the DSS. Mathew Collins observed that, "The popularization of the Scrolls and the prevalent public impression that they are in some manner the source of controversy and conspiracy has resulted in an arguably disproportionate degree of public interest and thus their widespread permeation into popular culture. These popular representations of the Scrolls often have little or no relation to any academic reflections upon the material" ("Scholarly and Popular Reception," 64).

6. This is why the "four kingdoms" count of Daniel 7 interprets the imperial past to understand current crisis and imminent deliverance. It's also why in the "little apocalypse" of Mark 13, the writer says, "Let the reader understand" (Mark 13:14; Matthew 24:15). This is a wink and nudge to the first-century CE reader/hearer living under Roman rule about the signs of the times. Apocalyptic literature's cryptic language lends itself to ongoing interpretation and revision in light of new political, social, or economic crises. This keeps hope always on the horizon, even if the apocalyptic dawn never breaks.

7. The parallel passages include Matthew 3:3, Mark 1:3, and John 1:23. Similarities such as this between the Gospels suggest that the writers were in conversation with earlier oral traditions or written sources. New Testament scholars refer to the task of discerning relationships between this network of texts and traditions as the "Synoptic Problem," which is really an opportunity. Note that the quoted passage in Luke sounds a little different from the form of Isaiah cited above. This is because the writers of the New Testament predominantly quote from the Greek LXX, which, as we saw in a previous chapter, included both textual and translational differences from other text traditions

of the Hebrew Scriptures. For more on the uses of the LXX by New Testament writers, see Law, *When God Spoke Greek*, 99–116.

8. In fact, 1 Thessalonians 4:13–5:11 includes sound bites of a conversation between Paul and his communities over the problem of believers passing away before the arrival of the imminent eschaton he advertised (see also 1 Corinthians 15).

9. Lawrence Schiffman's work signaled a major course change in Qumran studies in this direction. Core to his call for reorientation was the recognition that the Jewish DSS have been overread, or misread, through the lens of Christian terms and traditions. See especially his two summaries of the Qumran community's structure, lifestyle, and belief (*Reclaiming the Dead Sea Scrolls*, 18), which juxtapose a Christianized description with one from the perspective of Jewish tradition and practice.

10. For a sampling of these and other minor uses, see Leviticus 4:3; Numbers 3:3; 1 Samuel 26:9; 2 Chronicles 6:42; Psalms 105:15; and Habakkuk 3:13. In one remarkable case, the prophet Isaiah called the Persian King Cyrus "anointed"—literally a messiah of God—for his support in restoring, resettling, and rebuilding Jerusalem after the Babylonian exile (Isaiah 45:1).

11. See the *War Scroll* 11:6 and *Damascus Document* 7:18–19 at Qumran; Philo (*Praem. Poen.* §95); the Aramaic Targums (*Tg. Onq.* to Numbers 24:17); the New Testament (Revelation 22:16); and rabbinic literature (y. Ta'an. 4.7 fol. 68d). The bibliography of articles and books on messianism could drown Moby Dick in the Dead Sea. For an authoritative and accessible introduction, see Collins, *The Scepter and the Star.*

12. Oegema, *The Anointed and His People*, 22.

13. In fact, as early Christian scribes continued to copy ancient Jewish writings from this period, they sometimes intervened into ancient Jewish texts to assert the messianic identity of Jesus. Josephus's original remarks on Jesus are amplified to underscore that "he was the Christ" (*Ant.* 18.63). Similarly, the Latin tradition of 4 Ezra 7:28 switched the original "my son the messiah" to read "my son Jesus." These examples, of course, are all theologically motivated and impose Christian messianic identifications on earlier Jewish traditions.

14. Bird, *Are You the One Who Is to Come?*, 32.

15. This insight was included in a guest lecture George Nickelsburg delivered at Trinity Western University in 2008. I have been unable to find a published version of this observation—but it is brilliant and needs to be in the written record.

16. Two messianic figures are included in the *Testament of Naphtali* 5:3–5, a later Greek text received in Christian tradition. Although the text is fragmentary and of uncertain relation to the later Greek Naphtali tradition here, a Hebrew *Testament of Naphtali* (4Q215) was discovered in Qumran Cave 4. However, the messianic element is either lost or was not part of this Hebrew writing among the DSS.

17. The example of Hebrews invites another conversation partner from Qumran, 11QMelchizedek. Both Hebrews and 11QMelchizdek draw upon and extend the idea of a priestly order of Melchizedek in Psalm 11:4 in different directions. For the New Testament text, it provided a way of identifying Jesus as a member of an otherworldly priestly order in the heavenly temple. In the Cave 11 writing, however, Melchizedek is projected into the future as an authoritative judge and agent of deliverance from the domain of Belial, the chief evil being in the Qumran worldview.

18. Collins, *The Scepter and the Star*, 155. Fitzmyer noted, however, that we cannot be sure this similarity is coincidental, perhaps due to the common cultural setting of both writers (Fitzmyer, *The Dead Sea Scrolls*, 61). As we'll see below, this isn't the only place Luke seems to have been up on his cultural knowledge and terms derived from Jewish Aramaic sources. There is also a debate around whether *Aramaic Apocalypse* uses these terms to refer to a positive eschatological agent or a negative apocalyptic agitator. The first option is the most natural reading of the text. For arguments behind both views and a bibliography, see Perrin, *The Dynamics of Dream-Vision Revelation*, 222–23.

19. Shelby Bennett has brilliantly characterized this ancient tale as a #MeToo story ("Silenced Voices," 11). Ancient literary narratives such as this, of course, can be reread in view of the contemporary movement and watershed cultural moment now documented in Kanto and Twoney, *She Said*, as well as the wider recognition of many more such stories and experiences disclosed or unknown. I would add that the Danielic tale of Susannah in the LXX Additions to Daniel is another such example.

20. The translation here is from Machiela, *The Dead Sea Genesis Apocryphon*, 75.

21. Fitzmyer, *The Genesis Apocryphon*, 213; Machiela, "Luke 13:10–13."

22. Romans 2:15; 3:20, 27, 28; Galatians 2:16 (twice); 3:5, 10.

23. The passages noted above, as well as the history of interpreters hinted at here, connect to a much larger scholarly debate on precisely which perspective we should take when studying Paul. The so-called "new perspective" on Paul, though not particularly new anymore, took the novel approach by profiling Paul as an ancient Jew rather than seeing him through the theological lens of Reformation thinkers. As it relates to the

term ἔργων νόμου, the big question was whether Paul understood this category and the practices within it as having some value for attaining merit, or whether such items were identity markers that distinguished different social groups. New perspective readers of Paul have tended toward the latter approach. For an engaging treatment of the arc of Pauline interpretation and a refreshing original contribution, see Westerholm, *Perspectives Old and New on Paul*. For comment on the growing diversity of contextualization efforts on Paul, with a focus on readings informed by Second Temple Jewish, Hellenistic, and Roman settings, see Wright, *Paul: In Fresh Perspective*, 3–20.

24. Fraade, "To Whom it May Concern: 4QMMT and Its Addressee(s)," 509.

25. Abegg, "4QMMT C 27, 31 and 'Works Righteousness,'" 141.

26. Dunn, "4QMMT and Galatians," 151.

27. Scholars generally devise this date by reading in between the lines of 4QMMT's rhetoric, which seems to suggest correspondence from a community founder or authority to a group in Jerusalem from whom they were not yet estranged. This seems to fit with the politics around the high priesthood in the Hasmonean period, or mid–second century BCE.

28. Though commonly read as such, Revelation 22:19 isn't a claim about closing the canon of scripture or a caution against adding books to the Bible. Here again, a little homework in ancient scribal culture reveals that this postscript-type mechanism was meant to ensure the integrity of a given writing, not to lock down an entire anthology. David Aune provides some excellent comparative examples of this from ancient Jewish and classical writings in what he calls "integrity formulas" (*Revelation 17–22*, 1208–15).

29. This section is based on my open-access article, "Greek Gospels and Aramaic Dead Sea Scrolls."

30. While Luke is unique in the New Testament for including both infancy narratives and a boyhood scene of Jesus, the *Infancy Gospel of Thomas* (second century CE) includes an imaginative and insightful set of stories about Jesus's youth. These are often read for the (super)natural tension they portray. What would it have been like growing up as a child with the power of the cosmos coursing through your veins? Equally intriguing in these tales is how often Joseph is the first responder on the scene, having to explain, deescalate, apologize, or even discipline Jesus. Like in the *Infancy Gospel of Thomas* 4–5, when Joseph hauls Jesus off by the ear after the lad's temper tantrum resulted in another child falling dead in the marketplace. For an introduction and translation, see Burke, "The Infancy Gospel of Thomas (Syriac)."

Bibliography

Abegg, Martin G., Jr. "4QMMT C 27, 31 and 'Works Righteousness.'" *Dead Sea Discoveries* 6 (1999): 139–47.

Abegg, Martin, Jr., Peter Flint, and Eugene Ulrich. *The Dead Sea Scrolls Bible: The Oldest Known Bible Translated for the First Time into English*. New York: HarperSanFrancisco, 1999.

Allegro, John. *The Dead Sea Scrolls: A Reappraisal*. 2nd ed. Harmondsworth: Penguin Books, 1964.

Allen, Leslie C. *Psalms 101–150*. Word Biblical Commentary 21. Rev. ed. Nashville: Thomas Nelson, 2002.

Anderson, Robert T. and Terry Gils. *The Samaritan Pentateuch: An Introduction to Its Origin, History, and Significance for Biblical Studies*. Atlanta: SBL Press, 2012.

Aune, David E. *Revelation 17–22*. Word Biblical Commentary 52c. Nashville: Thomas Nelson, 1998.

Avigad, Nahman and Yigael Yadin. *A Genesis Apocryphon: A Scroll from the Wilderness of Judea*. Jerusalem: Magness Press and Heikhal Ha-Sefer, 1956.

Bakan, Joel. *The Corporation: The Pathological Pursuit of Profit and Power*. New York: Penguin Books, 2004.

Baltzer, Klaus. *Deutero-Isaiah: A Commentary on Isaiah 40–55*. Hermeneia. Minneapolis: Fortress, 2001.

Barthélemy, D. and J. T. Milik, eds. *Qumran Cave 1*. Discoveries in the Judean Desert 1. Oxford: Clarendon, 1955.

Bauckham, Richard. *The Jewish World around the New Testament*. Grand Rapids: Baker Academic, 2010.

Beaulieu, Paul-Alain. *The Reign of Nabonidus, King of Babylon (556–539 BCE)*. Yale Near Eastern Researches 10. New Haven: Yale, 1989.

Bennett, Shelby. "Silenced Voices: Hearing Biblical Women through the Genesis Apocryphon Scroll." M.A. thesis, Trinity Western University, 2021.

Bernhard, Andrew. "The *Gospel of Jesus' Wife*: Textual Evidence of a Modern Forgery." *New Testament Studies* 61 (2015): 335–55.

———. "Postscript: A Final Note About the Origin of *The Gospel of Jesus' Wife*." *New Testament Studies* 63 (2017): 305–17.

Berthelot, Katell and Daniel Stökl Ben Ezra. "Aramaica Qumranica: Introduction." In *Aramaica Qumranica: Proceedings of the Conference on the Aramaic Texts from Qumran in Aix-en-Provence, 30 June–2 July 2008*, edited by Katell Berthelot and Daniel Stökl Ben Ezra, 1–12. Studies on the Texts of the Desert of Judah 94. Leiden: Brill, 2011.

Bird, Michael F. *Are You the One Who Is to Come? The Historical Jesus and the Messianic Questions*. Grand Rapids: Baker Academic, 2009.

Black, Matthew. *An Aramaic Approach to the Gospels and Acts*. 3rd ed. Oxford: Oxford University Press, 1967.

Borodkin, Lisa J. "The Economics of Antiquities Looting and a Proposed Legal Alternative." *Columbia Law Review* 2 (1995): 377–417.

Breed, Brennan W. *Nomadic Text: A Theory of Biblical Reception History*. Indiana Series in Biblical Literature. Bloomington: Indiana University Press, 2014.

Brooke, George J. *The Dead Sea Scrolls and the New Testament*. Minneapolis: Fortress, 2005.

———. "Power to the Powerless: A Long-Lost Song of Miriam." *Biblical Archaeology Review* 20.3 (May/June 1994): 63–64.

Brooke, George et al., eds., in consultation with James C. VanderKam. *Qumran Cave 4.XVII: Parabiblical Texts, Part 3*. Discoveries in the Judean Desert 22. Oxford: Clarendon, 1996.

Brown, William P. *A Handbook to Old Testament Exegesis*. Louisville: Westminster John Knox, 2017.

Bruce, F. F. *Second Thoughts on the Dead Sea Scrolls*. Rev. and enl. ed. Grand Rapids: Paternoster, 1955.

Burke, Tony. "The Infancy Gospel of Thomas (Syriac)." In *New Testament Apocrypha: More Noncanonical Scriptures, Volume One*, edited by Tony Burke and Brent Landau, 61-68. Grand Rapids: Eerdmans, 2016.

Burrows, Millar. *The Dead Sea Scrolls*. New York: Viking Press, 1955.

Buth, Randall and Chad Pierce. "*Hebraisti* in Ancient Texts: Does Ἑβραϊστί Ever Mean Aramaic?" In *The Language Environment of First Century Judea: Jerusalem Studies in the Synoptic Gospels—Volume Two*, edited by Randall Buth and R. Steven Notley, 66–109. Jewish and Christian Perspectives Series 26. Leiden: Brill, 2014.

Casey, Maurice. *An Aramaic Approach to Q: Sources for the Gospels of Matthew and Luke.* Cambridge: Cambridge University Press, 2005.

Collins, John J. *The Apocalyptic Imagination: An Introduction to Jewish Apocalyptic Literature.* 3rd ed. Grand Rapids: Eerdmans, 2016.

———. *Beyond the Qumran Community: The Sectarian Movement of the Dead Sea Scrolls.* Grand Rapids: Eerdmans, 2010.

———. *Daniel.* Hermeneia. Minneapolis: Fortress, 1994.

———. *The Dead Sea Scrolls: A Biography.* Lives of Great Religious Books. Princeton: Princeton University Press, 2013.

———. "Epilogue: Genre Analysis and the Dead Sea Scrolls." *Dead Sea Discoveries* 17 (2010): 418–30.

———. *The Scepter and the Star: Messianism in Light of the Dead Sea Scrolls.* 2nd ed. Grand Rapids: Eerdmans, 2010.

Collins, Matthew A. "Scholarly and Popular Reception." In *T&T Clark Companion to the Dead Sea Scrolls*, edited by George J. Brooke and Charlotte Hempel, 59–73. London: Bloomsbury T&T Clark, 2019.

Davies, A. Powell. *The Meaning of the Dead Sea Scrolls: The Documents that Shed a Brilliant New Light on Christianity.* The New American Library. Mentor Books: New York and Scarborough, 1956.

Davila, James R. "Liturgical Works from Qumran." In *Eerdmans Dictionary of Early Judaism*, edited by John J. Collins and Daniel C. Harlow, 890–92. Grand Rapids: Eerdmans, 2010.

Davis, Kipp. *The Cave 4 Apocryphon of Jeremiah and the Qumran Jeremianic Traditions: Prophetic Persona and the Construction of Community Identity.* Studies on the Texts of the Desert of Judah 111. Leiden: Brill, 2014.

———. "Caves of Dispute: Patterns of Correspondence and Suspicion in the Post-2002 'Dead Sea Scrolls' Fragments." *Dead Sea Discoveries* 24 (2017): 229–70.

———. "Palaeographical and Physical Features of the Dead Sea Scrolls in the Museum of the Bible Collection: A Synopsis." In *Dead Sea Scrolls Fragments in the Museum Collection*, edited by Emanuel Tov, Kipp Davis, and Robert Duke, 19–35. Publications of the Museum of the Bible 1. Leiden: Brill, 2016.

Davis, Kipp and Torleif Elgvin. "1QDan^{b} (1Q72) with MS 1926/4b (Dan 3.26–27)." In *Gleanings from the Caves: Dead Sea Scrolls and Artefacts from The Schøyen Collection*, edited by Torleif Elgvin, Kipp Davis, and Michael Langlois, 257–70. Library of Second Temple Studies 71. London: Bloomsbury T&T Clark, 2016.

Diamond, Michael and Adam Harovitz. *Beastie Boys Book*. New York: Spiegel & Grau, 2018.

Dimant, Devorah. "From the Book of Jeremiah to the Qumranic *Apocryphon of Jeremiah*." *Dead Sea Discoveries* 20 (2013): 452–71.

——. "The Qumran Aramaic Texts and the Qumran Community." In *Flores Florentino: Dead Sea Scrolls and Other Early Jewish Studies in Honour of Florentino García Martínez*, edited by Anthony Hilhorst, Émile Puech, and Eibert J. C. Tigchelaar, 197–205. Journal for the Study of Judaism Supplements 122. Leiden: Brill, 2007.

Duke, Robert, Daniel Holt and Skyler Russell. "Daniel 10:18–20 (INV. MOTB. SCR.003170)." In *Dead Sea Scrolls Fragments in the Museum Collection*, edited by Emanuel Tov, Kipp Davis and Robert Duke, 200–209. Publications of the Museum of the Bible 1. Leiden: Brill, 2016.

Dunn, James D. G. "4QMMT and Galatians." *New Testament Studies* 43 (1997): 147–53.

Elgvin, Torleif, Kipp Davis, and Michael Langlois, eds. *Gleanings from the Caves: Dead Sea Scrolls and Artefacts from The Schøyen Collection*. Library of Second Temple Studies 71. London: Bloomsbury T&T Clark, 2016.

——. "Texts and Artefacts." In *Gleanings from the Caves: Dead Sea Scrolls and Artefacts from The Schøyen Collection*, edited by Torleif Elgvin, Kipp Davis, and Michael Langlois, 51–60. Library of Second Temple Studies 71. London: Bloomsbury T&T Clark, 2016.

Elgvin, Torleif and Årstein Justnes. "1QDan[a] (1Q71) with MS 192/4a (Dan 2.4–5)." In *Gleanings from the Caves: Dead Sea Scrolls and Artefacts from The Schøyen Collection*, edited by Torleif Elgvin, Kipp Davis, and Michael Langlois, 247–56. Library of Second Temple Studies 71. London: Bloomsbury T&T Clark, 2016.

Elgvin, Torleif and Michael Langlois. "Looking Back: (More) Dead Sea Scrolls Forgeries in The Schøyen Collection." *Revue de Qumran* 31 (2019): 111–33.

Elledge, C. D. *Resurrection of the Dead in Early Judaism: 200 BCE–CE 200*. Oxford: Oxford University Press, 2019.

Eshel, Hanan. *Qumran: Scrolls, Caves, History*. Carta Field Guides. Jerusalem: Carta, 2009.

Feldman, Ariel. "The Song of Miriam (4Q365 6a ii + 6c 1–7) Revisited." *Journal of Biblical Literature* 132 (2013): 905–11.

Fields, Weston W. *The Dead Sea Scrolls: A Full History, Volume 1*. Leiden: Brill, 2009.

Fitzmyer, Joseph A. *The Dead Sea Scrolls and Christian Origins*. Grand Rapids: Eerdmans, 2000.

——. *The Genesis Apocryphon of Qumran Cave 1 (1Q20): A Commentary*. Biblica et Orientalia 18/B. 3rd ed. Rome: Editrice Pontificio Istituto Biblico, 2004.

——. *A Guide to the Dead Sea Scrolls and Related Literature*. Grand Rapids: Eerdmans, 2008.

Flannery-Dailey, Frances. *Dreamers, Scribes, and Priests: Jewish Dreams in the Hellenistic and Roman Eras*. Journal for the Study of Judaism Supplements 90. Leiden: Brill, 2004.

Flint, Peter W. "The Daniel Tradition at Qumran." In *The Book of Daniel: Composition and Reception*, edited by John J. Collins and Peter W. Flint, with the assistance of Cameron VanEpps, 329–67. 2 volumes. Vetus Testamentum Supplements 83. Formation and Interpretation of Old Testament Literature 2. Leiden: Brill, 2001.

——. *The Dead Sea Psalms Scrolls & The Book of Psalms*. Studies on the Texts of the Desert of Judah 17. Leiden: Brill, 1997.

——. *The Dead Sea Scrolls.* Core Biblical Studies. Nashville: Abingdon, 2013.

——. "The Greek Fragments of Enoch from Qumran Cave 7." In *Enoch and Qumran Origins: New Light on a Forgotten Connection*, edited by Gabriele Boccaccini, 224–33. Grand Rapids: Eerdmans, 2005.

Fraade, Steven D. "To Whom it May Concern: 4QMMT and Its Addressee(s)." *Revue de Qumran* 19 (2000): 507–26.

Fröhlich, Ida. "Medicine and Magic in Genesis Apocryphon: Ideas on Human Conception and its Hindrances." *Revue de Qumran* 25 (2011): 177–98.

García Martínez, Florentino. "Aramaica Qumranica Apocalyptica?" In *Aramaica Qumranica: Proceedings of the Conference on the Aramaic Texts from Qumran in Aix-en-Provence, 30 June–2 July 2008*, edited by Katell Berthelot and Daniel Stökl Ben Ezra, 435–50. Studies on the Texts of the Desert of 94. Leiden: Brill, 2011.

Goldingay, John. *Psalms, Volume 3: Psalms 90–150.* Grand Rapids: Baker Academic, 2008.

Goldman, Liora. "Damascus Document (D)." In *T&T Clark Companion to the Dead Sea Scrolls*, edited by George J. Brooke and Charlotte Hempel, 306–9. London: Bloomsbury T&T Clark, 2019.

Goodacre, Mark. "How Reliable is the Story of the Nag Hammadi Discovery?" *Journal for the Study of the New Testament* 35 (2013): 303–22.

Halton, Charles and Saana Svärd. *Women's Writing of Ancient Mesopotamia: An Anthology of the Earliest Female Authors*. Cambridge: Cambridge University Press, 2018.

Harrison, R. K. *The Dead Sea Scrolls: An Introduction*. New York: Harper Torch Books, 1961.

Hellholm, David. "The Problem of Apocalyptic Genre and the Apocalypse of John." In *Early Christian Apocalypticism: Genre and Social Setting*, edited by Adela Yarbro Collins, 13–64. Semeia 36. Decatur: Scholar's Press, 1986.

Hoffman, Adina and Peter Cole. *Sacred Trash: The Lost and Found World of the Cairo Genizah*. New York: Shocken, 2011.

Horst, Pieter W. van der. "Bitenosh's Orgasm (1QapGen 2:9–15)." *Journal for the Study of Judaism 43* (2012): 613–28.

Hossfeld, Frank-Lothar and Erich Zenger. *Psalms 3: A Commentary on Psalms 101–150*. Hermeneia. Minneapolis: Fortress, 2011.

Jobes, Karen H. and Moises Silva. *Invitation to the Septuagint*. Grand Rapids: Baker Academic, 2000.

Johnston, Philip S. *Shades of Sheol: Death and Afterlife in the Old Testament*. Downers Grove, IL: IVP Academic, 2002.

Justnes, Årstein. "Fragments for Sale: Dead Sea Scrolls." *Marginalia*, June 22, 2018. https://themarginaliarewview.com/fragments-for-sale.

Kalman, Jason and Jaqueline S. du Toit. *Canada's Big Biblical Bargain: How McGill University Bought the Dead Sea Scrolls*. Kingston and Montreal: McGill-Queens University Press, 2010.

Kanto, Jodi and Megan Twohey. *She Said: Breaking the Sexual Harassment Story That Helped Ignite a Movement*. New York: Penguin Books, 2020.

Klein, Ralph W. *1 Samuel*. Word Biblical Commentary 10. Waco: Word Books, 1983.

Kloppenborg, John S. *Excavating Q: The History and Setting of the Sayings Gospel*. Minneapolis: Fortress, 2000.

Knoppers, Gary N. *Jews and Samaritans: The Origins and History of their Early Relations*. New York: Oxford, 2013.

———. "Toward a Critical Edition of the Samaritan Pentateuch: Reflections on Issues and Methods." In *Reading the Bible in Ancient Traditions and Modern Editions: Studies in Memory of Peter W. Flint*, edited by Andrew B. Perrin, Kyung S. Baek, and Daniel K. Falk, 163–88. Early Judaism and Its Literature 47. Atlanta: SBL Press, 2017.

Kottsieper, Ingo. "Physicality of Manuscripts and Material Culture." In *T&T Clark Companion to the Dead Sea Scrolls*, edited by George J. Brooke and Charlotte Hempel, 167–77. London: Bloomsbury T&T Clark, 2019.

Kraft, Robert A. "The Weighing of the Parts: Pivots and Pitfalls in the Study of Early Judaism and their Early Christian Offspring." In *The Ways that Never Parted: Jews and Christians in Late Antiquity and Early Middle Ages*, edited by Adam H. Becker and Annette Yoshiko Reed, 87–94. Minneapolis: Fortress Press, 2003.

Lange, Armin. "In the Second Degree: Ancient Jewish Paratextual Literature in the Context of Graeco-Roman and Ancient Near Eastern Literature." In *In the Second Degree: Paratextual Literature in Ancient Near Eastern and Ancient Mediterranean Culture and Its Reflections in Medieval Literature*, edited by Philip Alexander, Armin Lange, and Renate Pillinger, 3–40. Leiden: Brill, 2010.

Law, Timothy Michael. *When God Spoke Greek: The Septuagint and the Making of the Christian Bible*. New York: Oxford, 2013.

Leuchter, Mark. "The Pen of Scribes: Writing, Textuality, and the Book of Jeremiah." In *The Book of Jeremiah: Composition, Reception, and Interpretation*, edited by Jack R. Lundbom, Craig A. Evans, and Bradford A. Anderson, 3–25. Vetus Testamentum Supplements 178. Leiden: Brill, 2018.

Levine, Amy-Jill and Marc Zvi Brettler, eds. *The Jewish Annotated New Testament*. NRSV. 2nd ed. New York: Oxford University Press, 2017.

Lim, Timothy H. "Biblical Quotations in the Pesharim and the Text of the Bible—Methodological Considerations." In *The Bible as Book: The Hebrew Bible and the Judean Desert Discoveries*, edited by Edward D. Herbert and Emanuel Tov, 71–79. London: The British Library & Oak Knoll Press, in association with the Scriptorium: Center for Christian Antiquities, 2002.

———. "The Emergence of the Samaritan Pentateuch." In *Reading the Bible in Ancient Traditions and Modern Editions: Studies in Memory of Peter W. Flint*, edited by Andrew B. Perrin, Kyung S. Baek, and Daniel K. Falk, 89–104. Early Judaism and Its Literature 47. Atlanta: SBL Press, 2017.

———. *The Formation of the Hebrew Canon*. Anchor Yale Bible Reference Library. New Haven: Yale University Press, 2013.

———. "The Qumran Scrolls, Multilingualism, and Biblical Interpretation." In *Religion in the Dead Sea Scrolls*, edited by John J. Collins and Robert A. Kugler, 57–73. Grand Rapids: Eerdmans, 2000.

Lönnqvist, Minna and Kenneth Lönnqvist. "Parallels to Be Seen: Manuscripts in Jars from Qumran and Egypt." In *The Dead Sea Scrolls in Context: Integrating the Dead Sea Scrolls in the Study of Ancient Texts, Languages, and Cultures*, volume 2, edited by Armin Lange, Emanuel Tov, and Matthias Weigold, 471–87. Vetus Testamentum Supplements 140. Leiden: Brill, 2011.

Machiela, Daniel A. "The Compositional Setting and Implied Audience of Some Aramaic Texts from Qumran: A Working Hypothesis." In *Vision, Narrative, and Wisdom in the Aramaic Texts from Qumran: Essays from the Copenhagen Symposium, 14–15*

August 2017, edited by Mette Bundvad and Kasper Siegismund, 168–202. Studies on the Texts of the Desert of Judah 131. Leiden: Brill, 2019.

———. *The Dead Sea Genesis Apocryphon: A New Text and Translation with Introduction and Special Treatment of Columns 13–17*. Studies on the Texts of the Desert of Judah 79. Leiden: Brill, 2009.

———. "Luke 13:10–13: 'Woman, You Have Been Set Free From Your Ailment'—Illness, Demon Possession, and Laying on Hands in Light of Second Temple Period Jewish Literature." In *The Gospels in First-Century Judea: Proceedings of the Inaugural Conference of Nyack College's Graduate Program in Ancient Judaism and Christian Origins, August 29th, 2013*, edited by R. Steven Notley and Jeffrey P. García, 122–35. Jewish and Christian Perspectives Series 29. Leiden: Brill, 2015.

Mackenzie, Simon, Neil Brodie, Donna Yates, and Christos Tsirogiannis. *Trafficking Culture: New Directions in Researching the Global Market in Illicit Antiquities*. New York: Routledge, 2019.

Magness, Jodi. *The Archaeology of Qumran and the Dead Sea Scrolls*. 2nd ed. Grand Rapids: Eerdmans, 2021.

Marti, D. Karl. *Das Buch Daniel*. Kurzer Hand-Commentar zum Alten Testament 18. Tübingen: Mohr Siebeck, 1901.

McCarter, P. Kyle, Jr. *1 Samuel: A New Translation with Introduction, Notes and Commentary*. Anchor Bible 8. Garden City: Doubleday, 1980.

McCready, Wayne O. and Adele Reinhartz, eds., *Common Judaism: Explorations in Second-Temple Judaism*. Minneapolis: Fortress Press, 2008.

McDonald, Lee Martin. *The Biblical Canon: Its Origin, Transmission, and Authority*. Grand Rapids: Baker Academic, 2007.

Metso, Sarianna. *The Serekh Texts*. Library of Second Temple Studies 62. London: T&T Clark, 2007.

Metzger, Bruce M. and Bart D. Ehrman. *The Text of the New Testament: Its Transmission, Corruption, and Restoration*. 4th ed. New York: Oxford, 2005.

Mizzi, Dennis. "Archaeology of Qumran." In *T&T Clark Companion to the Dead Sea Scrolls*, edited by George J. Brooke and Charlotte Hempel, 17–36. London: Bloomsbury T&T Clark, 2019.

Moore Cross, Frank, Jr. *The Ancient Library of Qumran*. Anchor Books. Garden City: Doubleday, 1958. Rev. and repr. 1961.

———. "Reminiscences of the Early Days in the Discovery and Study of the Dead Sea Scrolls." In *The Dead Sea Scrolls: Fifty Years after their Discovery: Proceeding of the*

Jerusalem Congress, July 20-25, 1997, edited by Lawrence H. Schiffman, Emanuel Tov, and James C. VanderKam, 932–43. Jerusalem: Israel Exploration Society and The Shrine of the Book, 2000.

Mroczek, Eva. *The Literary Imagination in Jewish Antiquity*. New York: Oxford University Press, 2016.

———. "Moses, David and Scribal Revelation: Preservation and Renewal in Second Temple Jewish Textual Traditions." In *The Significance of Sinai: Traditions about Sinai and Divine Revelation in Judaism and Christianity*, edited by George J. Brooke, Hindy Najman, and Loren T. Stuckenbruck, 91–115. Themes in Biblical Narrative 12. Leiden: Brill, 2008.

———. "True Stories and the Poetics of Textual Discovery." *Bulletin for the Study of Religion* 45 (2016): 26–31.

Myer, Marvin W. *Gnostic Discoveries: The Impact of the Nag Hammadi Library*. New York: HarperOne, 2009.

———, ed. *The Nag Hammadi Scriptures: The Revised and Updated Translation of Sacred Gnostic Texts Complete in One Volume*. New York: HarperOne, 2010.

Newsom, Carol A. "Apocalyptic and the Discourse of the Qumran Community." *Journal of Near Eastern Studies* 29 (1990): 135–44.

———. "Why Nabonidus? Excavating Traditions from Qumran, The Hebrew Bible, and Neo-Babylonian Sources." In *The Dead Sea Scrolls: Transmission of Traditions and Production of Texts*, edited by Sarianna Metso, Hindy Najman, and Eileen Schuller, 57–79. Studies on the Texts of the Desert of Judah 92. Leiden: Brill, 2010.

Novakovic, Lidija. "Text-Critical Variants in the Pesharim, Other Commentaries, and Related Documents." In *The Pesharim and Qumran History: Chaos or Consensus?*, edited by James C. Charlesworth, 129–58. Grand Rapids: Eerdmans, 2002.

O'Callaghan, Jose. "New Testament Papyri in Qumran Cave 7?" Translated by W. L. Holladay. *Journal of Biblical Literature* 91 (1972): 1–14.

Oegema, Gerbern S. *The Anointed and His People: Messianic Expectations from the Maccabees to Bar Kochba*. Journal for the Study of the Pseudepigrapha Supplements 27. Sheffield: Sheffield Academic Press, 1998.

Oswalt, John N. *The Book of Isaiah: Chapters 40–66*. New International Commentary on the Old Testament. Grand Rapids: Eerdmans, 1998.

Pagels, Elaine. *The Gnostic Gospels*. New York: Vintage Books, 1979.

Patrich, Joseph. "Archaeology." In *Encyclopedia of the Dead Sea Scrolls*, edited by James C. VanderKam and Lawrence H. Schiffman, 57–63. 2 volumes. Oxford: Oxford University Press, 2000.

Paul, Shalom M. *Isaiah 40–66: Translation and Commentary*. Eerdmans Critical Commentaries. Grand Rapids: Eerdmans, 2012.

Penner, Ken M. et al., eds. *The Lexham English Septuagint*. Bellingham, WA: Lexham Press, 2019.

Perrin, Andrew B. "The Aramaic Imagination: Incubating Apocalyptic Thought and Genre in Dream-Visions among the Qumran Aramaic Texts." In *Apocalyptic Thinking in Early Judaism: Engaging with John Collins' The Apocalyptic Imagination*, edited by Sidnie White Crawford and Cecilia Wassen, 110–40. Supplements to the Journal for the Study of Judaism 182. Leiden: Brill, 2018.

———. "Capturing the Voices of Pseudepigraphic Personae: On the Form and Function of Incipits in the Aramaic Dead Sea Scrolls." *Dead Sea Discoveries* 20 (2013): 98–123.

———. "Charting Constellations of Aramaic Jewish Pseudepigrapha at Qumran." In *The Dead Sea Scrolls in the Context of Hellenistic Judea Proceedings of the Tenth Meeting of the International Organization for Qumran Studies (Aberdeen, 5–8 August, 2019)*, edited by Pieter B. Hartog and Andrew B. Perrin, 113–40. Studies on the Texts of the Desert of Judah 142. Leiden: Brill, 2023.

———. *The Dynamics of Dream-Vision Revelation in the Aramaic Dead Sea Scrolls*. Journal of Ancient Judaism Supplements 19. Göttingen: Vandenhoeck & Ruprecht, 2015.

———. "From *lingua franca* to *lingua sacra*: The Scripturalization of Tobit in 4QTob[e]." *Vetus Testamentum* 66 (2016): 117–32.

———. "Greek Gospels and Aramaic Dead Sea Scrolls: Compositional, Conceptual, and Cultural Intersections." *Open Theology* 6 (2020): 440–56.

———. *The Horizons of Ancestral Inheritance: Commentary on the Levi, Qahat, and Amram Qumran Aramaic Traditions*. Library of Second Temple Studies 100. London: Bloomsbury, 2022.

———. "Redrafting the Architecture of Daniel Traditions in the Hebrew Scriptures and Dead Sea Scrolls." *Journal of Theological Studies* 72 (2021): 44–71.

———. "Symptoms and Symbols, Prayers and Portents: Diagnostic Physiognomy and the Diviner in the Aramaic Prayer of Nabonidus (4Q242)." In *Science in Qumran Aramaic Texts*, edited by Ida Fröhlich, 43–64. Ancient Cultures of Science and Knowledge 1. Göttingen: Mohr Siebeck, 2022.

Perrin, Andrew B. and Loren T. Stuckenbruck, eds. *Four Kingdoms before and beyond the Book of Daniel.* Themes in Biblical Narrative 28. Leiden: Brill, 2021.

Pietersma, Albert and Benjamin G. Wright, eds. *A New English Translation of the Septuagint and the Other Greek Translations Traditionally Included under that Title.* Oxford: Oxford University Press, 2007.

Popović, Mladen. *Reading the Human Body: Physiognomics and Astrology in the Dead Sea Scrolls and Hellenistic-Early Roman Period Judaism*. Studies on the Texts of the Desert of Judah 67. Leiden: Brill, 2007.

Pummer, Reinhard. *The Samaritans: A Profile*. Grand Rapids: Eerdmans, 2016.

Reed, Annette Yoshiko. "The Modern Invention of 'Old Testament Pseudepigrapha.'" *Journal of Theological Studies* 60 (2009): 403–36.

Sabar, Ariel. *Veritas: A Harvard Professor, A Con Man and the Gospel of Jesus's Wife*. New York: Doubleday, 2020.

Said, Edward W. *Orientalism*. New York: Pantheon Books, 1978.

Sanders, E. P. *Judaism: Practice & Belief, 63 BCE–66 CE*. London: SCM Press; Philadelphia: Trinity Press International, 1992.

Sanders, J. A. *The Dead Sea Psalms Scroll*. Ithaca: Cornell University Press, 1976.

Sanders, Paul. "The Ashkar-Gilson Manuscript: Remnant of a Proto-Masoretic Model Scroll of the Torah." *Journal of Hebrew Scriptures* 14 (2014): 1–22.

Schiffman, Lawrence H. *Reclaiming the Dead Sea Scrolls: The History of Judaism, the Background of Christianity, and the Lost Library of Qumran*. Anchor Bible Reference Library. New York: Doubleday, 1994.

Schniedewind, William M. "Qumran Hebrew as an Antilanguage." *Journal of Biblical Literature* 118 (1999): 235–52.

Schøyen, Martin. "Acquisition and Ownership History: A Personal Reflection." In *Gleanings from the Caves: Dead Sea Scrolls and Artefacts from The Schøyen Collection*, edited by Torleif Elgvin, Kipp Davis, and Michael Langlois, 27–32. Library of Second Temple Studies 71. London: Bloomsbury T&T Clark, 2016.

Schuller, Eileen. *The Dead Sea Scrolls: What Have We Learned?* Louisville: Westminster John Knox, 2006.

———. "Hodayot (1QH and Related Texts)." In *The Eerdmans Encyclopedia of Early Judaism*, edited by John J. Collins and Daniel C. Harlow, 747–49. Grand Rapids: Eerdmans, 2010.

Schuller, Eileen and Marie-Theres Wacker, eds. *Early Jewish Writings*. The Bible and Women 3.1. Atlanta: SBL Press, 2017.

Schwartz, Seth. "Language, Power and Identity in Ancient Palestine." *Past & Present* 148 (1995): 3–47.

Shanks, Hershel. "An Interview with John Strugnell: Ousted Chief Scroll Editor Makes His Case." *Biblical Archaeology Review* 20, no. 4 (July/August 1994): 40–46, 57.

Strack, H. L. and Günter Stemberger. *Introduction to the Talmud and Midrash*. Translated by Markus Bockmuehl. Minneapolis: Fortress Press, 1992.

Strugnell, John. "Notes en marge du Volume V des 'Discoveries in the Judean Desert of Jordan.'" *Revue de Qumran* 7 (1969–71): 163–276.

Stuckenbruck, Loren T. "The Dead Sea Scrolls and the New Testament." In *Qumran and the Bible: Studying the Jewish and Christian Scriptures in Light of the Dead Sea Scrolls*, edited by Nóra Dávid and Armin Lange, 131–70. Contributions to Biblical Exegesis and Theology 57. Leuven: Peeters, 2010.

———. "The Formation and Reformation of Daniel in the Dead Sea Scrolls." In *The Bible and the Dead Sea Scrolls: The Princeton Symposium on the Dead Sea Scrolls, Volume One: Scripture and the Scrolls*, edited by James H. Charlesworth, 101–30. Waco: Baylor University Press, 2006.

Stuckenbruck, Loren T. and Daniel M. Gurtner, eds. *T&T Clark Encyclopedia of Second Temple Judaism*. 2 volumes. London: Bloomsbury T&T Clark, 2019.

Sukenik, Eleazer L. *The Dead Sea Scrolls of the Hebrew University*. Jerusalem: Magness Press, 1955.

Teeter, Andrew. "The Hebrew Bible and/as Second Temple Literature: Methodological Reflections." *Dead Sea Discoveries* 20 (2013): 349–77.

Tervanotko, Hanna. *Denying Her Voice: The Figure of Miriam in Ancient Jewish Literature*. Journal of Ancient Judaism Supplements 23. Göttingen: Vandenhoeck & Ruprecht, 2016.

Tigchelaar, Eibert. "The Dead Sea Scrolls." In *The Eerdmans Encyclopedia of Early Judaism*, edited by John J. Collins and Daniel C. Harlow, 163–80. Grand Rapids: Eerdmans, 2010.

Tov, Emanuel. "Introduction, Text Editions, the Collection of the Museum of the Bible, Textual and Orthographic Character, Relation to Other Fragments from the Judean Desert." In *Dead Sea Scrolls Fragments in the Museum Collection*, edited by Emanuel Tov, Kipp Davis, and Robert Duke, 3–18. Publications of the Museum of the Bible 1. Leiden: Brill, 2016.

———. "The Jeremiah Scrolls from Qumran." *Revue de Qumran* 14 (1989): 189–206.

———. "New Fragments of Amos." *Dead Sea Discoveries* 21 (2014): 3–13.

———. "Reflections on the Many Forms of Hebrew Scripture in Light of the LXX and 4QReworked Pentateuch." In *Textual Criticism of the Hebrew Bible, Qumran, Septuagint: Collected Essays*, 3–19. Vetus Testamentum Supplements 167. Leiden: Brill, 2015.

———. *Scribal Practices and Approaches Reflected in the Texts Found in the Judean Desert*. Studies on the Texts of the Desert of Judah 54. Leiden: Brill, 2004.

———. *Textual Criticism of the Hebrew Bible*. 3rd ed. Minneapolis: Fortress Press, 2012.

Tov, Emanuel, Kipp Davis, and Robert Duke, eds. *Dead Sea Scrolls Fragments in the Museum Collection*. Publications of Museum of the Bible 1. Leiden: Brill, 2016.

Trever, John C. "Completion of the Publication of Some Fragments from Qumran Cave 1." *Revue de Qumran* 19 (1965): 323–34.

——. *The Dead Sea Scrolls: A Personal Account*. 2nd ed. Grand Rapids: Eerdmans, 1977.

——. "1QDan[a]: The Latest of the Qumran Manuscripts." *Revue de Qumran* 26 (1970): 277–86.

——. "Preliminary Observations on the Jerusalem Scrolls." *Bulletin of the American School of Oriental Research* 111 (1948): 3–16.

——. *Scrolls from Qumrân Cave I from Photographs by John C. Trever*, with a foreword by Frank Moore Cross. Jerusalem: The Albright Institute of Archaeological Research and the Shrine of the Book, 1972.

——. *The Untold Story of Qumran*. Westwood, NJ: Fleming H. Revell Company, 1965.

Ulrich, Eugene. "The Bible in the Making: The Scriptures Found at Qumran." In *The Bible at Qumran: Text, Shape, and Interpretation*, edited by Peter W. Flint, 51–66. Grand Rapids: Eerdmans, 2001.

——. *The Biblical Qumran Scrolls: Transcriptions and Textual Variants*. Vetus Testamentum Supplements 134. Leiden: Brill, 2010.

——. *The Dead Sea Scrolls and the Developmental Composition of the Bible*. Vetus Testamentum Supplements 169. Leiden: Brill, 2015.

——. "The Text of Daniel in the Dead Sea Scrolls." In *The Book of Daniel: Composition and Reception, Volume II*,dited by John J. Collins and Peter W. Flint, 573–85. 2 volumes. Formation and Interpretation of Old Testament Literature. Leiden: Brill, 2002.

——. "Variant Editions of Biblical Books Revealed by the Qumran Scrolls." In *Reading the Bible in Ancient Traditions and Modern Editions: Studies in Memory of Peter W. Flint*, edited by Andrew B. Perrin, Kyung S. Baek, and Daniel K. Falk, 13–34. Early Judaism and Its Literature 47. Atlanta: SBL Press, 2017.

Ulrich, Eugene et al., eds. *Qumran Cave 4.VII: Genesis to Numbers*. Discoveries in the Judean Desert 12. Oxford: Clarendon, 1994.

——. *Qumran Cave 4.X: The Prophets*. Discoveries in the Judean Desert 15. Oxford: Clarendon, 1997.

——. *Qumran Cave 4.XI: Psalms to Chronicles*. Discoveries in the Judean Desert 16. Oxford: Clarendon, 2000.

VanderKam, James C. *The Dead Sea Scrolls and the Bible*. Grand Rapids: Eerdmans, 2012.

——. *The Dead Sea Scrolls Today*. 2nd ed. Grand Rapids: Eerdmans, 2010.

———. *An Introduction to Early Judaism*. Grand Rapids: Eerdmans, 2001.

VanderKam, James C. and Peter W. Flint. *The Meaning of the Dead Sea Scrolls: Their Significance for Understanding the Bible, Judaism, Jesus, and Christianity*. New York: HarperSanFrancisco, 2002.

Vermes, Géza and Martin D. Goodman. *The Essenes According to the Classical Sources*. Oxford Centre Textbooks 1. Sheffield: JSOT Press, 1989.

Wacholder, Ben Zion. *The Dawn of Qumran: The Sectarian Torah and the Teacher of Righteousness*. Monographs of Hebrew Union College 8. Cincinnati: Hebrew Union College Press, 1983.

Weitzman, Steve. "Why Did the Qumran Community Write in Hebrew?" *Journal of the American Oriental Society* 119 (1999): 35–45.

Westerholm, Stephen. *Perspectives Old and New on Paul: The "Lutheran" Paul and His Critics*. Grand Rapids: Eerdmans, 2003.

White Crawford, Sidnie. "4Q364 & 365: A Preliminary Report." In *The Madrid Qumran Congress: Proceedings of the International Congress on the Dead Sea Scrolls, Madrid 18–21 March, 1991*, edited by Julio Trebolle Barrera and Luis Vegas Montaner, 217–22. 2 volumes. Studies on the Texts of the Desert of Judah 12. Leiden: Brill, 1992.

———. *Scribes and Scrolls at Qumran*. Grand Rapids: Eerdmans, 2019.

Wise, Michael, Martin G. Abegg Jr., and Edward Cook. *The Dead Sea Scrolls: A New Translation*. Rev. ed. New York: HarperSanFrancisco, 2005.

Wright, Benjamin G., III. "Ben Sira." In *T&T Clark Encyclopedia of Second Temple Judaism*, edited by Loren T. Stuckenbruck and Daniel M. Gurtner, 130–34. 2 volumes. London: Bloomsbury T&T Clark, 2019.

Wright, N. T. *Paul: In Fresh Perspective*. Minneapolis: Fortress, 2009.

Yadin, Yigael. *The Message of the Scrolls*. University Library 135. New York: Grosset & Dunlap, 1957. Rev. and repr. 1962.

Zahn, Molly M. *Genres of Rewriting in Second Temple Judaism: Scribal Composition and Transmission*. Cambridge: Cambridge University Press, 2020.

———. "The Samaritan Pentateuch and the Scribal Culture of Second Temple Judaism." *Journal for the Study of Judaism* 46 (2015): 285–313.

Subject & Author Index

Scripture & Ancient Sources Index

Old Testament

Genesis

Exodus

Leviticus

Numbers

Deuteronomy

Joshua

New Testament

Dead Sea Scrolls

Apocrypha

Pseudepigrapha

Classical Sources

Ancient Near Eastern Texts

Rabbinic Writings

LEXHAM
GEOGRAPHIC
COMMENTARY
on the Pentateuch
BARRY J. BEITZEL
EDITOR